A2
Revise
PE
for OCR

second edition

by
Dennis Roscoe
Jan Roscoe

A2 Revise PE for OCR
second edition

by
Dennis Roscoe
Jan Roscoe

Jan Roscoe Publications Ltd
An imprint of Heath Books Ltd

Text copyright to Dennis Roscoe, Jan Roscoe, Bob Davis, graphics copyright to Jan Roscoe Publications.

First edition published in 2010 by Jan Roscoe Publications.
Second edition January 2018.

Heath Books Ltd
Willow House, Willow Walk
Sutton
Surrey
SM3 9QQ
United Kingdom

tel: 020 8644 7788
fax: 020 8641 3377
email: orders@heathbooks.co.uk

A Catalogue record for this book is available from the British Library.

ISBN   978-1-911-24106-5.

Cover designs by Roscoe-Rutter.

Published via Adobe InDesign, CorelDraw 10.410, Adobe Illustrator 9.0, Smartdraw 6.0, laid out and typeset by Dennis Roscoe.

Printed and bound by

Hobbs the Printers Limited
Brunel Road
Totton
Hampshire
SO40 3WX
United Kingdom

tel: 023 8066 4800
fax: 023 8066 4801

email: estimating@hobbs.uk.com

INTRODUCTION

This 'A' level PE book has been written to address the changes in content and style of the OCR Level 3 Advanced Year 2 GCE Physical Education (H555) syllabus which commenced in September 2017.

These Physical Education syllabuses are multi-disciplinary in nature, covering applied anatomy and exercise physiology, skill acquisition and sports psychology, and historical and contemporary studies in sport. These subject areas have generated a substantial quantity of specialist literature each with its own specific language. At times you may be overwhelmed by the amount of material covered, however this book addresses the problem of dealing with copious notes by summarising the content of the subject matter and attempting to explain in simple language what are sometimes complicated concepts or issues.

Practice questions are provided at the end of each chapter, and answers can be downloaded by going to the following link: http://www.jroscoe.co.uk/downloads/a2_revise_pe_ocr/ on the JRP website. The answers will amplify the subject matter and provide clues as to how the exam itself should be approached. A continuing feature is that there will be a number of multiple choice questions on each exam paper, and we include a small number of such questions at the end of each chapter along with the practice questions. There is also a requirement that the final exam questions on each section of the syllabus shall include an essay type answer worth 20 marks. This allows students to express their ability and knowledge in the context of properly written language (prose) with attention to grammar and punctuation. Question assessment guidelines and use of terminology are included immediately before the index section in this book.

Materials are presented in a concise and visual approach for effective and efficient revision. Modern terminology, nomenclature and units have been used wherever possible. At the end of the book there is a comprehensive index for easy reference.

Please note that students are recommended to have a clear understanding of the content as outlined in the OCR specification, and not to rely solely on this guide.

HOW TO USE THIS REVISION GUIDE

The ideal use of this Revision Guide would be to purchase it at the start of the course and relate each of the summary pages to the specific areas of the syllabus as an aide memoire. The inclusion of specific questions and full answers (to be found on the following link: http://www.jroscoe.co.uk/downloads/a2_revise_pe_ocr/) provide a means of self-testing. Each chapter has its own link specified on the questions pages. Don't be tempted to find out the answers before attempting a question.

In reality, whole examination questions contain a much broader content than those given in this guide. Examiners will attempt to examine more than one small area of the syllabus within the context of one full question and therefore it is important that you revise all aspects of your syllabus.

The main use of the Revision Guide should be during the final revision period leading up to your examinations, as it should help you to understand and apply concepts i.e. link summary content with examination question.

The aim of this book is to provide an aid that enhances syllabus analysis, and to raise your level of success in examinations.

THE QUALITY OF AUTHORS

The authors are experts in the physical education field and have considerable experience in teaching 'A' Level Physical Education. They have written examination syllabuses, and have set and marked examination questions within this subject area and taught at revision workshops throughout the UK. Much of the material within this book has been thoroughly student tested.

The authors hope that this Revision Guide will prove useful to staff and students. Jan Roscoe Publications will welcome any comments you would wish to make about the book's utility or layout. Thank you for using this work.

Dennis Roscoe
Jan Roscoe

ACKNOWLEDGMENTS

The authors wish to thank Bob Davis for his contribution in the Historical and Contemporary Issues elements of this book. Thanks are also due to Helen Roscoe-Rutter and David Roscoe-Rutter for their contributions as cover designers and photographers, Debbie Francis of Heath Books as proof reader, and Lois Cresswell, Jenny Pacey, Helen Roscoe-Rutter and Osian Jones for their patience as photographic models. The authors wish to thank members of the Belgian Olympic Athletics Squad for permission to use their images. **Dennis Roscoe** - *Editor*

ACKNOWLEDGMENTS FOR GRAPHICS

p. 14 figure 1.5 Eric Van Leewen/ Wikimedia Creative Commons.org,

p. 19 figure 1.12 Maxisport/Shutterstock.com, figure 1.13 Snap2Art/Shutterstock.com,

p. 20 figure 1.15 S.Kuvona/Shutterstock.com, p. 29 figure 1.27 Chuck Wagner/Shutterstock.com,

p. 35 figure 2.1 Lukas Budinsky/Shutterstock.com, p. 38 figure 2.5 Michaelpuche/Shutterstock.com,

p. 41 figure 2.9 WorldPress.com, p. 43 Maxisport/Shutterstock.com, p. 48 figure 3.2 Praisaeing/Shutterstock.com,

p. 50 figure 3.5 orthoinfo.aaos.com, p. 52 figure 3.6 Singaporeoesteopathy/Pinterest.com,

p. 58 figure 3.11 Oliveromg/Shutterstock.com,

p. 60 figure 3.14 Aircast ankle brace, figure 3.15 Loughborough University Sport Technology Institute,

p. 65 figure 3.20 news.co.au, figure 3.21 England Rugby, p. 67 figure 3.25 well photo/Shutterstock.com,

p. 70 figure 3.28 medicaldaily.com, p. 71 figure 3.30 sylv1rob1/Shutterstock.com, p. 73 figure 3.33 PhysioRoom.com,

p. 74 figure 3.36 Aircast ankle brace, p. 76 figure 3.38 fibromyjianewtoday.com,

p. 81 figure 4.4 Jim Lamberson/Wikimedia Creative Commons.org, p. 87 figure 4.17 A. Richardo/Shutterstock.com,

p. 89 figure 4.20 Dmitry Morgan/Shutterstock.com, p. 101 figure 5.14 Wth/Shutterstock/com,

p. 102 figure 5.18 Wikipedia Commons.org, p. 107 figure 6.4 Chris VanLennep Photo,

p. 108 figure 6.5 Mitch Gunn/Shutterstock.com, p. 109 figure 6.6 Shahjehan/Shutterstock.com,

p. 111 figure 6.9 Michael Krinke/istock.com, p. 113 figure 6.10 Sergey Nivens/Shutterstock.com,

p. 117 figure 7.3 Leonard Zhukovsky/Shutterstock.com,

p. 119 figure 7.7 Ligfo/Shutterstock.com, figure 7.8 maradon333/Shutterstock.com,

p. 121 figure 7.11 Anton Ivanov/Shutterstock.com, p. 122 figure 7.12 Shahjehan/Shutterstock.com,

p. 123 figure 7.15 Jimmy48 photography/Shutterstock.com, p. 127 figure 8.2 K Richardson-Walsh@katewalsh11,

p. 129 figure 8.5 David Rogers/Getty images, p. 131 figure 8.7 Monkey Business Images/Shutterstock.com,

p. 144 figure 9.4 Leonard Zhukovsky/Shutterstock.com,

p. 145 figure 9.5 Marcos Mesa Sam Worldey/Shutterstock.com, figure 8.17 Yoann Morin/Shutterstock.com,

p. 147 figure 9.8 Andrew Safonov/Shutterstock.com, figure 9.9 Wikimedia Creative Commons.org,

p. 150 figure 9.12 Vlad1988/Shutterstock.com, p. 151 figure 9.13 Alberto Girotto/Shutterstock.com,

p. 160 figure 10.4 Sport England, figure 10.5 legacycompany.co.uk,

p. 161 figure 10.6 mmichaelangelo/Shutterstock.com,

p. 162 figure 10.8 Michaelpuche/Shutterstock.com, figure 10.9 Leonard Zhukovsky/Shutterstock.com,

p. 163 figure 10.10 Wikipedia Creative Commons.org, p. 173 figure 11.3 Air images/Shutterstock.com,

p. 178 figure 11.10 BOA/Andy Ryan, p. 179 figure 11.12 domhnall doda/Shutterstock.com,

p. 180 figure 11.13 well photo/Shutterstock.com, p. 184 figure 12.2 Mikael Damkier/Shutterstock.com,

p. 185 figure 12.3 Elvar Palsson/Wikipedia Creative Commons.org, figure 12.4 Day Owl/Shutterstock.com,

p. 186 figure 12.6 Ben Jeayes/Shutterstock.com.

All other photographs or graphics are by Helen Roscoe-Rutter, David Roscoe-Rutter, Jan Roscoe, Dennis Roscoe, Bob Davis or other free sources.

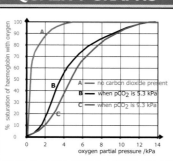

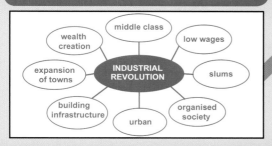

CONTENTS

A2 Revise PE for OCR

Part 1

Applied anatomy and exercise physiology

Part 2

Exercise physiology

Part 3

Biomechanics

CONTENTS

APPLIED ANATOMY AND EXERCISE PHYSIOLOGY

CHAPTER 1: *Energy for exercise*

Energy definitions

Energy is the capacity to do work, and work has a mechanical definition, namely **work = force x distance** moved in the direction of the force. Energy and work are measured in joules (J).

Chemical energy is energy that is produced by a complex series of chemical reactions, which can then be made available as **kinetic energy** and **potential energy**. Chemical energy in the form of ATP is the most useful form of energy in living systems because it is used to run almost all functional processes.

figure 1.1 – kinetic energy in motion

All chemical reactions either give out energy (**exothermic reaction**) or take in energy (**endothermic reaction**). The clever way that the biological system works is to **take in** energy (endothermic) with a series of chemical reactions from food and fuel, and **give out** the same energy (exothermic) with a **different** series of chemical reactions in order to provide energy for muscular contractions and other bodily functions. In muscle tissue, **chemical energy** is converted into **mechanical energy** when the muscle contracts.

Kinetic energy is energy due to the movement or motion of an object, observed by the constant moving of an object or living thing, for example, a person running (figure 1.1) or walking and a bouncing ball.

Potential energy is stored energy that has the potential or capacity to do work but is not presently doing so. For example, your leg muscles have potential energy when you sit still in a chair. When potential energy is released it is converted into kinetic energy.

Mechanical energy is energy directly produced by forces which do work in moving matter. For example, when you ride a bike, your legs provide the mechanical energy for moving the pedals and propelling the bike (figure 1.2).

figure 1.2 – mechanical energy converting to kinetic energy

Electrical energy results from the movement of charged particles. In the human body, electrical currents are generated when charged particles called ions move along and across cell membranes. The nervous system uses electrical currents called nerve impulses to transmit messages from one part of the body to another.

STUDENT NOTE

Refresh your memory on the transmission of an action potential down an axon of a motor neurone, by referring to AS/A1 Revise PE for OCR A Student Revision Guide ISBN 9781901424911, Chapter 1 page 27.

Power is the **rate** at which energy is used, or the energy used per second which is measured in watts (W). Power can be calculated using the formula:

$$\text{power} = \frac{\text{energy (in joules)}}{\text{time (in seconds)}} \quad \text{(answer in watts)}$$

Energy transfer in the body

We derive our energy from food, namely carbohydrates (CHO), fats, and to a lesser extent proteins.

The energy derived from carbohydrates, fats and proteins is stored in bodily tissues in the form of a high energy compound called **adenosine triphosphate** (ATP), which can be generated via three different processes:

- **ATP-PC** system (also called the alactic anaerobic system).
- **Anaerobic glycolytic** system also known as the **lactic acid** system (which is also anaerobic).
- **Aerobic** system.

ATP - adenosine triphosphate

ATP is the compound which stores energy and is therefore the energy currency linked to **intensity** and **duration** of physical activity. ATP exists in every living tissue and its breakdown gives energy for all life functions - this includes the action of the liver and the brain for example, as well as the contraction of muscle tissue. All muscular activity requires the availability and breakdown of ATP (figure 1.3).

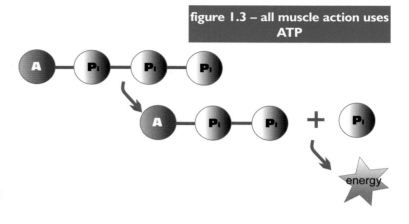

figure 1.3 – all muscle action uses ATP

The energy released during tissue respiration is stored in the chemical bonds in ATP, and this energy is released (an exothermic reaction) during the reaction:

$$ATP \rightarrow ADP + P_i + energy$$

Resynthesis of ATP from ADP (**adenosine diphosphate**) uses the reaction:

$$energy + ADP + P_i \rightarrow ATP$$

This is an **endothermic** reaction since energy is **given** to the molecule to enable the reaction to happen. This energy will be derived from **food fuels**.

The enzymatic catabolism (breakdown) of fat within the muscle cell mitochondria is termed **beta-oxidation**. Energy derived from the breakdown of **free fatty acids** (FFAs) is the preferred fuel food for long duration, low intensity exercise. The fatty acid molecule transforms into **acetyl-CoA** in the mitochondria. This reaction involves the successive splitting of 2-carbon acyl fragments from the long chain of the fatty acid.

Anaerobic energy systems

The ATP-PC system

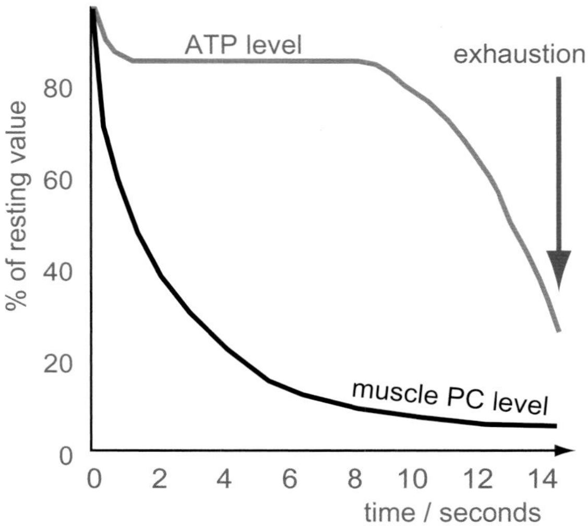

This system of replenishing of ATP from ADP is the predominant one for activity which lasts between 3 and 10 seconds, which means for high intensity maximum work, for example, flat out sprinting - the 100 metre sprint.

No oxygen is needed - the process is **anaerobic**. The chemical reactions within this system are a **coupled reaction** in which ATP is resynthesised via **phosphocreatine** (PC) stored in muscle cell sarcoplasm.

The following reactions take place: $\quad$ **PC** $\rightarrow$ **P$_i$ + C + energy**

$$energy + ADP + P_i \rightarrow ATP$$

The two reactions together are called a **coupled reaction** and are facilitated by the enzyme **creatine kinase** (CK).

The net effect of these two coupled reactions is:

$$PC + ADP \rightarrow ATP + C$$

figure 1.4 – changes in muscle ATP and PC

ATP level

exhaustion

% of resting value

80

60

40

20

0

0 2 4 6 8 10 12 14

time / seconds

muscle PC level

PC is re-created in muscle cells during the recovery process, which requires energy and is an **endothermic** reaction.

During intense exercise, peak anaerobic power is attained within the first 5 seconds, and depletion of PC occurs between 7 and 9 seconds (figure 1.5, page 14).

Look at the graph in figure 1.4 showing changes in muscle ATP and PC. After an initial small fall, the ATP level is maintained, then falls as the PC is used up because the energy from PC is being used to resynthesise ATP.

The ATP-PC system

This causes PC levels to fall rapidly to zero after about 10 seconds. The capacity to maintain ATP production at this point depends on the anaerobic glycolytic or lactic acid system.

STUDENT NOTE

This process does not directly require glucose as an energy source - but the re-creation of PC during recovery will do so.

Anaerobic glycolytic system or the lactic acid system

Glycolysis (figure 1.6) is anaerobic (without the presence of oxygen) and takes place in the **muscle cell sarcoplasm**.

- Carbohydrate, from the food we eat, is stored as **glycogen** in muscle and liver tissues.

- Glycogen is converted into **glucose** by the hormone glucagon, released when blood glucose levels fall (when glucose is used during tissue respiration).

- The breakdown of glucose provides the energy to rebuild ATP from ADP.

- This is facilitated by enzymes such as **glycogen phosphorylase** (GPP) and **phosphofructokinase** (PFK).

- The whole process produces **pyruvic acid**.

- Pyruvic acid is then converted to **lactic acid** by the enzyme **lactate dehydrogenase** (LDH).

- Rapid glycolysis allows ATP to form quickly without oxygen, generating **2 ATPs** per molecule of glucose.

As work intensity increases, lactic acid starts to accumulate above resting values, which produces **muscle fatigue** and pain. The resultant low pH inhibits enzyme action and cross-bridge formation, hence muscle action is inhibited and physical performance deteriorates.

The lactic acid system is the predominant one used to resynthesise ATP in sport or activities in which the flat-out effort lasts up to 30-60 seconds. For example, a 400 metre run or a 100 metre swim.

After exercise stops, extra oxygen is taken up to remove lactic acid by changing it back into pyruvic acid - this is the **EPOC** (**Excess Post-exercise Oxygen Consumption**, sometimes called the oxygen debt), see page 21 for the details of EPOC.

Aerobic energy system

The aerobic energy system releases stored energy from **muscle glycogen**, **fats** and **proteins**.

The aerobic system (figure 1.7, page 15) relies on the presence of oxygen to completely break down stored energy (from muscle glycogen, fats and proteins) into carbon dioxide, water and energy.

The energy yield is high – one molecule of glucose yields 36 molecules of ATP (note that in the lactic acid process the yield is two molecules of ATP). This process will continue indefinitely until energy stores run out.

figure 1.5 – triple jump - under 7 seconds to complete

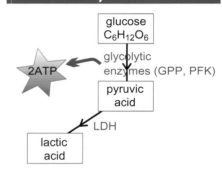

figure 1.6 – anaerobic glycolytic system

glucose $C_6H_{12}O_6$

2ATP

glycolytic enzymes (GPP, PFK)

pyruvic acid

LDH

lactic acid

Stage one - glycolysis

The first stage of the aerobic process is the same as that in the anaerobic glycolytic system namely glycolysis, i.e. the conversion of glycogen into two molecules of pyruvic acid (page 14), two ATP molecules and a number of hydrogen atoms. This process occurs via a series of 10 chemical reactions within the cell sarcoplasm.

From this point on, all chemical reactions involved in the aerobic system take place within the muscle cell mitochondria. The mitochondrion is often referred to as the power house of the cell, since it is the site of most energy production.

ATP regenerated = 2ATP per molecule of glucose.

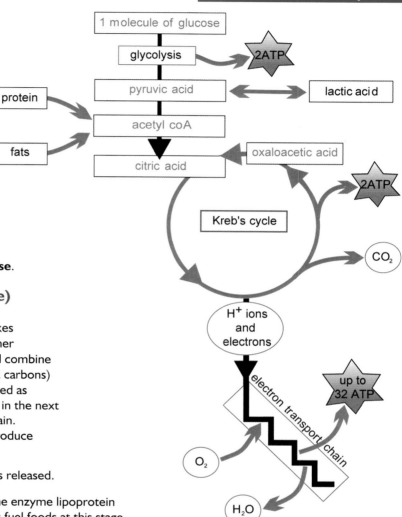

figure 1.7 – the aerobic system

Stage two - Kreb's cycle (citric acid cycle)

This stage occurs in the **presence of oxygen**, and takes place in the **muscle cell mitochondria** within the inner **fluid filled** matrix. Here, 2 molecules of **pyruvic acid** combine with **oxaloacetic acid** (4 carbons) and **acetyl coA** (2 carbons) to form citric acid (6 carbons). The citric acid is oxidised as hydrogen is removed from this compound to be used in the next stage of energy production, the electron transport chain. Carbon and oxygen are left behind and combine to produce carbon dioxide which is eliminated via the lungs.

In addition, energy sufficient to resynthesise **2 ATPs** is released.

Free fatty acids (FFA) from body fat, facilitated by the enzyme lipoprotein lipase, and protein (keto acids from muscle) can act as fuel foods at this stage, as indicated in figure 1.7 as exercise duration increases. Stored fat represents the body's most plentiful energy source.

Protein also serves as a potentially important energy substrate for long duration, endurance-type activities. The protein-to-energy pathways occur at two sites, acetyl-CoA and directly into Kreb's cycle. After nitrogen removal from the amino acid molecule during **deamination**, the remaining carbon skeleton enters the metabolic pathway to produce ATP aerobically or is converted to fat for further future energy needs.

Stage three - the electron transport chain

The **electron transport chain** occurs in the presence of oxygen within the **cristae** (inner part of the muscle cell mitochondria). The hydrogen given off at Krebs cycle is carried to the electron transport chain by **hydrogen carriers** (NADs and FADs). The hydrogen is split into **hydrogen ions** (H^+) and electrons (e^-). During a step-by-step chemical reaction, the hydrogen ions are oxidised to produce water (H_2O) and the electrons provide the energy to resynthesise ATP.

Aerobic respiration

In summary, the total effect of aerobic respiration is that it is an **endothermic** reaction:

$$\text{glucose} + \textbf{36ADP} + \textbf{36P}_i + \textbf{6O}_2 \rightarrow \textbf{6CO}_2 + \textbf{36ATP} + \textbf{6H}_2\textbf{O}$$

Fat fuels produce 2 ATPs less per molecule than glucose.

Energy transfer during long duration/lower activity exercise

The aerobic system requires carbohydrate in the form of **glucose** which is **derived from glycogen** stored in muscle cells (mostly slow twitch - SO type I) or in the liver.

The graph in figure 1.8 shows how the rate of usage of muscle glycogen is high during the first 30 minutes of steady exercise - which has to be replaced if a sportsperson is to continue at the same rate. Hence consumption of energy drinks and bananas during a long tennis match.

After the first 30 minutes of exercise, the body runs out of its glycogen stores and then turns mainly to what is left of the glucose in the blood and then finally to fatty acids and amino acids (derived from muscle protein).

By far the largest energy reserve in the human body is adipose tissue **triglycerides**, and these reserves are an important source of fuel during prolonged endurance exercise. As exercise progresses from low to moderate intensity, for example, 25-65% $\dot{V}O_{2max}$, the rate of total fat oxidation increases due to a relatively large use of intramuscular triglycerides.

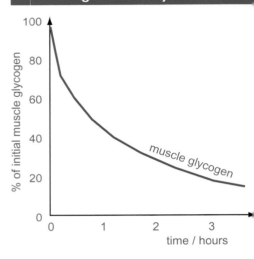

figure 1.8 – change in muscle glycogen during low intensity exercise

STUDENT NOTE

The abbreviation $\dot{V}O_2$ indicates oxygen uptake or consumption where the VO_2 denotes the volume consumed and the dot placed above the V expresses oxygen uptake as per minute.

Endurance athletes can utilise **free fatty acids** (FFAs) during prolonged exercise sooner than untrained people. This training adaptation enables the trained athlete to not use glycogen up immediately, but save it for later on in an exercise effort, or when the intensity of exercise increases. This is called **glycogen sparing**.

During exercise, the human body consumes large amounts of oxygen. The characteristics of oxygen uptake ($\dot{V}O_2$) kinetics differ with exercise intensity. When exercise is performed at a given work rate which is below lactate threshold (LT), $\dot{V}O_2$ increases exponentially to a **steady-state level**.

Figure 1.9 illustrates oxygen consumption during a 20 minute slow jog at a steady pace. At rest oxygen consumption is low, followed by a rapid increase during the first minute of the jog, to reach a relative plateau or steady state of aerobic metabolism between 4- 6 minutes. This steady state represents a balance between energy required by the body and rate of aerobic ATP production.

$\dot{V}O_{2max}$ is therefore a key component of aerobic endurance and is called **aerobic power** or **maximum oxygen uptake**, and so represents an accurate indicator of an athlete's fitness.

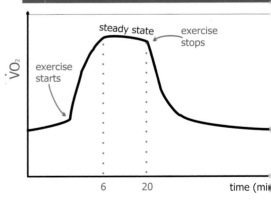

figure 1.9 – oxygen uptake during a slow jog

Energy continuum of physical activity

This describes the process by which ATP is regenerated via the different energy systems depending on the **intensity** and **duration** of exercise. Although **all** the systems contribute to ATP regeneration during any activity, one or other of the energy systems usually provides the major contribution for a given activity. Table 1.1 shows approximate proportions of ATP resynthesised via aerobic and anaerobic pathways for some sporting activities.

Table 1.1 – **percentage contribution of the aerobic and anaerobic energy systems to different sports**

sport or event	aerobic %	anaerobic (all) %
100m sprint	0	100
200m sprint	10	90
100m swim	20	80
boxing	30	70
800m run	40	60
hockey	50	50
2000m rowing	60	40
4000m cycle pursuit	70	30
3000m run	80	20
cross country run	90	10
marathon	100	0

figure 1.10 – variation in contribution of energy systems

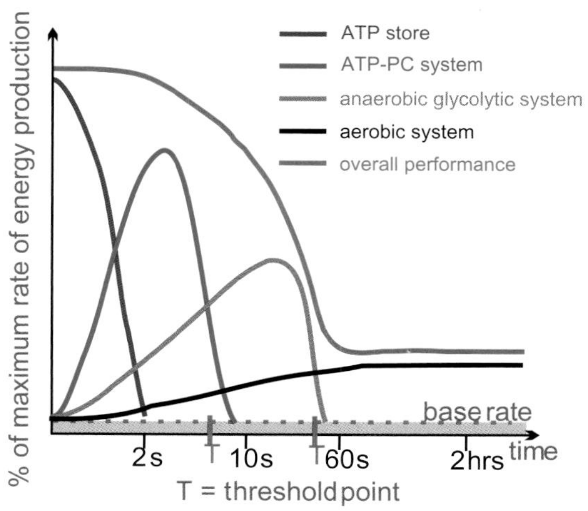

The graph in figure 1.10 shows how the different energy systems contribute resynthesis of ATP during flat-out exercise. Obviously, at reduced intensity of exercise, the contributions will be slightly different. But note that **all systems** are contributing from the start of exercise, only it takes some time for the lactic acid and aerobic systems to get going.

Short-term responses - thresholds

The concept of a **threshold** applies to the time at which one particular system of ATP regeneration takes over from another as the major regenerator of ATP during flat out exercise - marked as **T** in figure 1.10.

- For example, **ATP muscle stores** are depleted **within 2 seconds**, and towards the end of this period the ATP-PC system has risen enough to be able to provide the ATP necessary for the exercise.
- **Peak anaerobic power** is attained within the first 5 seconds of flat-out exercise, but depletion of PC occurs between 7 and 9 seconds.
- At this point, the lactic acid system has risen enough to be able to provide the ATP required for the next 40 seconds or so.

Hence the **threshold** between **ATP-PC and lactic acid** systems occurs between 7 and 9 seconds after the start of an exercise period. The lactate threshold occurs at the highest oxygen uptake or exercise intensity achieved with less than 1.0 mmol increase in blood lactate level concentration above the pre-exercise level.

Long-term training effects - thresholds

It is found that thresholds are **delayed** by training, so that the trained individual has a greater capacity for ATP-PC, has a greater lactic acid toleration, and more efficient ATP regeneration than the untrained person.

Differences in ATP generation in muscle fibres

Intensity and **duration** determine the energy system and hence metabolic mixture and muscle fibre type activation.

High powered activities, such as a 60 metre sprint, and other forceful muscular actions and stop and go activities or change of pace in sports such as basketball, netball, soccer and field hockey depend almost entirely on anaerobic metabolism for high energy release needed to activate the **fast twitch fibres**.

- High energy release is mainly due to **high glycolytic enzyme activity** and **myosin ATPase activity** within the anaerobic glycolytic system.
- Since only **2 ATPs** are produced per molecule of glucose, high powered exercise can only continue for a few seconds before fatigue sets in.
- **Fast twitch muscle fibre type IIb** have a **low aerobic capacity** and therefore quickly **fatigue** during maximal activity.

- **Fast twitch fibres type IIa** possess a relatively **higher aerobic capacity** when compared with type IIb, and so support **increased force** when needed, for example, when running up hills whilst maintaining a constant speed.

- **Slow twitch muscle fibres** generate energy for ATP resynthesis, predominantly by aerobic energy transfer, producing up to **36 ATPs** per molecule of glucose.
- High concentration of **mitochondrial enzymes** and **capillary density** support this fibre's aerobic capacity to **resist fatigue** and power-prolonged aerobic exercise.

- Activities at near maximum aerobic and anaerobic levels, like middle distance running, swimming or multiple sprint sports such as field hockey, soccer basketball and netball, activate both fast twitch and slow muscle fibre types and their relative energy production via both the anaerobic and aerobic pathways.
- Specific exercise training improves the energy-generating capacity of each fibre type.

STUDENT NOTE

Information on the classification and characteristics of muscle fibres types are located in the OCR AS/A1 Student Revision Guide ISBN 9781901424911, Chapter 1 page 30.

Fatigue

Effects of fatigue on performance

Performance can be affected by muscle fatigue, the depletion of energy stores in muscle (and the liver). Various factors contribute to this.

Muscle fatigue

Muscle fatigue can be described as a reduction of muscular performance, and an inability to maintain expected power output. Performance can often be continued at quite a high level in spite of fatigue, but the outcome of 'jelly legs' or 'jelly shoulders' will be well known to all sportspeople after an exhausting performance has been completed.

Depletion of energy stores

- Depletion of **PC** (phosphocreatine) and muscle and liver **glycogen** stores will be the major cause of fatigue.
- Fatigue in marathon runners is due to depletion of **muscle glycogen** in both ST and FT muscle fibres.
- **FT muscle fibres** have low aerobic capacity and therefore **quickly fatigue** during maximal activity. This is because stored ATP and PC are quickly used up (in under 7 seconds) during this sort of activity (weight training, sprinting for example).

figure 1.11 – fatigued athlete

Metabolic accumulation

During intense exercise lasting longer than 7 seconds and under 45 seconds, **accumulation of lactic acid** and CO_2 in muscle cells causes extreme fatigue and complete loss of muscle function. This is because increase in H^+ ions (decrease in pH due to the lactic acid acidity) inhibits both aerobic and anaerobic enzyme activity required for ATP regeneration.

Body fluid balance and dehydration

- Fluid loss **decreases plasma volume** which reduces blood pressure and hence produces a reduction in blood flow to skin and muscles.
- This means that the heart has to work harder, body temperature rises, and **fatigue** occurs.
- Hence **fluid intake is important** during endurance activities (figure 1.12).

Interplay of energy systems during intermittent exercise and factors that affect this interplay

Intermittent or interval exercise is characterised by periods of alternating exercise and rest by manipulating the following factors:
- **Intensity** of the exercise period.
- **Duration** of the exercise period.
- Number of **repetitions**/sets.
- **Length** of the recovery period.

Intensity of the exercise period
Energy production is both **time** (duration) and **intensity** related. Running at a very high intensity, as in sprinting, means that an athlete can operate effectively for only a very short period of time whereas running at a low intensity, as in gentle jogging, means that an athlete can sustain activity for a long period of time. Hence, there is a relationship between exercise intensity and the energy source.

Duration of the exercise period
If the exercise is high intensity and lasts over 2 minutes then both PC and muscle glycogen will become depleted and need repaying. Intensity of exercise will drop as the aerobic system becomes more dominant as observed in figure 1.10, page 17.

For example, the **anaerobic glycolysis** or **lactic acid system** would be predominantly used in netball when a centre works at a high intensity for duration of up to 40 seconds.

This could occur if a team fails to score, resulting in a prolonged period of play. Also during this time most of the PC stores would have been depleted, therefore the body would rely on the anaerobic glycolysis system for energy.

The aerobic system would be predominantly used by a centre in netball in medium to low intensity phases of play when the ball is out of play or when returning for a centre pass when a goal has been scored. An increased level of aerobic fitness would be mean the centre would take longer to reach anaerobic threshold and therefore would maintain anaerobic energy stores for longer which means a higher intensity can be maintained throughout the duration of the game. A higher level of aerobic fitness means that a player will take longer to reach the anaerobic threshold. $\dot{V}O_{2max}$ is a key physiological determinant of an athlete's aerobic fitness.

Length of the recovery period

Intermittent training involves the manipulation of sets and repetitions.

The length of recovery between repetitions is important in the recovery of power output through the resynthesis of PC. For example, during recovery from 6 second sprints, 80% recovery in **peak power output** (PPO) occurs within a one minute recovery and over 90% recovery of PPO in 3 minutes.

Once the PC stores are depleted the body resorts to stored glucose for ATP. The breakdown of glucose or glycogen in anaerobic conditions results in the production of lactate and hydrogen ions. The accumulation of hydrogen ions is the limiting factor causing fatigue in runs of 300 metres to 800 metres.

Sessions to develop this energy system:
- 5 to 8 × 300 metres fast - 45 seconds recovery - until pace significantly slows.
- 150 metre intervals at 400 metre pace - 20 seconds recovery - until pace significantly slows.
- 8 × 300 metres - 3 minutes recovery (lactate recovery training).

Other factors affecting the proportions of the energy systems

Fitness

Individual levels of both aerobic and anaerobic fitness will impact on the predominant energy system being used. Anaerobic training increases key **glycolytic enzymes**, such as phosphofructokinase (PFK), that increase flat-out sprint-power performance. The greater the anaerobic fitness the longer the performer can work in the anaerobic zone.

Aerobic training stresses the cardio-respiratory systems and the metabolic capacity of specific muscles. Trained athletes exercise at lower percentage of their $\dot{V}O_{2max}$ at a given work rate, with delayed OBLA, when compared with untrained individuals.

Fuel food utilisation

Endurance athletes can utilise **FFAs** during prolonged exercise sooner than untrained people. This training adaptation enables the trained athlete to delay the use of glycogen stores and save this energy supply for later on in an exercise effort, or when the intensity of the exercise increases. This is called glycogen sparing and is illustrated in figure 1.14.

A high CHO diet (figure 1.15) would assist replenishment of glycogen stores which would then be available for glycolysis.

Demands of player position

Player position does impact on the proportions of the energy systems used. For example, in a rugby game the front row forwards perform over three times more than outside backs. While the average duration of high intensity efforts are similar, at around five seconds, across all four positional groups, the average rest periods for the forwards are significantly shorter. Since both sets of forwards only get to enjoy around 35 seconds of recovery, their **PC stores** will not be replenished and so the glycolytic energy system will be very important for maintaining the work rate required.

Backs, by contrast, get plenty of recovery time between high-intensity efforts in order to replenish PC stores. Therefore the PC system will be most important for backs.

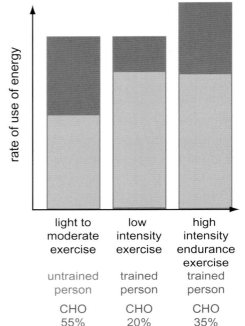

figure 1.14 – contribution of CHO and fats for trained and untrained people

rate of use of energy

light to moderate exercise	low intensity exercise	high intensity endurance exercise
untrained person	trained person	trained person
CHO 55%	CHO 20%	CHO 35%
fats 45%	fats 80%	fats 65%

figure 1.15 – CHO

Tactics and strategies

The 1500 metre running race produces the highest levels of blood and muscle lactate ever recorded in the human, which is a direct consequence of the utilization of the anaerobic energy system. Yet, these races still have an overall aerobic energy contribution of about 75 to 85% even though the phosphocreatine (PC) and lactic acid systems are also vital in race tactics and the final finishing drive to the tape.

Nevertheless, all three of these systems have to be considered, not only when trying to optimize overall speed and performance, but also when considering race tactics and final winning percentage.

Level of competition

Competitions often involve qualifying rounds, for example heats, semi-finals and final for a 400 metres race. Well-trained athletes are able to cruise through qualifying rounds and conserve their maximum effort until the final.

A team may take an early lead in a qualifying round and be able to ease off (increasing the contribution of the aerobic energy system) thus conserving their energy reserves for later matches. In contrast, the opposition team could be working at a higher rate of intensity (increasing the contribution of the anaerobic energy system) and so suffer from the effects of fatigue associated with OBLA (onset of blood lactate accumulation, page 23) sooner.

Size of playing area

Pitch size varies according to the sport. Basketball and netball are played on small courts and are higher intensity games, thereby increasing the contribution of the anaerobic energy systems.

Field hockey, rugby, lacrosse and soccer are played on much bigger pitches and have more players. These two factors enable players to recover quicker between bouts of high intensity exercise, such as a short sprint, and so the duration and intensity of play is predominantly aerobic.

Oxygen consumption during recovery

Bodily processes do not immediately return to resting levels after exercise ceases. The time taken for this to occur is called the **recovery period**. The recovery period is dependent on the intensity and duration of the exercise.

Excess post-exercise oxygen consumption (EPOC)

After every strenuous exercise (figure 1.16), there are **four** tasks that need to be completed before the exhausted muscle can operate at full efficiency again.

- **Replacement of ATP and phosphocreatine** (fast replenishment component).
- **Removal of lactic acid** (slow replenishment component).
- **Replenishment of myoglobin** with oxygen.
- **Replacement of glycogen**.

The first three require oxygen in substantial quantities, hence the need for rapid breathing and a high pulse rate to carry oxygen to the muscle cells.

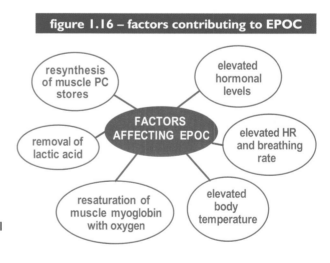

figure 1.16 – factors contributing to EPOC

resynthesis of muscle PC stores

elevated hormonal levels

FACTORS AFFECTING EPOC

removal of lactic acid

elevated HR and breathing rate

resaturation of muscle myoglobin with oxygen

elevated body temperature

The need for oxygen

The need for oxygen to rapidly replace ATP and remove lactic acid is known as the oxygen debt. The more modern term for oxygen debt is **excess post-exercise oxygen consumption** (EPOC) or oxygen recovery. This represents the elevation of the metabolic rate above resting values which occurs after exercise during the recovery period.

EPOC is the excess O_2 consumed following exercise needed to provide the energy required to resynthesise ATP used and remove lactic acid created during previous exercise. EPOC has **two** components (figure 1.17):

- **Alactic or alactacid.**
- **Lactic or lactacid.**

The **oxygen deficit** is the difference between the oxygen required during exercise and the oxygen actually consumed during the activity. The graph in figure 1.17 shows the relationship between oxygen consumption and the time before, during and after exercise.

As an athlete works from light to moderate to high intensities the oxygen deficit will increase. All-out physical effort demands a larger energy requirement than the aerobic processes can supply. Consequently anaerobic energy transfer increases and blood lactate accumulates, with considerable time required to achieve complete recovery to resting values.

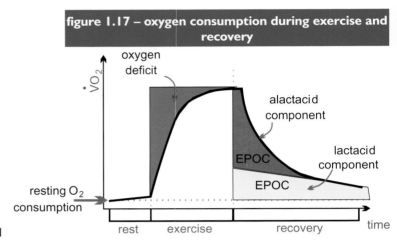

figure 1.17 – oxygen consumption during exercise and recovery

The alactacid component (without lactate build-up)

Figure 1.17 follows a single-component exponential curve termed the fast component of recovery oxygen uptake. This component involves the **conversion of ADP back into PC and ATP**, and is known as **restoration of muscle phosphagen**. This is a very rapid process (120 seconds to full restoration, figure 1.18) and is of size 2 to 3.5 litres of O_2.

Phosphagen recovery

Phosphagen recovery (figure 1.18) is achieved via **three** mechanisms:

- There is **aerobic** conversion of carbohydrates into CO_2 and H_2O to resynthesise ATP from ADP and P_i.
- Some of the ATP is immediately utilised **to create PC** using the coupled reaction: **ATP + C → ADP + PC**.
- A small amount of ATP is **resynthesised via glycogen,** producing small amounts of lactic acid.

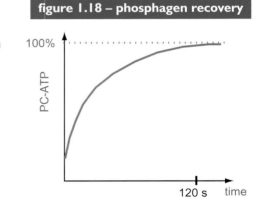

figure 1.18 – phosphagen recovery

Recovery oxygen uptake

During the **post-exercise period**, oxygen recovery is continuous. This is because:
- Muscle myoglobin recovers.
- Temperature falls.
- Hormone levels fall.

During the **recovery period**, temperature and hormone levels are higher than normal (although falling), which:
- Keeps metabolic rate high.
- Keeps respiratory rate high.
- Keeps heart rate high.
- Requires more oxygen than normal.
Hence **EPOC** increases.

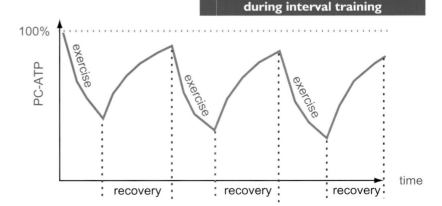

figure 1.19 – phosphagen recovery during interval training

The implications for interval training

- If there is only a short interval between bouts of exercise, the level of phosphagen stores gradually reduces (figure 1.19, page 22) thereby reducing the energy available for the later bouts.

- This stresses the ATP and PC storage and forces the muscle cells to adapt by storing more of these quantities.

- Also, cells will adapt by improving their ability to provide O_2, and hence increase the possible size of the alactic component.

- Anaerobic interval training studies have shown that 30 second bouts of exercise increase the activities of **glycolytic enzymes**, such as phosphorylase, phosphofructokinase and lactate dehydrogenase, from around 10% to 25%.

- This increase in **glycolytic capacity** will allow the muscle to develop greater tension for a longer period of time as the muscle tissue increases its **tolerance to lactate**.

OBLA (Onset of Blood Lactate Accumulation)

As discussed on pages 13 and 14, the anaerobic energy systems have a limited capacity of ATP production. As **work intensity** increases, **lactic acid** starts to **accumulate** above resting values. At a certain point (called the OBLA point) this produces muscle fatigue and pain, since the resultant low pH (high acidity) inhibits enzyme action and cross-bridge formation during muscle contraction. This means in turn that muscle action is inhibited and **physical performance deteriorates**.

The exact cause of OBLA remains controversial:

- It could be due to the point of **muscle hypoxia** or inadequate oxygen.

- It could be due to **muscle lactate accumulation** even in the presence of adequate muscle oxygenation.

- It could be due to **decreased total lactate clearance** or increased lactate production only in specific muscle fibres.

OBLA can be expressed as a percentage of $\dot{V}O_{2max}$ as shown in figure 1.20.

This point governs the **lactate aerobic threshold**.

- In the graph (figure 1.20), as exercise intensity increases and $\dot{V}O_2$ increases, untrained people have blood lactate which increases sharply at about 50% of $\dot{V}O_{2max}$.

- But trained athletes can exercise up to 70% of $\dot{V}O_{2max}$ before lactate concentration in the blood increases markedly.

- Hence **trained athletes** begin **OBLA at higher work intensities** - especially since trained athletes have higher values of $\dot{V}O_{2max}$ than untrained people in the first place.

- All this means that the **lactate aerobic threshold** moves to **higher values of $\dot{V}O_{2max}$**.

Hence OBLA effectively predicts endurance performance.

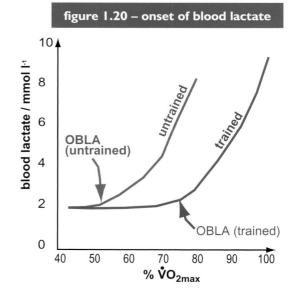

figure 1.20 – onset of blood lactate

Summary of factors affecting OBLA

- **Rate of blood lactate removal**: when removal and production are roughly equal, then blood lactate concentrations should stay constant. Only when production exceeds removal will lactic acid levels rise.

- **Exercise intensity**: as a performer works towards a higher intensity workload it is less likely to be performed aerobically and more likely to be performed **anaerobically** thereby producing lactic acid. Regular anaerobic physical activity increases the ability of the performer to tolerate higher levels of lactate and is able to remove lactic acid more quickly through a process called buffering (a chemical process that converts a strong acid to a weaker acid).

Summary of factors affecting OBLA

- **Muscle fibre type recruited**: slow twitch muscle fibres produce less lactic acid at the same intensity as fast twitch fibres due to increased mitochondria density.

- **Type of fuel being used**: **respiratory exchange ratio** (RER which is an indicator which estimates the fuel type - CHO, fat or protein - being used within a given activity). The closer the value is to 1, the more glycogen is being used and the more likely lactic acid is to be produced.

- **Training status of muscles**: trained muscles will have adaptive responses including more mitochondria, greater capillary density, improved used of FFAs as fuel, and higher myoglobin content, increasing aerobic capacity of muscle and reducing lactic acid production.

Lactacid oxygen recovery

High intensity exercise up to about 60 seconds creates **lactic acid**, and **oxygen is needed** to remove this lactic acid. This process begins to restore muscle and liver glycogen, and is relatively slow with **full recovery** taking up to 1 hour (figure 1.21).

Relatively large amounts of lactic acid (15 to 20 times the resting value of 1 to 2 mmol litre^{-1}) are produced during high intensity exercise, which is removed according to the proportions listed in table 1.2.

A small proportion of EPOC resynthesises lactate to glycogen. This **gluconeogenic** mechanism would probably progress faster during activity in trained individuals, for example an elite 400 metre sprinter.

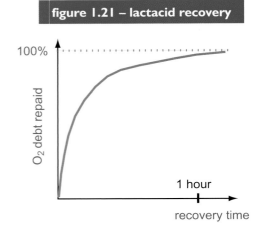

figure 1.21 – lactacid recovery

Removal of the lactic acid

Table 1.2 – **removal of the lactic acid**

oxidation into CO$_2$ + H$_2$O	65%
conversion into glycogen then stored in muscle and liver (Cori cycle)	20%
conversion into protein	10%
conversion into glucose	5%

The lactate shuttle

During the recovery process after intense exercise, a small proportion of the lactic acid produced is recycled back into glucose in the muscle cell. This is the reverse process to glycolysis and requires energy from ATP breakdown.

Buffering

A **blood buffer** is a chemical substance which resists abrupt changes in **hydrogen ion** (H$^+$) concentration. For example, when H$^+$ concentration increases as a result of intense exercise, H$^+$ reacts with oxyhaemoglobin (buffer) to form haemoglobinic acid.

These ions are released when H$^+$ concentration falls. So this is a temporary solution to rapid changes in acidity or alkalinity which would otherwise cause rapid fatigue symptoms.

Restoration of muscle glycogen stores post-exercise and nutrition

- During short duration high intensity exercise, restoration of glycogen takes up to 2 hours, and after prolonged low intensity aerobic exercise, restoration can take days.

When an athlete completes a hard training session, **glycogen depletion** will have taken place. It is essential that a **restoration** of energy stores is completed for recovery of the athlete prior to the next session or competition. Refer to page 29 for post-competition or training nutrition.

Restoration of myoglobin

Muscle myoglobin (an iron protein molecule similar to haemoglobin located in skeletal muscle) serves as a storage site for O_2, and has a temporary but greater affinity for O_2 than haemoglobin. Hence it acts as a **carrier of O_2** from HbO_2 (in blood) to mitochondria (in a muscle cell). Myoglobin is reoxygenated within 2 minutes.

Restoration of muscle myoglobin is important for recovery from high intensity exercise.

During high intensity exercise an increase in the recruitment of low-efficiency type IIb fibres (the fibres involved in the slow component) can cause an increase in the oxygen cost of exercise. A change in the pattern of motor unit recruitment, and thus less activation of type IIb fibres, may also account for a large part of the reduction in the slow component of $\dot{V}O_2$ observed after physical training.

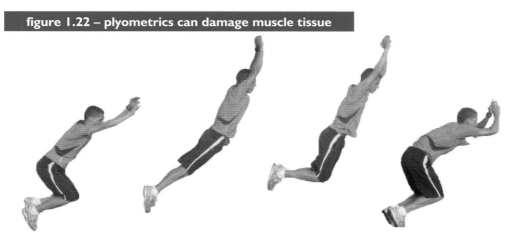

figure 1.22 – plyometrics can damage muscle tissue

Delayed onset of muscle soreness (DOMS)

There is improved oxygen recovery as a result of long-term aerobic training because of **better muscle capillarisation**. If an efficient cool-down is used, **lactic acid removal** is improved, hence there is a reduction in **DOMS**.

Table 1.3 summarises the probable six phases in DOMS development that ultimately lead to an inflammatory process and subsequent recuperation. The soreness usually disappears within about 72 hours of appearing.

If treatment is desired, any measure that increases blood flow to the muscle, such as low-intensity activity, massage and hot baths may help to relieve the symptoms.

Table 1.3 - **the six-phase sequence for DOMS following unaccustomed exercise**

phase	
1	unaccustomed exercise using eccentric muscle actions (downhill running, slowly lowering weights)
2	high muscle force damage sarcolemma causing release of protein enzymes, such as creatine kinase and myoglobin
3	damage to muscle contractile myofibrils and noncontractile structures
4	metabolites (e.g. calcium) accumulate to abnormal levels in the muscle tissue to produce more cell damage and reduce force capacity
5	DOMS considered to result from inflammation, tenderness and pain, the inflammation process begins, the muscle cell heals
6	the adaptive process makes the muscle more resistant to damage from subsequent bouts of the same exercises

Implications of the recovery process on physical activity

Bodily systems do not immediately return to resting levels following most physical activity. How long recovery takes is dependent on the **intensity** and **duration** of the exercise. In light activity, for example, golf, walking and bowling, return to resting conditions takes place rapidly and often progresses unnoticed. Intense physical activity such as running an 800 metres or trying to swim 200 metres flat out requires considerable time for bodily processes to return to resting levels.

An elite athlete utilises the full range of preparatory and recovery techniques in order to reduce the effects of fatigue, thereby enhancing his or her recovery periods between training sessions and competitions.

Recovery is about **restoring balance**, also known as **homeostasis** (figure 1.23) to the body. **Technologies** such as iPhone apps (that measure physiological parameters such as heart rate recovery), and **tactics** and **strategies** are all part of the **training schedule** and lifestyle of an elite athlete.

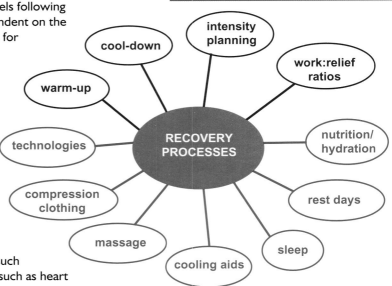

figure 1.23 – the recovery processes

intensity planning · cool-down · work:relief ratios · warm-up · nutrition/hydration · technologies · RECOVERY PROCESSES · rest days · compression clothing · massage · cooling aids · sleep

Warm-up and its role in improving recovery

As discussed on page 12, **all three energy systems** contribute to ATP regeneration during an activity.

A **warm-up** (figure 1.24) is intended to raise the **body temperature** and prepare an athlete **physiologically** and **psychologically** to train or compete in a competitive situation. The **intensity** and **duration** of a warm-up determines which fuel source is the predominant energy supplier.

A warm-up progresses from a light jog and general active stretching into a sport specific section (providing skill rehearsal for the activity). This will be from low to moderate intensity, and can increase muscle and core temperature without inducing fatigue or reducing immediate energy stores.

During the **sport specific** part of a warm-up, short, dynamic skill drills are often rehearsed and energy for this work will be provided via the ATP-PC system and regulated by blood serum creatine kinase (CK) levels (the primary enzyme responsible for regulating anaerobic metabolism).

A finely tuned warm-up will prepare the athlete by minimising the use of the **anaerobic glycolytic energy supply** as an energy source and the associated build up of lactic acid. In turn, the volume of oxygen (needed to pay back the oxygen deficit) will be reduced during the recovery period, resulting in the athlete recovering more quickly.

figure 1.24 – warming-up

Priming exercise and its role in warm-up

Priming exercise is a way of manipulating a warm-up to speed up how quickly the aerobic system starts at the onset of exercise by changing the intensity of the 'pulse raiser' element of the warm-up.

Physiologists refer to this as O_2 **uptake kinetics** (kinetics is the measuring and studying of the rates of reactions), which has recently shown to have predictable positive consequences for performance. There are three factors that are important in priming exercise:

The intensity of the priming exercise

There is some debate about the optimum intensity. Research showing positive benefits from priming has generally shown to be just below or just above the maximum steady state, provided there is a long enough gap between the end of the priming exercise and the start of the performance.

Maximal steady state is defined as the highest blood lactate concentration and work load that can be maintained over time without a continual blood lactate accumulation (figure 1.20, page 23). For priming exercise to improve performance, there is a balance between the effect of priming on the O_2 uptake kinetics. On the one hand this would be due to the predominance of energy supplied via the **aerobic** system, and on the other hand, the extent to which the anaerobic capacity has been depleted without the athlete experiencing **muscle fatigue**.

The intensity of the performance

Priming exercise is of most **benefit** to **anaerobic** activities since the increased oxygen delivery to active tissue cells will delay the onset of OBLA.

For example, a **traditional** track cyclist's warm-up may be anything up to an hour with intense efforts which can result in **significant fatigue** and impair the performance.
Switching on the aerobic energy system to just below maximum steady state (that monitors the intensity in relation to O_2 uptake kinetics by using a shorter and more controlled warm-up) will limit muscular fatigue by reducing the amount of energy sourced from the glycolytic system.

Heart rate and breathing rates will increase progressively, enabling more oxygen to be transported through the blood and used within the working muscles. With increased body temperature, the range of motion around joints will also improve and will get close to the athletes' optimal efficiency very quickly.

For **aerobic** activities, a less intense and shorter warm-up is recommended to prepare the body for steady state performance.

The gap between the end of the priming exercise and the start of the performance

Optimally, a competitive event or activity should begin within several minutes after the end of a warm-up to conserve energy stores and at the same time maintain the physiological benefits of the warm up. Somewhere **between 6 and 20 minutes** has been shown to be effective. Less than six minutes and performers seem to have some residual fatigue. The upper limit is more difficult to gauge but higher intensity priming exercise is still effective with a long break.

In global sporting events, athletes are often required to go to the call room anytime between **20-30 minutes prior** to their events. In this situation, athletes must attempt to **maintain** the effects of the warm-up, often in cramped spaces.

Cool-down following exercise

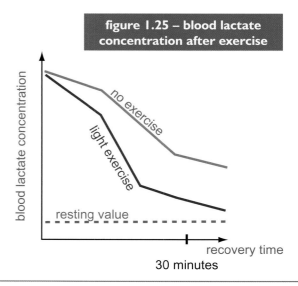

figure 1.25 – blood lactate concentration after exercise

Cool-down (the process of continuing low level exercise immediately after the end of a high intensity exercise bout) **continues to provide oxygen** to skeletal muscle. This therefore **enhances oxidation of lactic acid** and ensures that less lactic acid remains in tissue. Hence there is less muscle soreness (**less DOMS**).

Figure 1.25 shows how **blood lactate** falls after exercise, and that when an active cool-down is undertaken less lactate remains in muscle tissue.

How the immediate time after exercise is spent, is essential to muscle and tissue repair, strength building and overall recovery.

Cool-down prepares the body for the next exercise session.

Intensity planning, work:relief ratios

Work:relief ratio represents the ratio of the work and relief intervals, so a work-relief ratio of 1:2 means that the work interval is half as long as the relief interval (the time between a work interval and the next work interval or set). Knowledge of the recovery process helps in planning and structuring training sessions.

For speed and power athletes, such as jumpers and sprinters who predominantly rely on the ATP-PC system as their source of energy, the full restoration of the PC stores takes only 3 minutes and half is restored in 30 seconds, so a work:relief of 1:3 gives adequate time for ATP and PC stores to resynthesise between bouts of work.

Where athletes are predominantly working with the anaerobic glycolytic energy source, as is the case of an elite 400 metre athlete (figure 1.26), a work:relief ratio of 1:2 is recommended. This gives sufficient time for the athlete to recover before the next repetition and at the same time helps build up lactate tolerance levels. An active recovery, such as **light jogging**, will speed up the recovery process.

figure 1.26 – sprinters need active recovery

For aerobic, endurance-based athletes, such as a 10,000 metre runner, triathlete or long distance swimmer, a work: relief ratio of 1:1 will provide aerobic physiological adaptations (such as an increase in $\dot{V}O_{2max}$), and will also delay OBLA and muscle fatigue.

Short-term and long-term recovery

Short-term recovery

Short-term recovery is sometimes referred to as **active recovery** and occurs in the hours immediately after intense exercise. Active recovery refers to engaging in low-intensity exercise after workouts during both the cool-down phase immediately after a hard workout by maintaining elevated respiratory and cardiovascular levels, as well as during the days following the workout. Both types of active recovery are linked to performance benefits. **Cool-down** is a major way of reducing DOMS, by gradually returning the body to its former resting state. This is achieved by performing low intensity exercise such as jogging and stretching.

Long-term recovery

Most well-designed training schedules will include **recovery days** and **complete rest** from the athlete's chosen sport (particularly at the end of the competitive phase of the periodised year). This is also the reason why athletes and coaches vary a training programme throughout the **periodised year** by adding cross training, modifying workout types, and make changes in variables such as intensity, time, and distance. Both short and long-term recovery are important for optimal sports performance.

Rest, rest days and sleep for improved recovery

Ideal recovery plans include total **rest** and **active recovery**. Rest is an essential component of recovery (known as **passive recovery**), particularly following an intense training session. Most athletes know that getting enough rest after exercise is essential to high-level performance.

Building recovery time, including rest days, into any training programme is important because this is the time that the body adapts to the stress of exercise and the real training effect takes place. Recovery also allows the body to **replenish energy store**s and **repair damaged tissues**.

Exercise or any other physical work causes changes in the body such as muscle tissue breakdown and the depletion of energy stores (muscle glycogen) as well as fluid loss. Recovery time allows these stores to be replenished and allows tissue repair to occur. Without sufficient time to repair and replenish, the body will continue to breakdown from intensive exercise.

Symptoms of overtraining often occur from a lack of recovery time. Signs of overtraining include a feeling of general malaise, staleness, depression, decreased sports performance, and increased risk of injury.

Rest, rest days and sleep for improved recovery

Most elite athletes will train twice a day and have an afternoon nap, aimed at giving the body short-term recovery before the start of the second training session of the day. This is in addition to 8-9 hours sleep. During sleep, blood flow is redirected towards muscles and organs, and carries nutrients, such as amino acids and glucose, that support substantial tissue repair and muscle and liver glycogen restoration.

Nutrition/hydration for improved recovery

STUDENT NOTE

Details of nutritional aids to performance are covered in AS/A1 Revise PE for OCR, ISBN 9781901424911, Chapter 4, page 70 onwards.

figure 1.27 – sports drinks

When an athlete completes a hard training session, **glycogen depletion** will have taken place.
It is essential that a **restoration** of energy stores is completed for recovery of the athlete prior to the next session or competition.

Post-competition or **training nutrition** should consist of:
- A **hypertonic** sports drink (figure 1.27) immediately after exercise has finished.
- This begins **replenishment of blood glucose** and **glycogen** stores.
- A **high CHO** meal within 15 minutes of exercise ending (or as soon as possible) continues glycogen replenishment.
- For optimal recovery, carbohydrate mixed with protein enhances all-round recovery due to an increase in **protein synthesis** post-exercise.
- Many athletes regularly consume sports drinks that are designed to supplement the **energy**, **fluid** and **protein** needs of the athlete.

- **Protein supplements**, such as whey protein, enable muscle hypertrophy and muscle repair following hard training.
- This particularly applies to sports requiring large muscle mass, as in weight lifting and gymnastics.
- During a hard training session **micro muscle tears** occur and can cause **local inflammation**.
- Some foods contain **anti-inflammatory** agents as found in avocados, fish (mackerel and salmon), mixed nuts, seeds and garlic.
- **Avoid** pro-inflammatory foods, such as **processed foods** high in saturated fats, and foods containing trans fats found in cakes, pies and cookies.
- Eat foods that are rich in **vitamins** and **minerals**.

Cooling aids and recovery

STUDENT NOTE

Notes on cooling aids are located in AS/A1 Revise PE for OCR, ISBN 9781901424911, Chapter 4, page 69.

figure 1.28 – ice bath

Cooling aids such as ice baths (figure 1.28), cryotheraphy chambers (page 69) and wet ice towels are commonly used by elite athletes. Cooling aids decrease skin, subcutaneous and muscle temperature, causing narrowing of the blood vessels (vasoconstriction), thereby decreasing cellular metabolism and inflammation, pain and muscle spasm. Contrast water therapy (alternating between cold and warm water) is sometimes employed as a recovery strategy.

Oxygen aids and recovery

Hyperbaric oxygen therapy (HBOT, page 76) is commonly used as a regular recovery treatment within professional sports such as rugby, soccer, cricket.
HBOT delivers up to 25 times normal levels of oxygen to body tissues and so speeds up recovery from fatigue and from DOMS.

Compression clothing and its role in recovery

Compression clothing (figure 1.29) increases **venous return** and $\dot{V}O_{2max}$ during high intensity exercise. Recovery is improved and DOMS reduced. Products include socks, short and long tights and short-sleeve and long-sleeve tops. It is important that the compression garments fit well to get most benefit from wearing them.

Compression stockings are tight at the feet with a gradually looser fit on the leg (graduated compression). Compression stockings are known to decrease post-exercise soreness, by increasing circulation and reducing the lactic acid build-up during the exercise period, thereby reducing **DOMS**. Compression stockings are used to prevent medical conditions such as **deep vein thrombosis** (DVT).

figure 1.29 – compression tights

Massage and recovery

During **massage** (also used in rehab from injury), joints and associated muscles can be passively moved to full range. Massage helps reduce DOMS symptoms. Care must be taken that excessive forces are not applied to traumatised tissue.

Regularly using a **foam roller** offers a much cheaper way and has many of the same benefits as a sports massage, including reduced inflammation, scar tissue and joint stress, as well as improved circulation and improved flexibility (figure 1.30).

Rolling breaks down knots that limit range of motion, it preps muscles for stretching and so is a valuable part of a healthy runner's warm-up and cool-down.

figure 1.30 – roller massage

Modern technology and recovery

For example, **heart rate monitors** have been around for years, but some of the latest models are made with the tech-savvy user in mind (figure 1.31). They upload workout data to an online training log that may even synch with a smartphone to track peak exercise heart rate, average exercise heart rate, recovery heart rate and time spent in different training zones.

figure 1.31 – GPS, HR technology

Tactics and strategies used for recovery purposes

Team sports, such as football and hockey, involve intermittent exercise: with bouts of short, intense activity punctuating longer periods of low-level, moderate-intensity exercise.

High levels of blood lactate may sometimes be observed during a match, but the active recovery periods at submaximal exercise levels allow for its removal on a continual basis. Players can delay play by holding onto possession and by using **set plays** to increase recovery time following a high intensity period of play. The major aim is to maintain the required energy levels needed to complete a match.

Timeouts are one of the tactics which coaches have direct control over in sports such as basketball and netball. During this time, athletes can take on fluids and have tactical direction and be substituted, allowing fatigued players to take a short rest before returning to the match.

In individual sports, elite athletes are conscious of **conserving energy** during qualifying rounds, by just doing enough to qualify for the next round, for example during the heats or semi-final of a 400 metres.

Multi-event athletes, such as heptathletes, need to be able to cope with special technical and tactical demands even as they become fatigued.

Practice questions

1)   Which of the following reactions would liberate the most energy?
   a.   complete oxidation of a molecule of glucose to carbon dioxide and water.
   b.   conversion of a molecule of ADP to ATP.
   c.   respiration of molecule of glucose to lactic acid.
   d.   conversion of a molecule of glucose to carbon dioxide and water.

2)   Which activity below is fuelled primarily by the anaerobic energy system?
   a.   walking for 30 minutes.
   b.   jogging for 50 minutes.
   c.   taking part in an 400 metre race.
   d.   playing football.

3)   Mary runs up a hill for as hard as she can. After two minutes she is so tired she
        cannot continue to run. Physiologically what is happening?
   a.   Mary's aerobic system has been her predominant energy pathway during this bout of physical exertion.
   b.   ATP was produced to fuel muscle contraction using an anaerobic energy pathway and lactic acid has now
        accumulated as a result of this process and is causing her to stop exercising at such a high intensity.
   c.   ATP is being produced by the breakdown of fats and protein and her aerobic conditioning is inadequate
        to meet the demands of this exercise.
   d.   Mary's blood pressure has decreased to the point where she has to stop and this has allowed
        lactic acid to build up in her system.

4)   Which one of the following would result in the greatest decrease in muscle glycogen concentration?
   a.   four 30 second sprint intervals (total time = 2 minutes).
   b.   six 30 second endurance intervals at 100% $\dot{V}O_{2max}$.
   c.   4 minutes of continuous exercise at 100% $\dot{V}O_{2max}$.
   d.   60 minutes of continuous exercise at 75% $\dot{V}O_{2max}$.

5)   Which one of the following would have least effect on the maximal anaerobic capacity of a muscle?
   a.   an increase in muscle glycogen concentration.
   b.   an increase in phosphocreatine (PC) concentration.
   c.   an increase in muscle Na^+/K^+ pump capacity.
   d.   an increase in muscle buffering capacity.

6)   For which of the following sports would a training programme for
        increasing phosphocreatine (PC) stores be least important?
   a.   basketball.
   b.   100 metres track event.
   c.   high jump.
   d.   javelin throw.

7) a)   Define energy, and briefly describe how energy is released from food in the body.   5 marks

   b)   Identify the only form of usable energy in the body.   1 mark

   c)   What is meant by an exothermic reaction? Illustrate this definition with an example.   2 marks

   d)   What is meant by an endothermic reaction? Illustrate this definition with an example.   2 marks

8) Explain the specialist role of mitochondria in energy production.   4 marks

9) Explain the differences between chemical, potential and kinetic energy.   3 marks

Practice questions

10) During any event of low or high intensity, all three energy systems are used. However the physical demands of the event will determine the relative proportions of the energy system(s) being used. Complete the gaps in table 1.4 identifying the major energy systems and examples in sporting activities in relation to performance time. **8 marks**

Table 1.4

Area	Performance time	Major energy systems related to performance time	Examples of type of activity
1	Less than 10 s	ATP –PC	100m sprint / gymnastics vault / discus throw
2	10 –30 s		
3	20 s to 1.5 minutes		
4	1.5 –3 minutes		
5	greater than 3 minutes		

11) An elite swimmer performs a flat-out 100 metre freestyle swim in 50 seconds. Describe how most of the ATP is regenerated during the swim. Sketch a graph which shows the use of the appropriate energy systems against time during the swim. **10 marks**

12) a) Taking part in a triathlon involved swimming, cycling and running. Briefly describe how the aerobic energy system within the cell mitochondria supports this endurance event. **6 marks**

b) Construct a graph which illustrates the food fuel usage against time during a triathlon race lasting 2 hours. **3 marks**

13) Compare the relative efficiency of ATP production via the aerobic and anaerobic routes. Explain your answer. **3 marks**

14) Identify the predominant energy system being used in the following activities: shot put, 200 metres breaststroke, a game of hockey, 100 metres hurdles race, gymnastics vault and modern pentathlon. **6 marks**

15) Figure 1.32 illustrates the contribution of the anaerobic and aerobic energy systems to the total energy requirements for four different track events: 200 metres, 400 metres, 800 metres and 1500 metres.

a) Which column, grey or pink, represents the contribution from the anaerobic system? **1 mark**

b) With reference to the data provided, justify your answer. **3 marks**

c) What is the role of the anaerobic systems in the 1500 metres event? In your response, refer to the data provided. **2 marks**

16) Elite games players require high levels of fitness and psychological preparation, therefore regular fitness testing and after-match performance analysis are common. Using your knowledge of energy systems, outline and explain the relationship between energy sources and intensity of exercise. **20 marks**

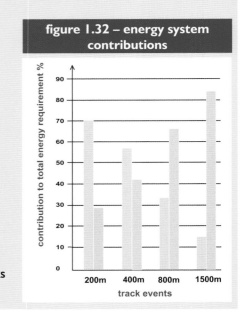

figure 1.32 – energy system contributions

Practice questions

17) The diagram in figure 1.33 is an energy continuum in relation to a variety of sports activities.

a)   Explain the concept 'the energy continuum'.   2 marks

b)   At each end of the continuum examples of sporting activities have been omitted. Give one example of a sporting activity that is predominantly anaerobic and one example of a sporting activity that is predominantly aerobic.   2 marks

c)   Suggest two factors that need to be considered in evaluating sports activities on the basis of their relative position on the energy continuum.   2 marks

d)   Explain, using specific examples, why a game of hockey has aerobic and anaerobic components.   4 marks

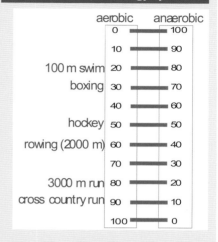

figure 1.33 – variation in contribution of energy system

18) Competitive swimmers will often compete in several events and suffer from fatigue due to limited recovery time. Explain the possible causes of fatigue during a race.   6 marks

19) Figure 1.34 shows oxygen uptake of an elite games player undertaking exercise followed by a recovery period.

a)   Using the appropriate letters, identify the oxygen deficit and Excess Post Oxygen Consumption (EPOC).   3 marks

b)   Why does the elite player incur an oxygen deficit during exercise?   2 marks

c)   Excess Post Oxygen Consumption (EPOC) is considered to have two components. State two aims of the first component and explain how this component is achieved.   4 marks

d)   Describe the process of ATP production that restores the oxygen debt or EPOC.6 marks

figure 1.34 – oxygen consumption during exercise and recovery

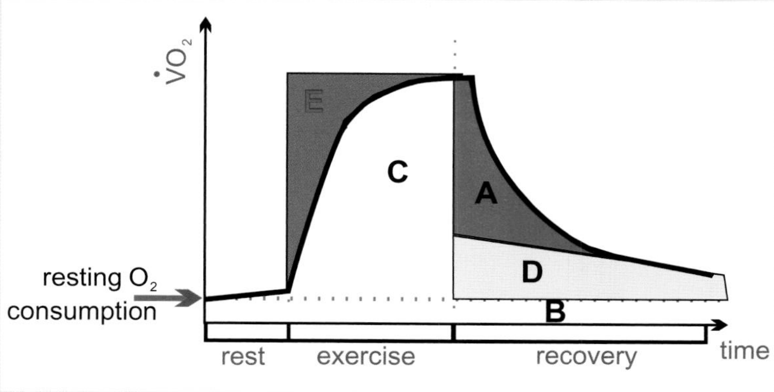

Practice questions

20) An elite games player performs an interval training session during which the rate of muscle phosphagen levels during the recovery period was recorded. Results from this training session are given in table 1.5.

a) Using the results in table 1.5, plot a graph of recovery time against the percentage of muscle phosphagen restored.   3 marks

b) What resting value would you recommend for a full recovery, and what would be the effect of restarting the exercise after 30 seconds?   2 marks

c) Part of the recovery mechanism after anaerobic exercise involves myoglobin. Explain the function of myoglobin during the recovery process.
          3 marks

Table 1.5 – **muscle phosphagen during recovery**

recovery time / s	muscle phosphagen restored / %
10	10
30	50
60	75
90	87
120	93
150	97
180	99
210	101
240	102

21) How could information on oxygen debt recovery be of use to an athlete and coach in designing training sessions?   5 marks

22) A high anaerobic capacity is important to any team player. Outline the physiological processes that will happen during a 30 minute recovery phase following an intense period of anaerobic exercise and discuss their implications when planning anaerobic interval training sessions.   20 marks

23) A friend comments 'I workout with free weights and swim regularly, yet on the odd occasion when I do some hill running, my leg muscles are sore a day or two after the event'. Explain why this is so.   4 marks

24) How can an understanding of the energy systems assist in the planning of a warm-up routine?   10 marks

25) How can priming for exercise assist an athlete in the planning of a warm-up routine?   6 marks

26) Discuss how elite athletes utilise recovery techniques as part of their training programmes.   20 marks

27) Discuss factors affecting the proportions of energy systems during low and high intensity exercise.   20 marks

28) How can a knowledge and understanding of excess post exercise oxygen consumption assist a coach in maintaining the training efficiency for his or her athlete?   10 marks

Answers link: http://www.jroscoe.co.uk/downloads/a2_revise_pe_ocr/OCRA2_ch1_answers.pdf

CHAPTER 2: *Environmental effects on body systems*

Exercise at altitude

STUDENT NOTE

Refresh your knowledge on gaseous exchange in relation to the oxyhaemoglobin curve located in AS/A1 Revise PE for OCR, ISBN 9781901424911, Chapter 3, page 52.

Altitude is the height of an object or point in relation to sea level.

Altitude training is the practice, used by endurance athletes, of training at high altitude for several weeks. The majority of altitude training centres for Olympic sports are located between 1600 and 2400 metres above sea level. Bekele's training camp in Ethopia is at 2566 metres above sea level.

The main interest for altitude training is its potential role on performance. On one hand, altitude training is absolutely necessary to complete performance in competitions or expeditions at altitude. On the other hand, the effect of altitude training and maximal work capacity are sustained by a basic knowledge of the physiological effects of altitude on the human body and the benefits derived for sea level competitions.

Hypoxia is a condition, experienced at altitude, in which the body or a region of the body is deprived of adequate oxygen supply at the tissue level. When athletes are exposed to hypoxia at an altitude greater than 1200 metres, their aerobic potential becomes limited.

$\dot{V}O_{2max}$ is significantly reduced at an altitude as low as 600 metres above sea level in elite-endurance athletes who will suffer from arterial hypoxemia (oxygen deficiency in arterial blood) during maximal and submaximal exercise.

figure 2.1 – effects of altitude

Effects of altitude on the cardiovascular and respiratory systems

The physiological response to altitude is centrally governed in response to oxygen availability. The higher the altitude (figure 2.1), the more an aerobic performance is affected by lack of oxygen pressure in the air.

This is because pO_2 (partial pressure of oxygen in the atmosphere, which relates to the density of oxygen molecules in the atmosphere) decreases proportionately to the decrease in barometric pressure ascending to higher elevations.

Reduced pO_2 and accompanying hypoxia precipitate the immediate adjustments to altitude and the longer-term process of acclimatisation. The inherent nature of the **oxyhaemoglobin dissociation curve** dictates only a small change in haemoglobin's percentage saturation with decreasing pO_2 until 3048 metres.

However this small drop significantly impedes physical performance. When an athlete exercises at altitude (figure 2.1) he or she will have to work harder (the aerobic system will be taxed that much harder) to achieve the same sea level performance (figure 2.2).

figure 2.2 – effects of altitude

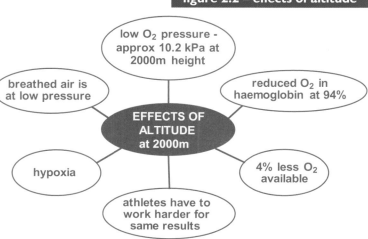

The physiological responses to altitude exposure

Immediate adjustment to altitude hypoxia

Arrival at elevations of 2300 metres and higher, initiates two rapid **physiological** adjustments to compensate for thinner air and accompanying reduction in alveolar pO_2 and impaired muscle O_2 delivery:

Hyperventilation
* The body reacts quickly to hypoxia by increasing the ventilatory drive.
* **Hyperventilation** accounts for approximately two-thirds of the increase in tidal volume and one-third of the increase in breathing frequency in an attempt to maintain oxygen consumption.

* Hyperventilation increases the output of carbon dioxide without increasing its metabolic production.
* It results in a **decrease in alveolar pCO2** and a corresponding **increase in alveolar pO2**. This change in alveolar gas is one of the most important reactions of the body in the early stages of acclimatisation.

* Increasing the flow of fresh air through the lungs increases the rate at which CO_2 is lost.
* Because CO_2 is an acid gas, losing more of it from the blood leaves the blood relatively alkaline. At altitudes up to about 6000 metres the kidneys correct the alkalinity of the blood over a few days by removing alkali (in the form of bicarbonate ions, HCO_3^-) from the blood.

Increased cardiac response
* As soon as a person arrives at altitude, **resting heart rate** and **cardiac output** increase in line with the level of hypoxia, whilst stroke volume and maximum cardiac output remain the same or decrease slightly.
* During acclimatisation to altitude, cardiac output and resting heart rate decrease gradually and return to values close to those observed at sea level. **Blood pressure** generally stays within the normal limits.

Longer-term adjustments to altitude hypoxia

Acclimatisation is the process in which an individual adjusts to a change in its environment. The rate of altitude acclimatisation depends on the terrestrial elevation.

Vascular adaptations
* The first adaptation in the blood is an increase in **erythrocyte production** and **haemoglobin concentration**.
* **Hypoxia** induces the kidneys to release erythropoietin (EPO), which stimulates the proliferation of erythrocytes (red blood cells). These blood modifications increase haemoglobin-based oxygen transport.

* Another mechanism to increase oxygen transport by erythrocytes is via 2,3-diphosphoglycerate, a metabolic by-product that influences the oxygen-binding curves of haemoglobin, thereby improving oxygen extraction at the tissue level.

* Also, there is a reduction in plasma volume, a slower long-term adaptation to living at altitude.

* The effect of increased manufacture of red blood cells and reduced plasma volume is to increase the **haemoglobin concentration** in the blood flowing to active tissue, and hence the oxygen-carrying capacity of the blood.

* Sea level residents, who train at altitude, are found to adapt by producing more haemoglobin at a rate of 1% to 2% per week.

Vascular adaptations

Figure 2.3 summarises the oxygen transport system at sea level and at altitude, both before and after acclimatisation.

Figure 2.3 A represents the situation at sea level, for a normal unathletic person.

Figure 2.3 B represents the situation at altitude for someone not acclimatised.

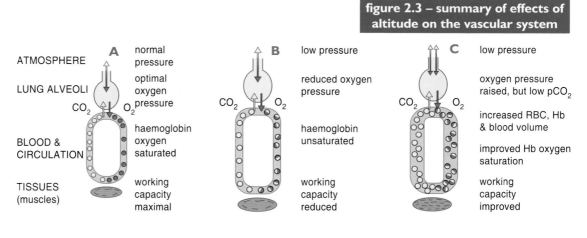

figure 2.3 – summary of effects of altitude on the vascular system

Figure 2.3 C represents the situation at altitude for an acclimatised person.

Muscular structure adaptations

• Skeletal muscles undergo a number of changes at altitude, depending on the duration and intensity of altitude exposure. These changes compensate for the lack of oxygen in the atmosphere.

• Hypoxia stimulates capillary growth around the muscle cells and a reduced distance between the capillary bed and the centre of the muscle-fibre surface which further improves the **oxygen diffusion** into the working tissue, and enhance the muscles' metabolic activity.

• It is thought that this phenomenon begins during very intense training at altitudes between 2000 and 3000 metres, contributing to the reduction in maximal force capacity.

Metabolic adaptations

There is an increased reliance on CHO oxidation, thought to be the result of increased circulation of **epinephrine** at the beginning of altitude exposure and increased insulin sensitivity to improve muscle glucose transport.

From a practical point of view, CHO plays a crucial role during recovery from training sessions at altitude and so increased intake of CHOs is highly recommended.

Figure 2.4 summarises aerobic tissue adaptation produced by exposure to altitude training.

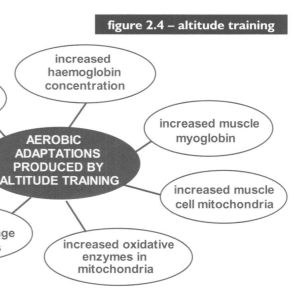

figure 2.4 – altitude training

• There is an increase of up to 16% in **myoglobin** content within muscle cells.

• There is also an increase in numbers of **mitochondria** and **oxidative enzymes** (such as **pyruvate dehydrogenase**) within the **mitochondria** to improve the working capacity of muscles.

• This happens because the efficiency of gaseous exchange improves **within muscle cells** for the sea level dweller that spends some time at altitude.

• Hence he or she would improve **aerobic** athletic performance and oxygen recovery after exercise.

Metabolic adaptations

This is why today's endurance athletes (long distance runners, cyclists and tri-athletes) try to spend a period of time before competitions living and training at altitude, before returning to sea level, where the extra oxygen carrying capacity of their blood would help improve the intensity and duration of their aerobic activity.

Anaerobic performances are not altered at altitude and they may even improve. For example, in speed events such as sprints and jumps, performance are favoured by the reduced air resistance.

Altitude training and acclimatisation

Athletes who travel to altitude for training purposes are at risk of suffering the detrimental effects of altitude. In addition to altitude sickness (hypoxia), weight loss, immune suppression and sleep disturbance may serve to limit athletic performance.

On arrival at altitude it is necessary to evaluate the different athletic capacities. For example, a progressive maximal running test can be used to evaluate aerobic capacity and short-term recovery until maximal running speed is regained.

Initially the principle is to double the recovery times between interval training sessions performed at sea level. Repeated testing during such a training period can be used to define the recovery time necessary for interval training sessions, and hence coaches can plan the recovery process needed by their athletes. Regular blood sampling will indicate changes in red blood cell count.

An altitude training programme needs to take in account the timing of altitude training in relation to the sea level competitive programme, all of which will be programmed into the athlete's periodised year.

The following points summarise a typical schedule for an elite endurance athlete:

figure 2.5 –
Sir Mo Farah

- Most elite athletes have a minimum of 2 **training blocks** or visits per year, one long training block of between 4-6 weeks during the preparation training phase, and then a shorter block of between 2-3 weeks just prior to a major competition. During a second visit the body adapts more quickly.

- Some elite athletes spend several weeks training at altitude. For example, Sir Mo Farah spends up to three months at a time training at altitude in Kenya's Rift Valley (2400 metres) and in Bekele's training camp in Ethopia (2,566 metres) preparing for key sea level events such as the London Marathon figure 2.5.

- **Short-term symptoms** to altitude exposure include headaches and dizziness and increased breathing and heart rates. The key is to adjust gradually (**acclimatise**) to higher altitude.
- During the first week of altitude training an elite athlete would normally work at between 60-70% of sea level intensity thus avoiding very hard lactate sessions.
- During the second week, the training would increase to full intensity (within days 10-14) and continue until returning to sea level. This would include 'tapering' or reducing the workload during the final couple of days just prior to a major competition. Paula Radcliffe chose to compete 2 days after returning to sea level.

- The process of altitude training will stimulate production of more **haemoglobin** and bigger increases in **myoglobin**, **mitochondria** and **oxidative enzymes** than at sea level in the way outlined above.

- Hence on return to sea level the sportsperson would have **increased** $\dot{V}O_{2max}$ and tissue cell respiration, leading to enhanced aerobic performance.

- The optimum time to compete is within 2 to 14 days of return to sea-level. After this, the adaptations gradually return to sea-level norms over a period of weeks, depending on the time spent at altitude and the individual's basic physiological state.

Acclimatisation to extreme altitude

An **acclimatisation schedule** is also necessary when ascending to extreme altitude. For example, acclimatising to the thin air at high altitude is necessary for a successful ascent of Mount Everest. It is recommended that climbers spend at least four weeks at Base Camp at around 5,000 metres. Once an ascent has started, climbers make use of different camps as they adjust to higher altitudes. From Base Camp, most climbers require about four days to ascend Mount Everest at 8,848 metres above sea level. More than 4,000 people have climbed Mount Everest, but fewer than 200 have done so without supplementary oxygen support.

Hypobaric chambers

Hypobaric chambers, such as a hypobaric house, represent an approach to creating an 'altitude' environment at sea level conditions. An athlete lives and sleeps in a hypoxic environment and trains and exercises outside the chamber. This has the effect of elevating EPO, red blood cells levels (hence haemoglobin), myoglobin, mitochondria and oxidative enzymes in a similar way to altitude training and hence the same physiological benefits.

Intermittent Hypoxia Training (IHT)

IHT is achieved using **aerobic** and **anaerobic interval training methods** alternating between low oxygen air and normal air, using a mask attached to an altitude generator. Although substantially different from sleeping at altitude, the goal of IHT is the same by improving aerobic performance.

Exercise in the heat

Thermoregulation

Thermoregulation is the ability to maintain body temperature within certain boundaries, even when the surrounding temperature is very different. The acceptable range is between 36.1 and 37.8°C.

The **thermoregulatory centre** is situated in the hypothalamus - in the brain. Changes in body temperature such as those caused by exercise, are sensed by central and peripheral receptors, and body temperature is maintained by balancing heat input and heat loss. Figure 2.6, and table 2.1 list the heat energy transfer methods from the human body.

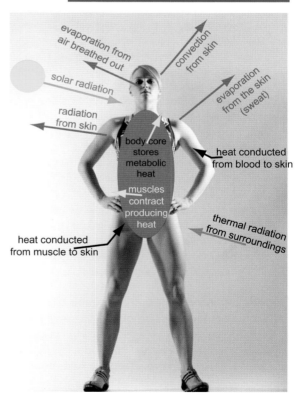

figure 2.6 – heat input and output

Table 2.1 – **heat energy transfer methods**

heat input	heat output
metabolic heat	radiation
exercise	conduction
shivering	convection
solar radiation	evaporation

The proportions of different methods of heat energy transfer are different between at rest and during exercise, and are set out in table 2.2.

Table 2.2 – **proportions of the different methods of heat energy transfer from the body**

mechanism of heat loss	% of total at rest	% of total during exercise
conduction & convection	20	15
radiation	60	5
evaporation	20	80

Thermoregulation

- Activity of the sweat glands is controlled by **autonomic nerves** which in turn are controlled by the thermoregulatory centre (figure 2.7).
- Increased **skeletal muscle activity** increases the core temperature by increasing **metabolic heat** production.
- Increased **sweat gland activity** decreases the core temperature by increasing **evaporative heat loss** (as in table 2.2).
- **Smooth muscle** in the **skin arterioles** can cause these vessels to **vasodilate** to direct blood to the skin for heat transfer out of the body, or **vasoconstrict** to retain heat energy deep within the body.

- The **amount of heat generated** during tissue respiration depends mainly on the volume (therefore the **mass**) of the body.
- Because most of the heat is lost through the skin, the **surface area of the skin** determines the amount of heat lost.
- Hence the effectiveness of the mechanisms of body temperature control depend on the **surface area to mass ratio** of the body.
- Small people (children, gymnasts, distance runners, jockeys) therefore will lose temperature much more quickly than large people (weight lifters, sumo wrestlers, throwers, rugby players).

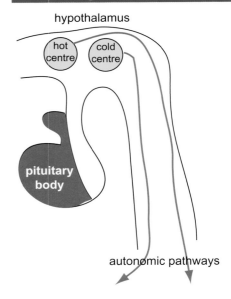

figure 2.7 – summary of main thermoregulatory mechanisms

hypothalamus

hot centre

cold centre

pituitary body

autonomic pathways

Exercising in hot conditions

Cardiovascular adjustments and evaporative cooling facilitate metabolic heat dissipation during physical activity, particularly in hot weather.

- Under hot conditions the surrounding temperature can exceed both skin and core temperature.
- This makes **evaporation** the predominant method of heat loss compared with conduction, convection and radiation.
- Skin cooling occurs when sweat evaporates, so exercising in hot dry climates feels more comfortable than in cooler but more humid tropical conditions.
- This is because in humid conditions the presence of high water vapour in the surrounding air suppresses evaporation even though large quantities of sweat bead on the skin.

- The practice of removing sweat with a towel before sweat evaporates will hinder evaporative cooling, since lack of moisture on the skin will mean that no evaporative cooling can take place.
- Sweating produces **loss of water** and **electrolytes** which initiates hormonal adjustments to conserve salts and fluids.

- Fluid conservation makes urine more concentrated during heat stress.
- The kidneys release the sodium-conserving hormone **aldosterone** that acts in the renal tubules to increase sodium reabsorption.
- **Vasopressin** (antidiuretic hormone) increases permeability of the collecting tubules of the kidneys to facilitate fluid retention.

- Hence a physically active person is vulnerable to the dangerous state of **dehydration** and **increased core temperature** (**hyperthermia**).
- The extreme result ends in circulatory failure, with core temperature increasing to lethal levels.

Adequate fluid intake before, during and after exercise is important. Fluid is needed to preserve plasma volume, maintain circulation and reduce the effects of the cardiovascular drift.

Cardiovascular drift

Two competitive cardiovascular demands exist when exercising in hot weather:

- Oxygen delivery to active muscles must increase to sustain energy metabolism.
- Peripheral blood flow to skin must increase to transport metabolic heat generated during physical activity for dissipation at the body's surface, with the blood no longer available to active muscles.

With **prolonged aerobic exercise**, at a constant exercise intensity such as marathon racing or **aerobic exercising in a hot environment**, stroke volume gradually decreases and heart rate increases, and hence cardiac output remains approximately constant as in figure 2.8. During this process arterial blood pressure declines. These responses are due to the need to transfer excess heat produced by active tissues from deep in the body (known as the core) to the skin where it has access to the outside environment. This heat is moved by the blood during **vasodilation** of blood vessels directly underneath the skin.

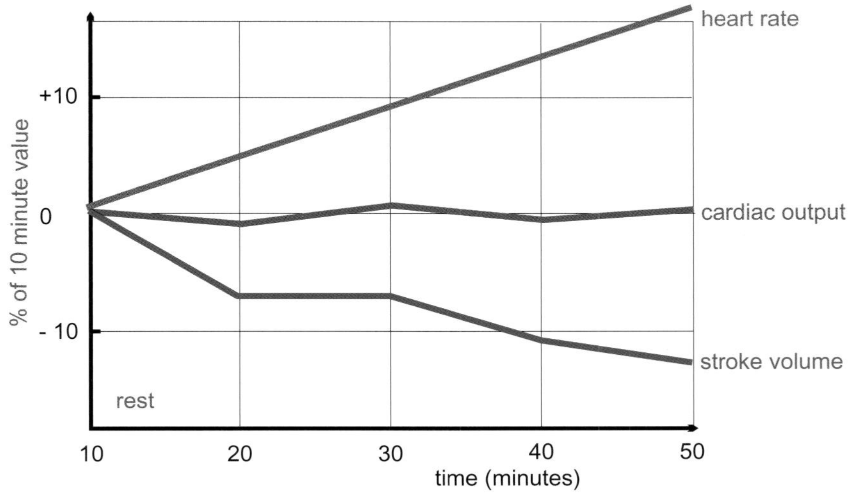

Evaporation is the primary route for heat dissipation and so as fluid or sweat evaporates heat is lost. Loss of fluid results in a reduced plasma volume and subsequent decreased venous return and stroke volume. A **reduced stroke volume** initiates a compensatory **heart rate increase** to maintain a **nearly constant cardiac output** as exercise progresses. All these circulatory responses are collectively referred to as the **cardiovascular drift**.

figure 2.8 – cardiovascular drift in response to moderate exercise

heart rate

cardiac output

stroke volume

% of 10 minute value

+10

0

- 10

rest

10   20   30   40   50

time (minutes)

Core temperature can increase as a result of heat generated by active muscles. A modest increase in core temperature is favourable in creating cardiovascular adjustments illustrated in figure 2.8. Arterial blood pressure remains constant during physical activity in hot temperatures.

The effects of heat and humidity are different for high intensity, short duration activities such as a sprint or jumps competition where there is little or no effect. Whilst the performance is unaffected, power athletes can take advantage of shade and liquid intake between rounds.

It is important for athletes to **rehydrate** (figure 2.9) with sports drinks (water containing a little sodium and glucose) during prolonged exercise periods or whilst performing aerobic exercise in a hot environment to minimise the loss of fluids and thus reduce the effects of the cardiovascular drift.

figure 2.9 – rehydrate in hot conditions

Effect of heat stress on the respiratory system

Exposure to heat stress is accompanied by marked alterations in breathing, especially by an increase in **breathing frequency** and a decrease in **tidal volume**. This ventilatory response results from an increase in central output from the hypothalamus (figure 2.7, page 40), an increase in peripheral output via skin temperature receptors, an increase in central or/and peripheral chemoreceptor output or sensitivity and can be also mediated through changes in thermoregulatory mechanisms.

As more moisture is drawn from the mucus membranes to moisten dry air, the nasal membrane can dry out quickly. This reaction causes the mucus membranes to create mucus faster than it can be processed, causing a backup of mucus in the nasal cavities. As the cavity fills up, it blocks off the air passageway, causing difficulty breathing through the nose. This leads to **dehydration** and **constriction of the airways**, resulting in a decrease in **pulmonary volume** (required for gaseous exchange) which is unable to match the oxygen cost of the physical activity.

Effect of heat stress on the respiratory system

During recovery from exercise, the resistance of the respiratory tract to airflow remains significantly lower when compared with recovery in cooler temperatures, hence recovery takes longer.

Sunlight and high temperatures can aid the conversion of air pollutants to different substances, for example, nitrogen oxide to nitrogen dioxide. **Nitrogen dioxide** impacts on the respiratory system causing **inflammation** of the airways, thus making breathing more difficult. Marathon runners may experience the effects of this type of chemical pollution when taking part in a city marathon in a hot climate where traffic density is high.

High temperatures can cause air to become stagnant (not move) in the lungs, and can trap pollutants in the air, which can also cause an asthma flare-up, coughing and wheezing.

Dehydration and heat stress

figure 2.10 – heat stress

Dehydration occurs when the body loses more fluid than it can take in. Athletes exposed to heat can sweat between one and two litres/hr^{-1}, and most athletes drink less than they sweat.

During prolonged exercise in the heat, water may be lost as a result of sweating (3-5%), and when dehydration exceeds 3% of total body water (2% of body mass) then aerobic performance is impaired, resulting in dehydration (figure 2.10). Changes in body weight indicate water loss and adequacy of rehydration during and following exercise in hot conditions. Dehydration is associated with dark yellow urine with a strong odour, whereas hydrated individuals typically produce large volumes of light-coloured urine without a strong smell.

Dehydration induced by 2 to 3 hours of intense physical effort in the heat often reaches levels that impede heat dissipation and severely comprises cardiovascular function and performance capacity.

Sweat rates during exercise in the heat vary dramatically depending on the metabolic rate, environmental conditions and heat acclimatisation status. Whilst values ranging from 1.0 to 1.5 l hr^{-1} are common for athletes performing vigorous exercise in hot environments, certain individuals can exceed 2.5 l hr^{-1}. For example, predicted sweating rates for an athlete weighing 70 kg running at 12.5 km hr^{-1}, dry temperature 18°C is 1.02 l hr^{-1}, as opposed to the same athlete running at the same speed, in dry heat of 28°C is 1.12 l hr^{-1}, an increase of 11.2% loss in body fluids.

Hot humid environments impede the effectiveness of evaporative cooling from high ambient air vapour pressure, with such environments promoting large fluid losses.

Consequences of dehydration and heat stroke

When plasma volume decreases as dehydration progresses, peripheral blood flow and sweating rate also decrease to make the body's control of thermoregulation progressively more difficult. This potentially can lead to heat stroke.

Performance fatigue can occur from reduced plasma volume, which in turn increases heart rate, electrolyte imbalance, perception of effort and core temperature.

Signs and **symptoms** of dehydration and heat stroke include:
- Intense thirst.
- Fatigue.
- Cramps.
- Lethargy.
- Irritability.
- Loss of coordination.
- Faintness/dizziness.
- Altered consciousness.

Treatment for heat stroke is to place the victim in a shady area, remove unnecessary clothing, apply cool or tepid water to the skin, fan the victim to promote sweating and evaporation, and place ice packs under the armpits and groin.

Heat stress and energy supply

The net response of the cardiovascular and respiratory systems to heat stress is that aerobic energy production decreases, whilst anaerobic respiration increases (which is reliant on the use of CHO as the main fuel food). This depletes glycogen stores more rapidly and increases fatigue levels thereby limiting the endurance capacity of the athlete.

Pre-exercise hydration

Resting and well-fed humans are generally well-hydrated, and the typical variance in day-to-day total body water fluctuates from 0.2% to 0.7% of body mass. When exposed to heat stress in the days preceding competition, it may, however, be advisable to remind athletes to drink sufficiently and **replace electrolyte losses** to ensure that rehydration (normal state of body water content) is maintained. Generally, drinking 6 ml of water per kg of body mass is advisable during this period every 2–3 h, as well as 2–3 hours before training or competition in the heat.

figure 2.11 – sports drinks

Exercise hydration

It is important for athletes to pre-hydrate and rehydrate with sports drinks (water containing a little sodium and glucose (figure 2.11) during prolonged exercise periods or whilst performing in a hot environment to minimise the loss of fluids.

In competition settings, hydration is dependent on several factors, including fluid availability and the specificities of the events. For example, while tennis players have regular access to fluids due to the frequency of breaks in a match, other athletes such as marathon runners, have less opportunity to rehydrate (figure 2.12).

figure 2.12 – taking in water throughout a marathon

Cooling strategies and heat stress

Skin cooling will reduce cardiovascular strain during exercise in the heat, while whole-body cooling can reduce organ and skeletal muscle temperatures and return the core temperature gradually.

Cooling garments

Ice-cooling jackets (packed with ice or chemical coolants - figure 2.13) are used to cool athletes before or during exercise by lowering skin temperature, and thus reducing cardiovascular strain and, eventually, heat storage. Cooling garments are practical in reducing skin temperature without reducing muscle temperature, and athletes can wear them during warm-up, in competitive situations or recovery breaks.

Wet-ice packs

Water is a much better conductor of heat energy than air or plastic. By being wet, the **wet-ice pack** allows for greater heat energy transfer out of the body compared to gel or chemical packs. For example, tennis players use wet-ice packed towels during match intervals in long hot matches.

figure 2.13 – use of ice jackets in a competitive situation

Cold fluid ingestion

Cold fluids can potentially enhance endurance performance when ingested before, but not during exercise.

Heat acclimatisation

Heat acclimatisation describes the improved tolerance as a result of physiological adaptive changes over the course of 7 to 14 days that are specific to the climatic heat stress and are beneficial to exercise in the heat and allow the body to better cope with heat stress. Today, many elite athletes can prepare for competitions by training in artificially hot indoor environment. The principle underlying any heat acclimatisation protocol is an increase in body (core and skin) temperature to induce profuse sweating and increase skin blood flow.

Main recommendations for heat acclimatisation

- Athletes planning to compete in hot ambient conditions should heat acclimatise (i.e. repeated training in the heat) to obtain biological adaptations lowering physiological strain and improving exercise capacity in the heat.
- Heat acclimatisation sessions should last **at least 60 min/day**, and induce an increase in body core and skin temperatures, as well as stimulate sweating.
- Athletes should train in the same environment as the competition venue, or if not possible, train indoors in a hot room.

- Early adaptations are obtained within the first few days, but the main physiological adaptations are not complete until a second week of heat exposure.
- Ideally, the heat acclimatisation period should pass 2 weeks in order to maximise all benefits.

- Athletes should wear suitable **clothing** that allows for heat dispersement.

- Athletes should **rehydrate** as much as possible using hypotonic and hypertonic solutions to replace fluids, glucose and electrolytes lost through sweat.

Table 2.3 - **summarises the main physiological adaptations that occur during heat acclimatisation**.

acclimatisation response	effect
improved cutaneous blood flow	transports metabolic heat from deep tissues (core) to shell
effective distribution of cardiac output	appropriate circulation to skin and muscles to meet demands of metabolism and thermoregulation resulting from greater blood pressure stability during exercise
lowered threshold for start of sweating	evaporative cooling begins early in exercise
more effective distribution of sweat over skin surface	optimum use of effective body surface for evaporative cooling
increased sweat output	maximises evaporative cooling dilute sweat preserves electrolytes in body fluid outside the cells
lower skin and core temperatures and heart rate for standard exercise	frees greater proportion of cardiac output to the active muscles
less reliance on CHO catabolism during exercise	glycogen sparing

Practice questions

1) Which one of the following will be encountered after an individual is acclimatized to high altitude?
   a. blood pH is higher than normal.
   b. there is an increase in red cell count.
   c. cardiac output at rest is higher than that at sea.
   d. periodic breathing may occur, especially during sleep.

2) Which one of the following is not an aerobic adaptive response to altitude training?
   a. improved working capacity of muscles.
   b. increased muscle myoglobin.
   c. increased utilisation of fast twitch motor units.
   d. increased haemoglobin concentration.

3) Which hormone is responsible for maintaining water and electrolyte balance in the human body?
   a. aldosterone.
   b. insulin.
   c. glycagon.
   d. human growth hormone.

4) A heat-acclimatized athlete and an untrained subject are exercising in the same room and at the same absolute power output. Which one of the following statements is true?
   a. to help prevent dehydration, the athlete allows her core temperature to increase to a greater extent than the untrained subject before she begins sweating.
   b. skin blood flow will increase earlier in the untrained subject than in the athlete.
   c. sweating and increased skin blood flow will occur earlier in the athlete than in the untrained subject.
   d. none of the above.

5) Which one of the following does not lead to an increase in body's core temperature?
   a. a reduction in plasma volume.
   b. a decrease in sympathetic nervous activity.
   c. a decrease in the amount of cutaneous blood flow.
   d. an increase in cardiac output.

6) Altitude training is used by some marathon runners as part of their physiological preparation for sea level racing. Discuss whether altitude training is always beneficial to marathon runners.   8 marks

7) a) Describe the conditions at altitude that could limit performance.   3 marks

   b) An elite group of endurance athletes spend three weeks training at 2400 metres. What major physiological responses and adaptations would they expect during this period of acclimatisation?   8 marks

8) Discuss immediate and longer-term physiological adjustment to altitude exposure.   10 marks

9) Discuss whether altitude training produces greater improvement than sea-level training on a sea-level exercise programme.   8 marks

10) a) Define what is meant by the term acclimatisation.   1 mark

    b) Discuss the importance of acclimatisation when exercising in a hot environment.   4 marks

    c) Identify three short-term physiological adaptive changes that improve heat tolerance, following a period of heat acclimatisation.   3 marks

Practice questions

11) The cardiovascular adjustment to heat stress is a phenomenon termed cardiovascular drift. Explain how the cardiovascular drift helps maintain a nearly constant cardiac output during submaximal activity, lasting more than 15 minutes in hot conditions. 5 marks

12) Discuss the role of the thermoregulatory centre in maintaining the core temperature of the body. 3 marks

13) a) What are the major avenues for loss of body heat energy? Which of these four pathways is important for controlling body temperature at rest, and during exercise? 6 marks

  b) What happens to the body temperature during exercise and why? 4 marks

14) How does the body regulate temperature when an elite athlete is training in a warm climate? 3 marks

15) What are the physiological effects of dehydration on an athlete and how does this affect exercise performance? 4 marks

16) List four environmental factors that limit the ability of an athlete to continue to exercise in hot conditions. 4 marks

17) Describe how an athlete is able to control his or her body temperature during a marathon race. 4 marks

18) Why is humidity an important factor when an athlete is performing at high temperatures? Why are wind and cloud cover important? 4 marks

19) a) Quantify fluid loss during hot-weather exercise, and indicate the consequences of dehydration on human physiology and performance. 6 marks

  b) How is body water balance maintained during prolonged aerobic exercise in hot weather? 3 marks

  c) What are the potential benefits of using sports drinks? 3 marks

20) Long-distance runners may experience difficulties with their temperature regulation during performance. Why may an increase in body temperature cause a problem and how is it regulated during performance? 6 marks

Answers link: http://www.jroscoe.co.uk/downloads/a2_revise_pe_ocr/OCRA2_ch2_answers.pdf

EXERCISE PHYSIOLOGY

CHAPTER 3
INJURY PREVENTION AND THE
REHABILITATION OF INJURY

CHAPTER 3: *Injury prevention and the rehabilitation of injury*

Types of injury

A **sports injury** is any kind of injury, pain or physical damage that occurs as a result of sport, exercise or physical activity.

Sports injuries are unfortunately inevitable, and are dependent on a performer's intensity of training, the preparation he or she makes to avoid injury, and the ways in which rest and recovery are planned into a training and competitive programme. Figure 3.1 outlines the factors influencing how injuries are caused and can be dealt with.

Sports injuries are:
* Most commonly associated with the musculo-skeletal system, which includes muscles, joints and their associated tissues such as ligaments and tendons.
* Commonly classified as **acute** or **chronic**.
* Mild, moderate or severe.
* Characterised by pain, swelling, tenderness, weakness and the inability to use or place weight on the injured area.
* **Acute** injuries refer to sports injuries that happen in a moment.
* **Chronic** injuries are characterised by a slow, sustained development of symptoms, that culminate in a painful inflammatory condition.

figure 3.1 – sports injuries

prevention of injury

causes of injury

SPORTS INJURIES

rehabilitation after injury

acute injuries

chronic injuries

Acute injuries

Common symptoms associated with acute sports injuries:
* Acute injuries require **immediate first aid treatment** at the scene of the injury.
* Sudden severe **pain**.
* **Stretching painful** in the case of a muscle strain.
* Swelling, **inflammation**, bruising or tenderness over injured area.
* **Restricted mobility** above and below injured area.
* Loss of **stability** in the case of leg injuries.
* Loss of **function** in the injured area.
* **Protruding bone** from the skin in the case of a compound fracture.
* **Deformity** around injured area.
* Cold **purple colouration** of skin indicating a lack of proper blood circulation in that injured part.

Common hard tissue injuries

Fractures

A bone fracture is a break in the bone and is caused by excessive external forces and so is classified as traumatic fracture. There are two major classes:
* **Simple fractures** (figure 3.2) are broken bones that remain within the body and do not penetrate the skin.
* **Compound fractures** are broken bones that penetrate through the skin and expose the bone and deep tissues to the exterior environment, creating an open wound with a risk of infection.

Dislocations

A **dislocation** is the result of a complete rupture of joint surface contact and is often associated with severe injury leading to surrounding ligaments and joint instability. Subluxation describes an incomplete or partial dislocation to the misalignment of a joint surface that has some overlap. This is often caused by damage to the ligaments and is a common injury in throwing and racket sports.

figure 3.2 – simple fracture

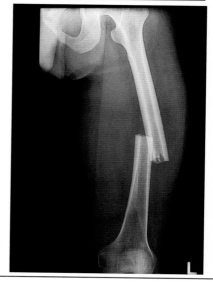

Dislocations

- For example, a shoulder dislocation occurs when a player's arm is forced outwards and upwards by a tackle or heavy landing and the shoulder joint pops out.
- Injuries can occur quite **easily** because the shoulder joint is a shallow ball and socket when compared to the hip joint.
- A dislocation is usually accompanied by a **sprain** (page 50).
- **Repeat dislocations** of the same joint are common because the initial dislocation stretches the joint capsule and ligaments, and results in joint hypermobility.

Common soft tissue injuries

A soft tissue injury occurs when **muscles**, **ligaments** and **tendons** are damaged. Common soft tissue injuries usually occur from a sprain, a strain or a one off blow resulting in a contusion or bruise. Soft tissue injuries can result in pain, swelling, bruising and loss of function.

Contusions and haematomae

- **Contusions** can be the result of direct impact from a player or object.
- For example, when athletes are playing wheelchair basketball, the wheel chairs come into close contact with each other and rapid evasive manoeuvres are necessary.
- The athlete's fingers can then be jammed both in and between wheelchairs. Such injuries are characterised by swelling and tenderness, and abrasions may be present.
- Contusions are common in contact sports such as rugby and boxing.

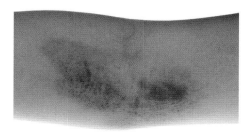

figure 3.3 – an haematoma

- The damaged tissue develops into an **haaematoma** (figure 3.3) which is an abnormal collection of congealed blood outside of a blood vessel and is often the result of severe contusions.
- It occurs because the blood vessel wall, artery, vein, or capillary, has been damaged to the extent that blood has leaked into surrounding tissues.
- Symptoms of hematomas include **swelling** and **discolouration** and depend upon their location, and whether adjacent structures are affected by the inflammation and swelling associated with the bleeding.

Abrasions

- An **abrasion** is a wound that tears or rubs off part of the skin.
- An example of an abrasion is a grazed knee resulting from a slide tackle in soccer.
- **Mild** abrasions only involve the epidermis, appear as grazes or scrapes and do not bleed or scar.
- **Deep** abrasions are lacerations to the subcutaneous layers and the skin.
- This degree of injury will need suturing and may lead to the formation of scar tissue.
- Abrasions should be cleaned and any debris, such as grit, removed.

Blisters

- A **blister** is a small pocket of body fluid (lymph, serum, plasma, blood, or pus) within the upper layers of the skin, typically caused by forceful rubbing (friction) usually shoes or socks rubbing against the skin.
- Heat and moisture intensify friction by making feet swell.
- That explains why many runners only suffer blisters during races, such as marathons.
- Blisters can be prevented by wearing synthetic socks that wick moisture away from the skin, and well-fitting sports shoes.

Strains

- Muscles can be damaged both by direct trauma (impact) or indirect trauma (overloading).
- A strain (pull or tear) refers to **damage to muscle fibres** or its attaching tendons caused by a sudden stretching force or a very forceful contraction of the muscle.
- The tearing of the muscle can also damage small blood vessels, causing local bleeding, or **bruising** (known as a **haematoma**), and pain caused by **irritation of the nerve endings** in the area.
- The most common muscle injuries occur in **high speed activities** such as sprinting and weight lifting, which load muscles such as the hamstrings, quadriceps, calf, back and biceps.
- Muscle tears range from a mild to moderate to severe strains or complete rupture.

Sprains and tears of ligaments

- A **ligament** is an extension of a joint capsule consisting of tough, fibrous connective tissue that provides stability by joining bone to bone positioned inside a joint (intrascapular) and outside of a joint (extracapsular).
- In a sprain, **ligaments** reinforcing a joint are **stretched** or torn.
- One of the most common knee injuries is an **anterior cruciate ligament** (ACL) sprain or rupture. The ACL runs diagonally across the middle of the knee and prevents the tibia from sliding out in front of the femur, as well as providing rotational stability to the knee.
- Athletes who participate in high demand sports like soccer, and basketball are more likely to injure their ACLs.
- About half of all injuries to the ACL occur along with damage to other structures in the knee, such as articular cartilage, meniscus or other ligaments.

Sprains and tears within joints

- Common sites of sprains are the ankle, knee and thumb joints.
- Sprains happen most often in the **ankle** (figure 3.4) in sports that involve twisting and turning movements, such as in netball.
- Knee sprains are common football injuries.
- Thumb sprains are common in skiing and contact sports such as judo.

Ice therapy is a common method used for acute joint and muscle injuries. Ice should be applied indirectly to the injured area for between 10-15 minutes, removed for 30 minutes (and repeat) to reduce internal bleeding, swelling and pain.

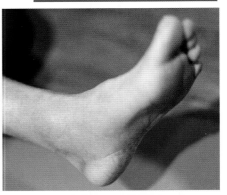

figure 3.4 – a sprained ankle

Ligament injuries

There are three graded categories for all ligament injuries:

Grade 1 sprain: the ligament is mildly damaged as it has been slightly stretched, but is still able to help keep the knee joint stable.
Grade 2 sprain: the ligament is stretched to a point where it becomes loose, and is commonly known as a partial tear of the ligament.
Grade 3 sprain: a complete tear of the ligament into two pieces. For example, a complete tear of the ACL creating an unstable knee joint (figure 3.5).

The ACL can be injured in several ways:
- Changing direction rapidly.
- Stopping suddenly.
- Slowing down while running.
- Landing from a jump incorrectly.
- Direct contact or collision, such as a football tackle.

A complete rupture leads to mechanical instability, which is partly the result of damage to the proprioceptive feedback mechanism.

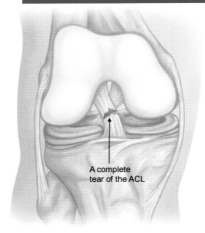

figure 3.5 – a complete ACL tear

A complete tear of the ACL

Symptoms of cruciate ligament injuries
- A 'popping' noise is associated with a ruptured ACL.
- The knee gives way and becomes unstable.
- Causing further damage to the cushioning cartilage (meniscus) of the knee.
- Pain and swelling within 24 hours.
- Loss of full range of motion.
- Tenderness along the joint line.
- Discomfort whilst walking.

- When a ligament is torn completely, it can be replaced with a graft, for example, the anterior cruciate ligament of the knee joint can be replaced using a hamstring tendon graft (page 72).

Concussion
- Concussion (or minor brain injury) is a temporary disturbance in the brain's functioning as a result of a blow to the head.
- The effects of concussion can leave people with symptoms including dizziness, nausea, confusion or an inability to process or retain information, sensitivity to light, and vision distortion.
- Concussion is common in body-contact sports, for example in a clash of heads, and in hard-ball games, for example a golf ball injury. Even adequate headgear may not entirely protect the head from a blow.
- The injured athlete must be removed from the activity and assessed by a medical professional.

This type of injury is discussed further on page 65.

Achilles tendon injuries

- A tendon is a tough cord or band of dense white fibrous connective tissue which connects a muscle to a bone and transmits the force which the muscle exerts.
- The Achilles tendon is located at the back of the ankle and connects the powerful calf muscles to the heel bone (calcaneus).
    - When the calf muscles contract, the Achilles tendon is tightened, pulling the heel.
    - This allows the foot to point and stand on tiptoe, vital to such activities as walking, running, and jumping.

- Tears of the Achilles tendon can be tiny (microtears), or large (macrotears), causing pain, swelling, and impaired movement.
    - Tears may occur suddenly (acute) during activity, or gradually over time (chronic).
    - A complete tear through the tendon, which usually occurs about 2 inches above the heel bone, is called an Achilles tendon rupture.
    - A rupture can occur when a significant load has been applied quickly and sustained without adequate warm-up.
- An Achilles tendon rupture is more common in those with pre-existing tendinitis of the Achilles tendon.
- By the age of thirty, tendons begin to lose their elasticity with increasing degenerative changes, but the process can be delayed by regular exercise.

- Total tendon ruptures often occur in a degenerated tendon and is especially common in older athletes who return to sport after some years' absence from training, and middle-aged men and women participating in recreational sports that require bursts of jumping, pivoting, and running.
- Most often these are in sports such as tennis, squash, basketball, and badminton.

Achilles tendon injuries

- A rupture is most likely to occur when an individual makes a **forceful push-off** by the thigh muscles whilst the knee is extended. One example might be preparing for a overhead shot during a badminton rally.
- Other common causes for a rupture can occur as a result of a sudden **trip** or **stumble** when the foot is thrust in front to break a fall, forcefully overstretching the tendon, or abruptly stepping into a hole.
- A complete rupture of the Achilles tendon may make a 'popping' sound, followed by pain and swelling of the lower leg.
- Figure 3.6 compares a ruptured and normal Achilles tendon.
- Treating an Achilles tendon rupture requires surgery or long-term immobilisation of the ankle.

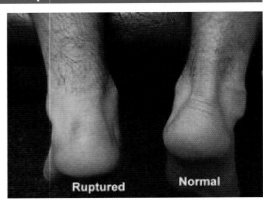

figure 3.6 – a ruptured and normal achilles tenndon

Ruptured   Normal

Chronic or overuse injuries

Common symptoms associated with chronic overuse sports injuries:
- Chronic injuries start off with **mild symptoms** that enable performer to ignore the injury and carry on with his or her activities.
- Followed by a gradual **increase of pain** and inflammation over a period of time resulting from continued **overuse**.
- Increase in pain during sporting activity.
- Mild swelling after completion of sporting activity.
- Constant **aching** at rest.
- Chronic injuries are also associated with fatigue.

Hard tissue injuries

Stress fractures
A **stress fracture** is a small crack in a bone resulting from **overuse**.
There are two theories about the origin of stress fractures:

- The **fatigue theory** states that during repeated protracted effort, such as running, the muscles pass their peak of endurance and are no longer able to support the skeleton during impact applied as the foot strikes the ground. The **load** is therefore transferred **directly to the skeleton**. Its tolerance is eventually exceeded causing a tiny crack or stress fracture.

- The **overload theory** is based on the fact that certain muscle groups contract in such a way that they cause the **bones** to which they are attached, to **bend**. For example, the contraction of the calf muscles causes the tibia to bend forward like a drawn bow. After repeated contractions the innate strength of the tibia is exceeded and it cracks.

More than 50% of all **stress fractures** occur in the weight-bearing bones of the foot and lower leg because of the repetitive forces they must absorb. Typically, runners sustain stress fractures of the lower third of the fibula and high jumpers of the upper third of the fibula.

Symptoms and diagnosis
- **Pain** is felt during training as intensity increase and eventually a dull ache which persists after the exercise period.
- Local **swelling** and **tenderness** can be felt over the fracture area.
- Stress fractures affect people of **all ages** who participate in repetitive sporting activities and are especially common in tennis players, runners, gymnasts and basketball players.

Symptoms and diagnosis

- Repeated use of **X-ray** examination is used to check the **process of healing**, whilst the athlete is resting and using prescribed crutches to relieve the injured part.
- If stress fractures are to be avoided, the athlete should pay particular attention to selecting appropriate **footwear**, **equipment** (page 59) and periodisation of training or load.

Soft tissue injuries

Shin splints (periostitis)

Shin splints are a type of **soft tissue injury** due to **inflammation** of the **periosteum** (a layer of connective tissue that surrounds bone), usually caused by repeated stress on the tibia. Shin splints are common in people who do a lot of running or other activities that involve repeatedly putting weight on the legs, such as tennis or basketball.

Shin splints can usually be treated at home as follows:
- **Rest**: stop the activity that causes shin splints for at least two to three weeks, then gradually resume normal activities.
- **Ice**: for around 10 minutes every few hours for the first few days. This helps to relieve pain and swelling.
- **Pain relief**: such as paracetamol and ibuprofen help to relieve the pain.
- **Switch to low-impact activities**: such as cycling, swimming and yoga.

Tendinopathy

Tendinopathy is the umbrella term for clinical conditions in and surrounding a tendon including tenderness on palpation and pain, often felt when exercising. **Tendonitis** is an acute tendon injury accompanied by swelling ('itis'), resulting from **excessive overuse**, and describes common elbow injuries experienced by tennis players, golfers and throwers.

The **elbow joint** is surrounded by muscles that move the elbow, wrist and fingers. The tendons in the elbow join the bones and muscles together, and control the muscles of the forearm.

Golfer's elbow is not as well known as its cousin, **tennis elbow**. Both are forms of tendinopathy. The difference is that **tennis elbow** stems from overusing tendon attachments to the **outside** of the elbow, while **golfer's elbow** is caused by overusing tendons on the **inside** of the elbow.

Golfer's elbow is a common overuse injury associated with playing golf and throwing activities such as javelin and bowling in cricket. It is caused by **overusing** the muscles in the **forearm** that allow the individual to grip, rotate the arm, and flex the wrist.

Repetitive flexing, gripping, or swinging can cause irritations to the tendons creating pronounced tenderness and pain when the medial epicondyle is subjected to pressure, and when the hand is flexed downwards (**palmer flexion**) at the wrist joint against a resistance.

Tennis elbow is a common overuse injury associated with racket sports such as squash, badminton and tennis. For example, in tennis it can be caused by repetitive faulty stroke technique, such as hitting backhand balls by using wrist movements instead of hitting backhand balls with a firm wrist and a movement of the whole arm and shoulder.

Top level tennis players may develop **lateral epicondylitis** despite having good playing technique and is usually caused by the serving action during which the wrist is bent at the same time as the forearm is turned inwards.

Elbow

Those who hit an exaggerated 'top spin' and in so doing rotate the forearm vigorously inwards (excessive pronation) can also be affected.
This was the injury sustained by Andy Murray (figure 3.7) at the beginning of the 2017 tennis season.
The flexor muscles, that are principally responsible for these movements, have their origins at the medial epicondyle of the elbow.

The **symptoms** are similar to those of golfer's elbow, but are located on the **outer aspect** of the **elbow joint**. If the muscles and tendons are irritated, it can cause thickening of the tendon and pain near the bony lump (the lateral epicondyle) on the outside of the joint.

General **tendonitis symptoms** include:
*   **Pain** which mainly affects the outside aspect of the elbow (tennis elbow) or inside of the elbow (golfer's elbow) that can radiate along the upper and lower arm.
*   **Weakness** in the wrist.
*   A **tender local hot** spot over the epicondyle.

figure 3.7 – wrist supination can cause elbow tendonitis

Injury prevention

Extrinsic and intrinsic risk factors affecting sports injuries

Table 3.1 outlines the intrinsic and extrinsic risk factors which affect sport injury. Intrinsic risk factors are those within the performer, and extrinsic risk factors are those derived outside the performer.

Table 3.1 – **intrinsic and extrinsic risk factors in sport injuries**

intrinsic risk factors	extrinsic risk factors
gender	training volume, overtraining
age increases injury risk as bone tissue loses strength	sport technique
body mass and body composition	playing surfaces
muscle balance/imbalance	equipment difficulties, eg selecting the perfect ski boots, skis and poles
joint flexibility (or lack of it)	clothing/footwear/equipment
orthopaedic and skeletal features	environmental conditions
conditioning	
nutrition	

Although the **chances of injury** in sport can never be fully eradicated, preventative measures and procedures can be put into place to minimise the risk of getting injured, as discussed in managing risks (page 60).

Intrinsic risk factor variables

Conditioning

Regardless of the sport involved, most athletes need **general muscle fitness** to reduce the risk of injury to the muscle-tendon unit itself and to the joints protected by muscle activity.
Weight training and **circuit training** are common training methods that are used improve the general **strength and conditioning** of muscles.

Athletes must be fit enough to be able to perform the skills needed to compete in their sport and so long-term preparation is needed in training for many activities, for example, running a marathon for which preparation can take several months.

Conditioning

When athletes become tired, performance levels can drop and injuries are more likely to occur due to fatigue.

A **core stability** conditioning programme benefits good **muscle balance** and **coordination** (figure 3.8). Good core stability involves the effective recruitment of the muscles that **stabilise** the **lumbo-pelvic-hip complex**, together with those that stabilise the shoulder girdle. Many athletes attend **pilates**, a body-conditioning technique that concentrates on strengthening the core postural muscles needed by all active sportspersons.

figure 3.8 – core stability

Variance in training avoids the overuse injuries associated with using the same exercises and movements year round, and builds the right foundation for achieving peak performance at the right time.

All training/competitive activities should begin with a **warm-up**. A warm-up takes the body from a non-active state to one ready for exercise. The absence of a warm-up or an inadequate warm-up is a common cause of injury.

Lack of flexibility can limit **range of movement** (ROM) and lead to sprain and strain injuries. **Hyper-mobility** enables joints to move beyond the normal range expected for that particular joint and can lead to poor joint stability and dislocations.

A **cool-down** gradually returns the body to its former resting state with reduced injury risk. A major physiological value of an active cool-down is to **flush out lactic acid** thereby preventing muscle soreness (**DOMS**).

Sport performers require **sports specific** training programmes aimed at developing those muscle fibres which are used most intensively in competition. These programmes should include a variety of skills, drills and techniques that should mimic the desired sporting action as closely as possible.

STUDENT NOTE

For reviews of antagonistic muscle action, and preparation and training methods refer to AS/A1 OCR ISBN 9781901424911, Chapter 1, page 20, Chapter 5, page 93 onwards.

Muscle balance

Human movement and function requires a **balance** of muscle **length** and **strength** between opposing muscles surrounding a joint. Normal amounts of opposing force between muscles are necessary to keep the bones centred in the joint during motion, to create muscle balance.

Muscle imbalance occurs when opposing muscles provide different **directions of tension** due to tightness and/or weakness. When a muscle is too tight, the joint tends to move in that direction and is limited in the opposite direction since this is typically the path of least resistance.

There are also two recognised causes of **muscle imbalance**:
* **Neuromuscular imbalance** due to the predisposition of certain muscle groups to be either tight or weak.
* **Biomechanical imbalance** resulting from poor technique.

Muscle imbalances can be characterised by either **side-to-side** (right versus left) or **front-to-back** (agonist versus antagonist) differences in muscle length or strength. Most musculoskeletal pain syndromes are caused by front-to-back differences, or imbalances of muscles surrounding a joint, rather than side-to-side differences (in the frontal plane).

Muscle balance

For example, the quadriceps and hamstrings of the knee joint perform opposite motion (antagonistic pairing), and so an imbalance between the two could put undue stress on the knee joint. A tight hamstring would not allow the joint to glide normally or fully extend, which could put extra stress on the quadriceps muscle and patella (knee cap) tendon.

Muscle imbalance can be the result of poor weight training techniques, or playing intense sports where one side of the body is used slightly more than the other as in the repetitive action of kicking in football.

When muscles are balanced the human body moves efficiently, requiring less energy and preventing unnecessary stress on the muscles, nerves, ligaments and joints. This synergy is known as **neuromuscular efficiency**, requiring the interaction of the neuromuscular systems.

It is important to know which muscles need to be **strengthened** and which muscles need to be **stretched** in order to create good muscle balance.

Good posture ensures that movements can be performed with minimal strain. For example, when the body leans slightly to one side, the nerves associated with the muscles and ligaments send messages to other muscles to help correct this movement by telling muscles to contract to regain muscle balance. If there are imbalances within this unit, problems can occur, such as **decreased performance**, muscle trauma and injury.

Running posture is an important technical aspect for both enhancing performance and minimising injury risk. Runners who lean forward (figure 3.9) to a greater extent are more economical (run faster for a given oxygen uptake) and less likely to suffer from knee injuries, the most common of which occurs at the **patellofemoral joint** (PFJ) - a joint between the patella and femur).

PFJ pain syndrome is often caused by imbalances in the muscles surrounding the knee, which affect the kneecap (patella) and cartilage within the joint. Symptoms include a **scratching**, **grinding** or **clicking** sensation in the knee, and non-specific knee pain.

Maintaining a **forward lean** without losing straight alignment over long distances requires certain level of **torso strength**, which is why **strength** and **mobility** exercises are fundamental in improving running performance and reducing injury risk.

Muscle balance assessment

A muscle balance assessment is a series of tests and observations that evaluate joint **range of movement** (ROM), strength and coordination, and muscle flexibility. Such assessments can establish what is working well or not so well.

For example, an **isokinetic lido leg strength test** can assess the strength ratio between the quadriceps and hamstring muscle groups. For good muscle balance the ideal ratio should be 2:1. If it is greater that this value, the hamstring muscle group becomes susceptible to injury.

STUDENT NOTE

Proprioceptors, such as Golgi tendon organs and muscle spindles, are specialised sensory receptors sensitive to stretch, tension and pressure located in tendon, joints and muscles.
They relay information about muscular dynamics, limb position and kinaesthesia (movement sense) to conscious and subconscious portions of the CNS.

Proprioceptive training methods

Proprioceptive training methods can improve muscle balance, as is the case with **plyometric** training. The emphasis is placed on making the ROM more stable, in particular in single limb tasks.

Proprioception is the ability to sense stimuli arising within the body regarding position, motion, and equilibrium.

For example, in an ideal **long-term athlete development** plan (LTAD) a coach could teach a young athlete to land bilaterally off low level drops, from horizontal jumps/bounding (figure 3.10) and jumps using a multi-directional approach.

To achieve a **softer landing**, the coach could tell the athlete that they need to land on the front of the foot, and then flex the knees into a squat position in order to dissipate the ground reaction force effectively.

This would **avoid** such **high peak forces** in shorter time frames on landing, which has been demonstrated as a most likely cause of knee and muscle/tendon injuries.

The aim is to be able to absorb and handle the impact of **eccentric loads** on landing and ground stroke in high velocity running.

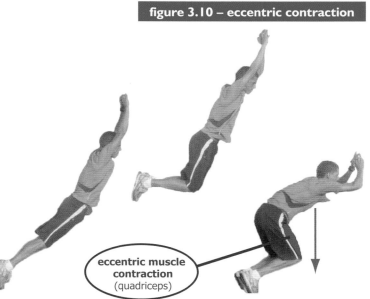

figure 3.10 – eccentric contraction

eccentric muscle contraction (quadriceps)

The progression within single leg landings would ensure the athlete can land softly to begin with, promoting good landing mechanics of holding and maintaining good **postural balance** by controlling the alignment of the knee and effective position of the trunk in a neutral position.

The proprioceptors therefore have to **adapt** to control these movements and keep a balanced athletic position on landing. Once achieved, the young athlete is ready to progress from low level muscle balance work through to **greater training loads**, thereby increasing the muscular strength and balance.

By improving an athlete's proprioceptive ability, he or she can gain the balance skills necessary to maintain stability for their sporting needs.

Muscle balance is enhanced by having a **strong core** as discussed above.

Age

- People lose bone mass or density as they age, especially women after menopause. The bones lose calcium and other minerals.
- **Muscle weakness** contributes to fatigue, weakness and reduced activity tolerance.
- Joint problems ranging from mild stiffness to debilitating **arthritis** (osteoarthritis) are very common.
- The risk of injury increases because gait changes, and instability and **loss of balance** may lead to falls.
- Bone and muscle tissue respond to mechanical loads, therefore, the principle of **progressive overload**, which progressively places higher than normal demands on the working musculature, applies when training not only muscle but bone as well.
- With bone tissue proper applications of the principles of overload is the key to increasing density and strength.

Nutrition

Poor nutrition can contribute to stress, tiredness and capacity to work. Over time it can lead to eating disorders such as anorexia nervosa. The sports culture, with its emphasize on optimal body size or shape for optimal performance, is in many cases an influencing factor in developing such a condition.

By choosing the right diet and supplements injury prevention and recovery can be enhanced. For a full account of the effects of diet on recovery refer to page 29.

Extrinsic risk factor variables

Technique

If an athlete does not have a good technique he or she is more likely to sustain a sports injury. **Poor technique** can expose players to the risk of acute injury. For example, rugby tackling with the head in front of the ball carrier's leg rather than behind it.

figure 3.11 – a PE lesson

Injuries are not the only by-product of poor technique, **performance levels** will also be decreased by **poor technique** as this will prevent optimum strength, power and speed in the particular movement or shot.

In injury prevention, **good technique training** from a **coach** is vital and should start when athletes are young (figure 3.11). **Movement patterns** in technique training must be performed correctly right from the start as it can be difficult to correct a faulty pattern later (as illustrated in the example within the proprioceptive training methods).

Achieving optimal coordination requires **constant repetition** of the various elements of the movement. This is achieved by establishing good interaction between the muscles and the nervous system to produce good **muscular coordination**.

Technique training should be assigned to the **beginning** of the training session when it is easier to concentrate and the body is well-rested. All athletes should have a **solid technical foundation** before taking part in competition.

The coach is responsible for **planning** appropriate levels of **intensity**, **duration**, **frequency** and **variance** within a training programme to prevent **overtraining**.

Overuse injuries refer to injuries sustained from repeated action. For example, **repetitive**, **excessive overload** can cause microscopic injuries, leading to inflammation, which is the body's response to injury.

Repeated low level impacts can cause chronic injury, for example, Achilles tendinopathy if long-term measures, such as rest and strengthening are not taken.

Protective equipment and clothing

For some sports, protective equipment is important to prevent damage to participants. This is particularly relevant when the sport or activity involves physical contact with other players.

Protective equipment and clothing

Equipment in any sport may be inadequate, poorly designed or ineffective and not suitable for age, stature or ability. For example, generic trainers (footwear) will not provide the support and grip needed for throwing events.

Protective clothing can be faulty or insufficient to meet the needs of the sporting activity. Specialised protective clothing (figure 3.12) has been developed for many sports with well known examples from fencing, field hockey, cricket, baseball, American football and equestrianism.

figure 3.12 – specialist equipment for injury prevention

Boxing and other **martial arts** require **helmets** (with or without face guards), padding, boxes, strapping, gloves, mouth guards and so on, depending on the rules of the sport, and the damage allowed to be inflicted within the rules of the sport. All these pieces of equipment are designed to prevent injury to **vulnerable** parts of the body.

Specialist clothing is also required for **low and high temperatures** to maintain body temperature within a safe range.

Wicking fabrics (a mixture of cotton and man-made light and stretchy fibres) are used in a range of sports clothing. The wicking properties have the ability to soak up sweat then move it away from the body, thus saving energy on maintaining skin temperature, and **preventing hyperthermia** (heat exhaustion). In cold conditions such fabrics insulate the body thereby reducing hypothermia.

Energy absorbing plastics (also known as **shear-thickening**, energy absorbing materials, for example D30) are used as materials to create foam-filled clothes that cushion, absorb and dissipate the energy resulting from a high impact blows. The shear-thickening property means that greater the force acting on it, the more solid the material becomes. This material is used in **ski clothing** and sports such as **motor racing clothing** to provide significant protection from injury against high impact incidents.

Compression clothing (page 30) works by supporting and protecting body tissues, increasing circulation, assisting in the removal of lactic acid and thereby reducing DOMS.

Footwear, braces and strapping
Sports footwear is the most important item of equipment for most sports. When choosing sports footwear, several factors must be taken into consideration including the **sport** involved and the **surface** used.

figure 3.13 – Dan Hipkiss - with specially moulded shoes

For example, in long-distance running the **weight** of the shoes can be of importance. They should not, however, be so light that their **stability** is impaired.

Elite athletes are often provided with **bespoke footwear**. The foot is scanned to capture its shape, then footfall is analysed (using forceplate technology). This indicates how the foot lands and moves and leads to the development of personalised footwear, whose aim is to make movement more efficient, improve performance and reduce the likelihood of injury, (figure 3.13).

Proper fitting and sport-specific footwear reduce the risk of injury to the soft tissues, bones or joints of the lower limb.

The risk of a sprained ankle and other such injuries has been shown to significantly be reduced by wearing **braces** such as ankle supports (as worn by tennis star Andy Murray - figure 3.14, page 60).

Footwear, braces and strapping

There are a few items that can be used in training, but **not allowed** in competitive situations. For example, **strapping** a shot putter's fingers or hand helps prevent finger knuckle sprains, but is not allowed in competition.

There are many other examples of protective equipment, all of which contribute in the prevention of sports injuries.

The environment and safety hazards

A hazard is something that is potentially dangerous to an individual or activity or both. For example, if a sports hall roof leaks the floor may become wet and so it will need to be coned off and dried to prevent people slipping during a physical activity.

Low temperature and **wet and windy** conditions can also be responsible for injury. Cyclists should take particular care when cycling on wet, greasy roads.

The ability to perform vigorous exercise for long periods is limited by **hyperthermia** (over heating) and **loss of water and salt** in sweating. Athletes should know the hazards of vigorous exercise in hot, humid conditions particularly in ultra endurance events, and should be able to recognise the early warning symptoms that precede heat injury.

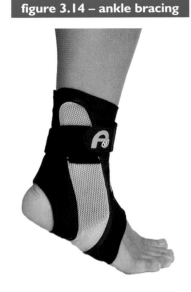

figure 3.14 – ankle bracing

Managing risks

Managing risks refers to the practice of identifying potential risks in advance, analysing them and taking precautionary steps to reduce/curb the risk. This is known as a **risk assessment**.

Injury prevention and management is an important component of a coaching programme for participants in many sports and activities. An important function of a coach is to **identify**, **evaluate** and **refine** an injury risk coaching strategy programme for everyone in the coaching group, in addition to managing injury recovery strategies.

Coaches must also take account of guidelines and assessment opportunities from national governing bodies, experts and their own prior experience when designing and delivering injury prevention and management strategies.

Scientific experts at Loughborough University Sport and Technology Institute have developed a running kinematics assessment facility that uses motion analysis technology (figure 3.15).

This technology objectively assesses the running efficiency of the athlete and so can identify poor running technical elements that could potentially injure the athlete.

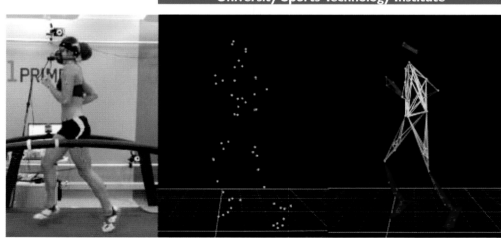

figure 3.15 – running kinematics, Loughborough University Sports Technology Institute

Managing risks

Another example of risk management, is that of physiotherapy **screening** services which are designed for sports persons of all ability. Standard tests are used to assess strengths and weaknesses in key areas, such as strength, flexibility (figure 3.16), core control and balance. This information can be used in exercise prescription for musculoskeletal conditioning, thereby decreasing the risk of getting injured.

figure 3.16 – sit and reach test

To be effective, injury prevention management has to be properly integrated into the participants' programme.

In summary there are several key progressive stages that will assist a coach and athlete to minimise the risk of injury as outlined in table 3.2.

Table 3.2 - **stages for prevention of injuries**

	progressive stages for injury prevention
1	analyse the athletes' current risk of injury in relation to their level of development, previous history and the demands of the sport
2	select and plan activities, information and advice that will help the athletes minimise the risk of injury
3	where necessary, seek the support of other specialist staff
4	ensure that the strategy for injury prevention effectively supports and integrates with other training programme components
5	provide planned activities, information and advice to minimise the risk of injury
6	evaluate and review the success of the strategy for injury prevention
7	monitor and refine the strategy for injury prevention as part of the athletes' programme

Screening and injury prevention

Screening is a search for a specific condition that can help to detect health risk factors, for example, undetected cardiac abnormality. Standard screening tests are used to assess strengths and weaknesses in key areas, such as strength, flexibility, core control and balance. This information can be used for exercise prescription for musculoskeletal conditioning thereby decreasing the risk of getting injured. Regular screening provides information about physical changes over time, which is particularly important in the growing athlete and for an athlete following long hours of training/competition.

Safety measures

Safety measures, which are intrinsic to sports coaching and teaching, include understanding the rules, having the kit and equipment appropriate to the sport and making use of technologies. Coaches, athletes, teachers and officials must abide by set rules that are intended to minimise the chances of getting hurt or injured, by taking precautionary measures.

Effectiveness of warm-up and cool-down

STUDENT NOTE

Refer to pages 26 and 27 for background notes on warm-up and cool-down and AS/A1 Revise PE for OCR ISBN 9781901424911, Chapter 6, page 97 onwards.

Warm-up

It is generally accepted that increasing the flexibility of a muscle-tendon unit promotes better performances and decreases the number of injuries.

The use of flexibility for reducing injuries depends upon the intensity of the sport. Sports involving bouncing and jumping activities with a high intensity of stretch-shortening cycles (SSCs), for example, football, require a muscle-tendon unit that is compliant enough to store and release the high amount of elastic energy that benefits performance in such sports.

If the participants of these sports have an insufficient compliant muscle-tendon unit, the demands in energy absorption and release may rapidly exceed the capacity of the muscle-tendon unit.

This may lead to an increased risk for injury of this structure. For example, Achilles tendon injuries are common in soccer.

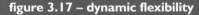

figure 3.17 – dynamic flexibility

Stretching

Stretching programmes can significantly influence the viscosity of the tendon and make it significantly more compliant, and when a sport demands SSCs of high intensity, stretching may be important for injury prevention. But which type of stretching is best suited during a warm-up and cool-down?

- **Dynamic stretching** involves movement and muscular effort for the stretch to occur. While static stretching takes a muscle to its full length and holds it there for 15 to 60 seconds.
- Dynamic flexibility (figure 3.17) has been shown to improve performance when done before an activity that requires a lot of power, strength or speed.

- For example, the sports specific front and trail leg drills performed and rehearsed by hurdlers prior to a training session or competition.
- These drills are performed slowly at first to activate the neural pathways and establish the required ROM.

- Then gradually build up speed in order to achieve the optimal balance, coordination and speed needed for the specific activity.
- **Static stretching** (figure 3.18) has long been used in a warm-up, with the aim of enhancing performance and reducing the risk of injury.
- Static stretching has been shown to compromise muscle performance by reducing peak power, eccentric muscle force production and the effectiveness of antagonistic muscle action, running speed, reaction and movement time.
- In addition, strength endurance is compromised, due to a decrease in the ability of muscle tissue to extract and utilise oxygen needed for explosive sports such as sprinting.
- 5-10 minutes spent doing static stretching can lead to muscle temperature dropping.

As such, muscles, although stretched, become less elastic and less powerful.

figure 3.18 – hold this static stretch

- For most sports, both **proprioceptive neuromuscular facilitation** (PNF) stretching and **ballistic stretching** have been shown to be detrimental to subsequent performance.
- However, static stretching and the use of PNF stretching techniques before activity, might increase performance in sports that require an increased range of movement, such as gymnastics.
- It is not unusual to observe a sports masseur working on joint mobility prior to a competitive performance.

Stretching

Given these findings, the use of static, PNF, and ballistic stretching in warm-up needs to be questioned in relation to the requirements of the sporting activity.

Based on current evidence, **dynamic stretching**, for most sports, would be the preferred option for stretching during a warm-up and the use of static stretching is best recommended during the cool-down phase, as discussed in the effectiveness of a cool-down.

Cool-down

A **cool-down** is a session of light exercise that immediately follows demanding physical activity. Depending on the intensity and duration of the session, a cool-down can last anywhere between 15-30 minutes and may include an ice bath (page 29) or an alternative form of cryotherapy treatment (page 69) .

The aim of a cool-down is to continue to provide oxygen to skeletal muscle tissue, until the body has returned to its resting state. This therefore enhances oxidation of lactic acid and ensures that less lactic acid remains in the tissue. Hence there is less muscle soreness (DOMS).

Recovering muscles will activate the skeletal muscle pump for venous return of blood to the heart thereby preventing **blood pooling** and dizziness (blood will remain in limbs if muscle action is stopped suddenly) and reduce blood lactate levels (page 27, figure 1.25) and muscle soreness (DOMS, page 25).

There are three key elements which should be included in a cool-down programme to ensure an effective and complete recovery:

- 10 minutes of **whole body activity** such as jogging, walking and biking to maintain venous return.

- 20 to 30 minutes of low-intensity, long-hold (30 to 60 seconds) static stretching.
- Many athletes make the mistake of stretching too hard or too vigorously during this part of the cool-down.
- The aim here is not necessarily to improve flexibility, it's to gently lengthen out those that have been constantly contracting during the training session or performance.

- **Re-fuel** with hypertonic sports drinks and protein drinks immediately after exercise has finished.
- This begins **replenishment** of blood glucose and glycogen stores and muscle tissue repaid respectively.
- A high **CHO meal** (figure 3.19) within 15 minutes of exercise ending (or as soon as possible) continues glycogen replenishment needed for complete recovery.

figure 3.19 – types of carbohydrate

Helen Roscoe Photography

A cool-down massage

A cool-down **massage** has several benefits.
- Encourages relaxation from the tensions as well as overuse, which usually takes place when an individual has undergone a physical exertion or strenuous activity.
- Will make the recipient feel much better both physically and mentally.
- Will assist in lessening the irritating pains as well as throbbing that generally result in serious injuries.

Responding to injuries and medical conditions in a sporting context

During any kind of physical activity there is a chance that somebody participating may get injured or hurt. The first job is for someone to **assess** the nature and **severity** of the injury and decide whether further medical assistance is needed. If this person has seen the incident happen, he or she is more likely to be aware of what procedures to undertake and have an idea of what the injury might be. Most official sporting events have first aid support, such as a St John's Ambulance crew, who can respond immediately once an injury has been sustained.

Assessing sporting injuries using SALTAPS

In most cases, a more specific sports-related method of assessing an injury is more relevant. One such technique is **SALTAPS.** The aim of the SALTAPS process is to make an accurate assessment of the type, location and severity of an injury by using the following procedure:

- **S**top the activity when an athlete gets injured and observe the injury.
- **A**sk questions about the injury such as where does it hurt and pain intensity.
- **L**ook for specific signs and indicators of injury, such as bleeding, swelling, distorted joints and bones.
- **T**ouch the injury site and decide the extent of the injury. This requires gentle palpations around the injured area to identify discomfort, pain, swelling and loss of skin sensation.
- **A**ctive movement of the injured area assesses if the athlete is able to move the injured part independently.
- **P**assive movement of the injured area assesses which movements the athlete can't make.
- **S**trength testing assesses if the athlete is stand up and walk and whether he or she can resume physical activity.

With increasingly serious injuries, it is important to cease the SALTAPS process at an appropriate stage. For example, never move an athlete with a suspected neck or spine injury or an unconscious athlete.

Acute management of soft tissue injuries using PRICE

Acute soft tissue injuries are most common in people who participate in sports and recreational activities where signs and symptoms such as bruising, heat and redness, pain and inflammation are common.

The **PRICE regime** (formally RICE) is another simple protocol that even somebody who is not trained in first aid can use to minimise the effects of immediate injury. The PRICE five-step process for treating a muscle or joint injury such as an ankle sprain is short for **P**rotection, **R**est, **I**ce, **C**ompression, and **E**levation.

- **P**rotection ensures that the injured person is safe from further damage and the first aider is also in a safe area. If the injury was sustained on the sports field, stop the game and protect the injured part with a bandage, padding or splint. If the patient can move, carefully transfer him or her to a safer area using a stretcher or a crutch, but if there is any doubt, do not move the patient.
- **R**est is needed as soon as the injury occurs to prevent making it any worse and allow adequate rehabilitation time for the injury to heal.
- **I**ce applied to the injured are for 10-15 minutes, then removed for 20 minutes (and repeat) will reduce internal bleeding, inflammation. It is advisable to wrap the ice pack in a cloth to prevent cold burns on the skin.
- **C**ompression reduces swelling, supports soft tissue, minimising further damage and so speeds up recovery. Using a stretchy bandage such as cohesive bandage, elastic adhesive bandage or tubular bandage will suffice.
- **E**levation, created by raising the injured area above the heart, aids the drainage of any liquid/leakage caused by the injury, thereby reducing swelling and inflammation.

Aims of PRICE

- Reduce temperature.
- Reduce pain.
- Limit and reduce swelling.
- Protect the damaged tissue from further injury.
- Promote good healing of the tissue.

PRICE is the key to the early management of most kinds of acute soft tissue injuries, but the patient may also need medication for pain and/or inflammation.

Although ice is an excellent anti-inflammatory, it may not be the best treatment for ligament and tendon injuries that are poorly supplied with blood vessels. Alternating hot and cold therapies (page 70) may provide better therapeutic benefits as heat brings healthy blood into an area, and ice helps to flush out inflammatory agents.

figure 3.20 – shoulder charge

Recognising concussion:
IRB's 'Recognise and Remove' 6 R's

Head injuries are common in body contact sports such as boxing and rugby, and in hard-ball games, such as cricket and rounders. (Figure 3.20 shoulder charge). **Concussion** (page 51) is a temporary unconsciousness or confusion caused by a blow on the head. When dealing with a concussed player it is important to be aware he or she may also have a serious head injury or spinal injury. If the player is unconscious, one should assume he or she may also have a head and spinal injury and manage the player accordingly.

The signs and symptoms of a concussion can be subtle and may not show up immediately. Symptoms can last for days, weeks or even longer and may include symptoms identified in figure 3.21.

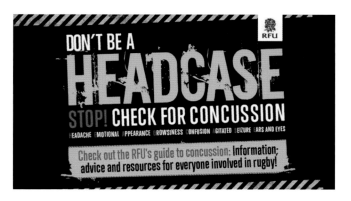

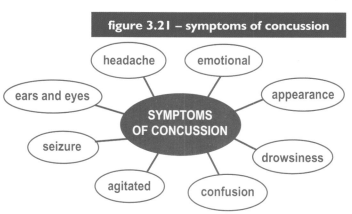

figure 3.21 – symptoms of concussion

SYMPTOMS OF CONCUSSION: headache, emotional, appearance, drowsiness, confusion, agitated, seizure, ears and eyes

The 6'Rs is a 'recognise and remove' campaign that was launched by World Rugby to help players recover from concussion:

- **Recognise**: learn the symptoms and signs of concussion.
- **Remove**: if a player has suspected concussion he or she should be removed from play immediately.
- **Refer**: to a qualified medical professional.
- **Rest**: players must rest from exercise until symptom free and then start a **Graduated Return to Play** (GRTP).
- **Recover**: full recovery from the concussion is required before return to play is authorized.
- **Return**: the player should complete the GRTP protocol before fully resuming his or her sport.

World Rugby's Graduated Return to Play Protocol (GRTP)

GRTP aims to return an injured player back to full playing fitness by using a graduated and progressive step-by-step rehabilitation exercise protocol providing the target for each progression is met. If not, the individual repeats the previous step until injury free.

Table 3.3 - **World Rugby's Graduated Return to Play Protocol (GRTP)**

Day 1: minimum rest period during which no concussive symptoms are experienced
Day 2: light aerobic exercise to increase heart rate
Day 3: sport specific exercise, such as running drills, excluding head impact activities
Day 4: non-contact training drills, stressing coordination and attention
Day 5: full-contact practice, resuming normal training activities
Day 6: return to play

There is some debate about the use of protective headgear in contact sports, since wearing a helmet cannot totally prevent concussion or eliminate the risk. **Protective headgear**, such as helmets and face guards, are used in many sports such as cricket, lacrosse (figure 3.22) and ice hockey. Energy absorbing plastics (for example D30, also known as shear-thickening) may offer better protection as this material absorbs and dissipates energy resulting from high impact blows. D30 helmet design is popular with elite alpine skiers and snow boarders.

figure 3.22 – lacrosse protective headgear

Boxing headgear, for male contests, was ditched in the 2016 Rio Olympic Games, since it is considered foam padding did little to protect against concussions and knockout blows. On the other hand, female boxers are still wearing headgear, due to lack of safety data.

Rehabilitation of sports injuries

Rehabilitation is the process of restoring full physical function after an injury has occurred.

A rehabilitation programme should be designed with individual short-term and long-term goals in mind. The **timescales** and **treatment options** involved in rehabilitation from injury depend upon the age of the person, severity of the injury, fitness levels and active daily lifestyles.

There are three recognised phases in a sports' rehabilitation programme:

Acute phase represents the initial healing phase. The treatment plan during this phase includes rest, pain reduction, swelling reduction and promotion of tissue healing.

Mid phase represents the mature healing process. During this phase the use of progressive overload training will promote strong healing of the injured tissue. For example, elastic resistance exercises that strengthens the rotator cuff musculature following a shoulder injury (figure 3.23).

figure 3.23 – Thera Band exercise

Later phase represents functional integration of drills and a variety of training modes, such as plyometric drills and weight training exercises. During this phase the injured body part is trained to work perfectly with the rest of the body by building up strength, endurance and coordination.

Stretching

Choosing the right type of stretching during a rehabilitation programme will have a tremendous effect on the speed of recovery, whilst choosing the wrong type could lead to further injury and a very slow recovery.

The **recovery process of a soft tissue injury** can be broken down into a number of phases and it is important that the right type of stretching is employed for each phase, as previously discussed.

Acute phase: avoid stretching during the first 72 hours. Using the **PRICE** protocol has been shown to provide an early base that significantly reduces recovery time as most of the initial swelling will have subsided.

Mid phase: recovery normally commences after 3 days and can last up to 2 weeks depending on the nature of the injury. Light, gentle active rehabilitation techniques can be started, by using a combination of 4 daily sessions of static and active controlled stretching, along with heat and massage treatments. Pain is the warning sign which should not be overlooked.

Later phase: of a rehabilitation programme can last anywhere between 2 and 5 weeks, again depending on the nature of the injury. Build up the static (passive) and active stretching programme started during mid phase recovery, alongside **PNF stretching** (Proprioceptive Neuromuscular Facilitation. The aim of this later phase of recovery is to work on joint ROM and muscle elasticity.

Once over the injury it is important to regain the fitness components that were lost during the injury process. This involves making the injured area stronger and more flexible that it was before the injury occurred. A combination of a dynamic and active stretching programme is recommended.

Massage

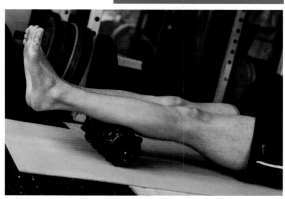

figure 3.24 – roller massage

Massage therapy involves **stroking**, **kneading**, and/or **striking** of the skin and underlying musculature for periods of time such that pressure and muscle distension are produced. Massage therapy is used to treat **mild** to **moderate muscle injuries**, for reduction of muscle soreness and for enhancement of post-exercise muscle recovery (DOMS) following intense anaerobic training.

Massage can be performed by a practitioner, such as a physiotherapist or sports masseur, or by using equipment, such as a roller tube (figure 3.24).

Massage techniques assist in soft tissue mobilisation, muscle function and local pain (figure 3.25).

figure 3.25 – medical support

When, when not and how to use massage therapy
* Massage can only be used for treatment during the acute stage to assist lymphatic drainage in order to reduce swelling.
* Massage is not advisable for tendon and ligament tissue repair or on open wounds or contusions.
* Rehabilitation massage treatments are mainly carried out at the repair or mid injury stage.
* Care should be taken that excessive forces are not applied to traumatised tissue.
* Muscles and joints can be **passively** moved to a full range and improve ROM.

Benefits of massage
* Massage reduces **inflammation**, beaks down **scar tissue**, reduces **joint stress** and improves **circulation** (and hence increased tissue metabolism) and **flexibility**.
* Benefits include a boost in interchange of nutrients and fluids between the cells of the tissue and the blood due to increased blood flow.
* When circulation is increased to these muscles, they can more quickly get rid of these toxins and recovery time between workouts can be shortened.
* Massage also helps the **body's muscle-building** process, and improves muscle elasticity and strength and prevents future injuries.

Heat, cold and contrast therapies

Heat therapies

Heat is an effective and safe treatment for most aches and pains following injury or hard training workouts. Heat can be applied in the form of a heat pad, deep heat cream, hot water bottle, infra-red heat lamp and therapies such as ultrasound.

Heat should not be used on an injury during the acute phase of recovery as it will increase bleeding under the skin around the injured area. The exception to this is back strains. A lot of the pain in this case is caused by muscle spasm rather than tissue damage, so heat is often helpful by providing an analgesic effect and relaxation effect for tight muscles.

Benefits of heat therapies
Heat therapy provides the following physiological responses that enhance injury recovery processes:
* Creates a **stress response** in the body. As temperature rises, the body responds by rerouting blood flow to increase blood vessel dilation and secreting a number of hormones, including the growth hormone (GH, or somatotropin) which assists in increasing the rate of musculoskeletal tissue repair.
* It has a direct **soothing** effect and helps to relieve pain and spasm and can ease stiffness by making the tissues more supple.
* **Reduces cellular oxidation rates** (high rates of oxidation may compromise the recovery rate and cause damage to cell membranes).
* **Stimulates heat-shock proteins**, which play a role in organising other proteins that are thought to play a role in the growth/repair of muscle tissue.
* Provides an ideal environment for **regaining the ROM** of joints and muscles, for example, increasing the range of motion of an ankle joint after injury.

Care must be taken to not push a joint through pain as this can actually reinjure the tissue.

Heat therapies are divided into **superficial** and **deep** heat therapies.

Superficial heat therapies
* Superficial heat therapies are those in which heat is transferred directly from the heat source to the body but the temperature increase only penetrates to a depth of a few centimeters.
* Examples of superficial heat therapies commonly used include dry and moist hot packs, hot whirlpool, hot tub or Jacuzzi, saunas and warm pools.
* For example, by applying a heat pack to painful joints and muscles, the heat stimulates sensory receptors to block the transmission of pain signals to the brain, resulting in an instant and effective pain relief.
* Superficial muscle strains can benefit from superficial heat therapy techniques.
* When muscle tissue is heated, it becomes more extensible and better able to stretch.
* Heat modalities should be used for 10-15 minutes, prior to stretching.
* After heating, a gradual and progressive pain-free stretch can be applied to the area.

figure 3.26 – a sauna

Deep heat therapies

Deep heat therapies deliver heat into deep tissues and muscles and are beneficial immediately following the acute stage of an injury. Deep heat may be used to treat a number of injuries, such as:

- Muscle spasms.
- Fractures, sprains, strains, and tendonitis.
- Arthritis and bursitis.

For example, the use of **ultrasound therapy** (by a physiotherapist):

- Provides gentle massage as it transmits heat energy into deep underlying tissue with no added strain to the injured area.
- Acts as a pro-inflammatory agent to stimulate the presence of macrophages (a type of white blood cell that engulfs and digests cellular debris).
- Increases in the extensibility of structures such as ligaments, tendons, fibrous scar tissue (resulting from the build up of mature collagen fibres which may form after the injury).
- Softens any scar tissue, within muscle tendons and/or ligaments, without any strain.

Hydrotherapy

Hydrotherapy is a therapeutic whole body treatment that involves moving and exercising in warm water. The temperature, pressure and movement of water are controlled and changed according to who's using the pool.

For example, **aquajogging** (figure 3.27) has proven to be a very good form of injury rehabilitation.

Warm water exercising avoids muscle soreness, enables full ROM of working joints and muscles and stress fractures to repair. In addition, the recovering athlete is able to maintain fitness during a rehabilitation programme.

figure 3.27 – aquajogging

Cryotherapy or cold treatments

Cryotherapy is the treatment by means of applications of **cold temperatures**, and can be used as soon as the wound has healed (i.e. no broken skin). Cryotherapy treatment decreases skin, subcutaneous and muscle temperature, causing narrowing of the blood vessels (**vasoconstriction**). Its goal is to decrease cellular metabolism, decrease **inflammation**, pain and muscle spasm. A variety of cold applications can be used to treat sports injuries.

Whole body cryotherapy (WBC)

WBC involves exposing individuals to extremely cold dry air (below -100°C) for two to four minutes in a **cryogenic chamber**.
Reduction in skin and muscle tissue temperatures reduces blood flow to the arms and legs (**vasoconstriction**) and diverts blood flow to the body's central core.

On leaving the chamber, blood flow returns to the arms and legs (**vasodilation**) reinstating normal oxygen levels, thus aiding the healing process.

WBC relieves muscle soreness and **inflammation** following high intensity training, as a result of reduced muscle metabolism, and is a popular recovery method used by professional sportspeople. WBC is a much quicker alternative to ice baths, but does require expensive specialist equipment.

Alternative cold therapy methods

Various alternative and cheaper cooling therapies are used in acute sports injuries as well as rehabilitation of the injured athlete, injury prevention and recovery from training and competitions. For example, ice packs, ice towels, ice massage and frozen gel packs.

Ice water immersion

Ice water immersion (figure 3.28) use the fact that **chilling** the affected area can **reduce local inflammation**. Ice bath immersion is thought to constrict blood vessels, flush waste products such as lactic acid and reduce swelling and tissue breakdown.

figure 3.28 – ice water immersion

Total cold water immersion

Studies have shown that total cold water **upright immersion** (at an optimal temperature of 10 degrees and up to 10 minutes immersion) **decreases inflammation** following injury and aids recovery from training. The effect is best when the water pressure is greatest. In addition, it gives the athlete a feeling of perceived freshness.

Precautions should be taken because prolonged application of very low temperatures could have detrimental effects.

Cryostretching

Cryostretching is a technique combining cryotherapy and stretching. Application of a cold pack is used to reduce muscle spasms and so increase flexibility.

This technique involves three phases:
- **Cold application** sufficient to produce a numbed response.
- Followed by **static stretching**, static stretches overcome the stretch reflex to reduce muscle spasm.
- Then the **contract-relax technique** (PNF). Muscle relaxation is often greater following a contraction than before. There should not be any pain throughout the procedure.

Contrast therapy

- Contrast therapy involves the alternating use of **cold** and **heat** applied to the injured, but recovering body part.
- For example, a leg recovering from a hamstring pull is placed in an ice bath, followed by a warm water bath. A cold-to-warm ratio of 1 to 3 min is recommended, based upon clinical observations and experience.
- The physiological effects of contrast therapy result from cycles of **vasoconstriction** (decreasing blood flow) and **vasodilation** (increasing blood flow) to the injured body part.
- The sharp sensory contrast between heat and cold appears to reduce pain and therefore muscle spasm. A decrease in pain and spasm, combined with active, pain-free range of motion, would in turn increase lymphatic drainage from the area and decrease swelling.

Contrast therapy is not recommended during the acute recovery phase when the injury is still swollen and bruised.

Anti-inflammatory drugs

Sporting injuries, including both acute trauma and chronic overuse injuries, are usually presented with clinical signs of swelling and pain.

Non-Steroidal Anti-Inflammatory Drugs (NSAIDs), such as aspirin and ibuprofen, are commonly used to reduce the pain, heat, swelling and redness that are associated with inflammation in an acute sports injury. Following an acute soft tissue injury, chemicals are released by the damaged cells that cause blood vessels to vasodilate and blood and cellular fluid to leak into the tissues. This causes swelling, pain, redness and a loss of function of the injured part. NSAID treatment is an attempt to inhibit this response, thus reducing the total rehabilitation time.

Anti-inflammatory drugs

In cases of chronic injuries, such as tendinopathy, an injection of corticosteroids (stronger anti-inflammatory agents) into an inflamed tendon can relieve pain in the short term up to 6 weeks, but there is no evidence they provide any benefit in the long-term. When prescribing NSAIDs for athletes, doctors should consider not only their efficacy, but also their toxicity, and bleeding risks.

Physiotherapy

The role of physiotherapy in sports medicine is one of participation in both **prevention** and **treatment** of injuries. The aim during injury rehab is to restore **original function** to the affected part.

Physiotherapy (administered by physiotherapists) uses a range of the physical recovery methods for musculoskeletal injuries:

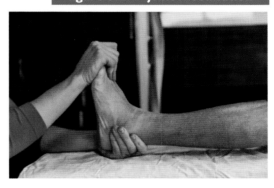

figure 3.29 – joint mobilisation

Joint mobilisation
Joint mobilisation is a passive hands-on movement technique and treatment varies depending on the joint stiffness/hypermobility and the pain associated with moving the joint. Joint mobilisation is generally very safe (figure 3.29).

Massage of soft tissues
Soft tissue massage involves direct physical action on the muscle and other soft tissues of the body, and targets muscles, tendons, ligaments, or other connective tissue such as fascia.
For further information see page 67.

Electro stimulation
Electro stimulation (ES) also known as **neuromuscular electrical stimulation** (NMES). It is a training technique used for injury prevention, injury treatment, toning, pain relief, muscular recovery and physical preparation.

Electrodes are placed on the muscle groups such as the abdominal muscles, hamstrings (figure 3.30), calf muscles, plantar arch muscles and lower back muscles. An electric current is produced which is sent to the nerve fibres causing a mechanical response in the muscle. The current settings can vary depending on the clinical pathology requirements.

figure 3.30 – electro stimulation

ES is thought to affect the body with associated **therapeutic benefits** that:
- Stimulate muscles to **contract**, by stimulating muscle fibre recruitment.
- Stimulate nerves to **decrease pain** by stimulating larger nerve fibres that can override the smaller nerve fibres that produce pain.
- Increase **blood flow** to speed healing.
- Reduce **inflammation**.

- Stimulate cells to reproduce and speed **healing**.
- Assist the **removal of lactic acid** following a training session or competition and hence reduce **DOMS**.

- ES can be used early on in the recovery process when a wound has healed but the injured body part is not ready for loading.
- ES in combination with physical activity, serves is to stimulate weaker muscles to contract and improve strength more quickly.

Exercise programmes to strengthen weakened muscles/joints.

- In the case of a planned surgical procedure, the physiotherapist can be valuable both before and after.
- For example, prior to an ACL or meniscus operation, it is essential for the patient to exercise his or her thigh muscles as they are responsible for stabilising the knee, and if they are well-trained before the operation, subsequent rehabilitation is facilitated.
- Assessing an individual's functional state is part of the physiotherapist's work. By analysing the causes and consequences of a functional impairment, the physiotherapist can draw up a programme for the treatment of muscles, joints and ligaments.
- The treatment methods used are flexibility, strength and coordination in prescribed portions, together with encouragement, rest and pain relief.

figure 3.31 – the plank

- One of the major detraining effects that occur during long-term injuries is **muscular atrophy** of the unused limb. It is therefore essential that these particular muscles increase in size back to normal. Within the early stages of muscle rehabilitation, muscular size can be increased by effective **electrical stimulation** to the muscle as described on page 71.

- As soon as an injured athlete can tolerate **loading**, he can progress through his rehab process back into a more traditional strength and conditioning programme (figure 3.31). For a recuperating athlete, an exercise programme will also include **sport specific activity** that is progressively overloaded to restore total bodily functioning required for that sport.

Rest and active rest

The physiotherapist will include **rest and active rest** to give stressed body parts time to recover prior to the next part of the rehabilitation programme.

- Modern rehab includes **rest** as essential recovery time after trauma.
- **Active rest** means that low level exercises are undertaken in order to improve the blood flow through affected areas without physical stress, and therefore to promote healing via blood carried nutrients, particularly oxygen.

- Cell to cell activation is really important, since it stimulates the healing process.
- This also has the effect of preventing a muscle or other soft tissue from healing at a shorter length than it was before the injury. This is because post-trauma muscle length is unpredictable depending on joint flexibility and nutrition.
- Low level activity also has the effect of keeping muscle fit enough to exert force once an injury is healed.

The role of the physiotherapist is to monitor the total exercise until the athlete no longer needs this supervision.

Surgery

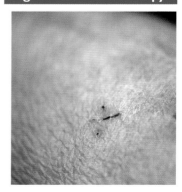
figure 3.32 – arthroscopy

Most sports injuries don't require surgery, but severe injuries, such as compound fractures and torn and stretched ligaments, may require corrective treatment.

Arthroscopy (keyhole surgery) is used to tidy up injuries such as torn menisci and ruptured ligaments (figure 3.32).

For example, a ruptured anterior cruciate ligament (ACL) is a common injury sustained in team sports such as soccer, rugby, netball, hockey and basketball. When it is torn it is unable to heal and the balance information it carries is lost. A reconstructed ligament involves replacing it with a graft taken from one of the hamstring tendons.

Surgery

- Following the immediate surgical reconstruction of the ACL, rest and regular application of a cryo-cuff (figure 3.33) on the knee provides iced water compression to help reduce pain and swelling.
- Within 24 to 48 hours following the operation the patient is encouraged to walk with the aid of crutches (used to off-load weight bearing on the injured leg) and a fully supporting leg brace and is discharged as an outpatient for regular outpatient physiotherapy appointments.
- Rehabilitation of the knee joint can take up to 6 months after which the athlete will be able to return to **non-contact sport/training** and have a final review at the clinic if all is good. Return to contact sport is recommended when the damaged leg is at least 85% the strength of the other.

figure 3.33 – cryocuff

Compound fractures

More severe injuries, such as compound fractures, require open surgery that has significant scarring (figure 3.34), takes longer to heal and is more susceptible to infection. During this type of procedure, the bone fragments are first repositioned into their normal alignment.

They are held together with special screws and metal plates attached to the outer surface of the fractured bone. Plates and screws are routinely used to provide additional support and strength to the repaired bone (figure 3.35), and enable the patient to recover more quickly (up to 6 months) from the operation.

Both keyhole and open surgery are performed under a general anaesthetic.

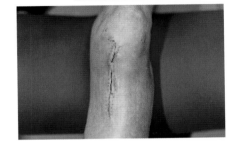

figure 3.34 – operation scars

Treatment of common sporting injuries

Fractures
- Flush open wounds associated with compound fractures with clean, fresh water and cover them with a dry dressing.
- Use **PRICE protocol** to decrease swelling and to relieve pain.
- In the short-term immobilise and if possible realign the joint above and below the fracture by using a splint, with wrapping tape around the splint.

- For example, if a forearm is broken, the splint should run from across the wrist to the hand and across the elbow to the upper arm, supporting the forearm without repositioning it.
- Monitor the extremity near the fracture assessing any loss of sensation, decreased temperature, and pulse.
- Administer anti-inflammatory pain relief medication.
- Medical professionals normally place a plaster cast to assist the healing process.
- Bone generally takes between 6 and 12 weeks to heal.

A **stress fracture** is a common overuse injury often experienced by runners and jumpers (page 52) and occurs significantly in the weight-bearing bones of the foot.

In addition to the PRICE protocol and anti-inflammatory medication, a doctor may recommend the **use of crutches** to keep weight off the stress fracture until the pain and inflammation subsides.

It typically takes from 6 to 8 weeks for a stress fracture to heal. **Non-weight-bearing activities**, such as aquajogging (page 69, figure 3.27) closely mimics the movement of running, provides a neuromuscular workout that, in addition to stimulation of the aerobic system, benefits and keeps running-specific muscles active.

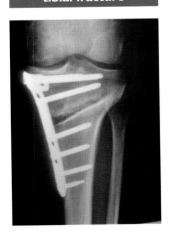

figure 3.35 – plates and screws supporting tibial fracture

Joint injuries

Dislocations

Use **PRICE protocol** to decrease swelling and to relieve pain. In some cases, the dislocated joint might go back into place naturally after this treatment. If the joint doesn't return to normal naturally, a doctor may use one of the following treatments:

- **Manipulation** or repositioning the joint back into place performed by a doctor.
- **Immobilization**, such as wearing a sling for a shoulder dislocation. The length of time the joint needs to be immobile will vary, depending on the joint and severity of the injury.
- **Medication** may be prescribed as a pain reliever or a muscle relaxant, however most of the pain should go away after the joint returns to its normal position.
- **Surgery** may be needed if nerves and blood vessels are damaged.
- **Rehabilitation** begins once the joint is into the correct position and the sling or splint has been removed. The goal of rehabilitation is to gradually increase the joint's strength and restore its range of motion. Exercises that progressively overload and mobilise the joint will strengthen the ligaments, tendons and surrounding musculature.

Sprains

Most sprains can be managed at home using painkillers, such as ibuprofen, to ease any pain and reduce swelling.

- If the injury is a **grade 1 sprain**, use the **PRICE therapy** treatment protocol.
- If is an ankle sprain, use crutches to remove weight bearing load on the injured foot.
- Within two to three days commence stretching and strengthening exercises, providing pain can tolerated.

- For a **grade 2 sprain**, use the same treatment protocol as outlined for a grade 1 sprain, but allow more time for healing to occur.
- In the case of a sprained ankle, the doctor may also use a device such as a boot or a splint to immobilize the ankle and may also prescribe physical therapy to regain full use of the ankle joint.

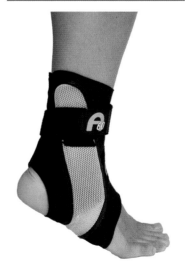

figure 3.36 – ankle bracing

- **Grade 3** or a severe sprain involves a complete tear or rupture of a ligament and takes considerably longer to heal.
- It is treated with immobilization of the joint followed by a longer period of physical therapy for range of motion, stretching, and strength building.
- Surgery will be considered for reconstructing the torn ligaments.

- On average, the initial treatment of a sprain includes resting and protecting the ankle until swelling goes down for about one week. That is followed by a period of one to two weeks of exercise to restore range of motion, strength, and flexibility. For a severe sprain, it can take several more weeks to gradually return to normal activities.

- Equipment, such as an ankle brace (figure 3.36), can provide additional support during the healing process, in addition to significantly reducing injury risk. Proper fitting and sports-specific footwear will also reduce the risk of injury to soft tissues, bones and joints of the lower limb.

There are many secondary therapies used to treat sports injuries that can assist the primary treatment received, for example, from a physiotherapist or doctor.

Hyperbaric oxygen therapy (HBOT page 76) assists in the recovery of acute traumatic injury to muscle contusions and sprains and strains thereby reducing recovery time.

Torn cartilage

Cartilage is a tough, flexible tissue found throughout the body. It covers the surface of joints, and acts as a shock absorber and allows bones to slide over one another. Cartilage damage is a relatively common type of injury. It often involves the knees, although joints such as the hips, ankles and elbows can also be affected. Cartilage has no blood vessels or nerves. It therefore heals very slowly after an injury because the cells and nutrients, necessary for tissue repair, cannot reach the damaged area very easily.

Cartilage within the knee joint can become damaged as a result of a sudden injury to the menisci (two large C-shaped cartilages that are positioned on the top of the tibia bone of the knee), caused by a sudden twisting movement, or slowing down too quickly from a flat-out sprint.

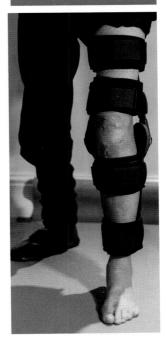

figure 3.37 – hinged knee bracing

During a prolonged extreme load on the knee joint, as experienced in downhill skiing, the articular cartilage of the patella is vulnerable to injury. Long-term overuse by gradual wear and tear is also responsible for cartilage injuries. When some of the cartilage covering the ends of the bones, gradually roughens and becomes thin it is known as **osteoarthritis**.

The treatment plan depends on the severity of the injury:
- **Self-care measures**, using the PRICE protocol and medication, are usually recommended as the first treatment for minor cartilage injuries.
- Minor cartilage injuries may get better on their own within a few weeks, but more severe cartilage damage may require surgery.

A number of surgical techniques can be used, with the help of arthroscopy, also known as key hole surgery (figure 3.32, page 72) including:
- **Trimming** the jagged/torn edges and cleaning out floating debris from inside the joint is sufficient to clear up a minor tears and recovery is anywhere between 3 to 6 weeks.
- Where cartilage damage is extensive, drilling small holes in the nearby bone (microfracture surgery) encourages the growth of new cartilage.
- Replacing the damaged cartilage with healthy cartilage taken from another part of the joint.
- The recovery period with these last two techniques includes at least 3 months of **non-loading activity**. Initial rehabilitation, following surgery, often involves the use of supports, such as crutches and hinged knee bracing (figure 3.37) and **physiotherapy** that will include exercises that gradually strengthen the surrounding musculature and balance activities.

Exercise induced muscle damage (EIMD)

- During a hard training session, such as eccentric to concentric **plyometric training** (figure 3.10, page 57) sarcomeres can be stretched beyond their optimum functional length thus creating muscle tissue instability, weakness, and micro tears that can cause local inflammation.

- **Protein enzymes** such as **creatine kinase** (CK), and **myoglobin** may leak from damaged membranes into the blood circulation causing potential pain and inflammation.

- This acute inflammation is known as **exercise induced muscle damage** (EIMD).

- The prominent symptoms of **EIMD** are pain, swelling, stiffness, reduced strength and fatigue.

- Most of these symptoms are related to the **delayed onset of muscle soreness** (DOMS).

- Treatments for EIMD include cold therapies, massage, anti-inflammatory medication and sufficient rest between hard training sessions.

Multi-purpose modalities used in injury rehabilitation

- **Climate chambers** replicate different climates that control altitude, temperature and humidity.

- **Hypobaric chambers** (containing a reduced amount of oxygen in the air compared with sea level atmospheric pressure) can assist in the recovery of fractures and general healing processes.

- **Hypoxic stimulation** occurs in cells and tissues that are in a hypoxic state and so is responsible for a number of adaptive responses that enable to body to make better use of the limited oxygen available.

- The main adaptive response is an increase in manufacture of red blood cells (erythropoietin production), alongside increases in myoglobin, mitochondria, oxidative enzymes levels.

- In the case of fracture healing, recovery is also enhanced by stimulating the repair of a variety of proteins, fibroblasts, endothelial cells and osteoblasts.

- These responses support an increased oxygen and nutrient delivery to body tissues undergoing repair. This is of great value to the rehabilitation process from injury, particularly when the athlete is exercising during the active phase of rehab.

- Hypoxic sessions can commence as soon as the injured athlete has recovered from the initial sedentary treatment phase to the active recovery phase of rehab.

- **Hyperbaric oxygen therapy** (HBOT) is a treatment which enhances the body's natural healing process by inhalation of 100% oxygen in a total body chamber, (figure 3.38).

- HBOT sessions can commence as soon as the injured athlete has recovered from the initial treatment phase.

HBOT benefits

- Delivers up to 25 times normal levels of oxygen to body tissues.
- Stimulates the **growth of new blood vessels**, thus improving blood flow to areas with an arterial blockage that may have resulted from an impact injury.
- Reduces **fatigue** from inadequate oxygen supply to body tissues.
- Speeds up **recovery** from fatigue such as DOMS.
- Boosts **immune** system function by stimulating white blood cell activity, thereby controlling infection.
- Decreases swelling and **inflammation**.
- Promotes **regeneration** of injured tissues.
- Decreases ligament and tissue **healing time**.
- Aids the **repair** of stress fractures and breaks.

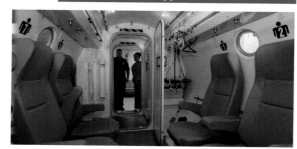

figure 3.38 – hyperbaric chamber

HBOT is an example of a **secondary therapy** used to treat sports injuries and its purpose is to assist the primary treatment received, for example, from a physiotherapist or doctor. HBOT assists in the recovery of acute traumatic injury to muscle contusions and sprains and strains thereby reducing recovery time.

Practice questions

1) Injury to the medial meniscus of the knee joint is common amongst:
   a. hockey players.
   b. boxers.
   c. footballers.
   d. track and field athletes.

2) Elevation of an injured body part helps reduce injury by:
   a. helping support the weight of the limb.
   b. allowing white blood cells to be released to fight infection.
   c. reducing blood flow to the area.
   d. increasing blood flow to the area.

3) Overuse of tendons in physical activity can cause problems.
   Which one of the following is associated with tendon overuse?
   a. inflammation.
   b. arthritis.
   c. hypertrophy.
   d. bruising.

4) Which one of the following is not a method of reducing risks of injury when participating in physical activities?
   a. wearing shin pads when playing hockey or football.
   b. making sure you warm up before participating in an exercise class.
   c. playing with others of similar ability in a rugby match.
   d. wearing fashionable sports equipment when going to the gym.

5) A sprain during a sport activity is to be immediately attended to by:
   a. application of ointment.
   b. elevation of affected body part.
   c. cold compression.
   d. massage.

6) Which of the following would you recommend to prevent inflammation of the joints during or after physical activity?
   a. rub massage oil into your joints before and after exercise.
   b. use carbo-loading to increase energy levels.
   c. stretch your muscles thoroughly before exercising.
   d. do not do too much activity at any one time.

7) Why are joint sprains a particular problem? 2 marks

8) Sports injuries can be broadly classified as either acute or chronic injuries.
   Explain what is meant by these two classifications, using examples where appropriate. 4 marks

9) Playing kit and equipment are major factors that an athlete needs to consider in injury prevention. Identify the key factors that affect the selection of their use. 4 marks

10) Discuss the principles and guidelines for injury prevention. 5 marks

11) Why should stretching be part of an injury preventative training programme? 2 marks

Practice questions

12) Hyperbaric oxygen chambers and ice baths are aids to rehabilitation for elite performers. Briefly describe how each of these therapies assist in this process.   **6 marks**

13) Describe the use of the PRICE protocol for the immediate treatment of acute injuries.   **5 marks**

14) What are the signs and symptoms of concussion and how is this condition treated?   **4 marks**

15) Warm-up and cool-down are useful in preventing injury and in aiding the recovery process after intense exercise.
    a) What activities would you include in the warm-up and why?   **3 marks**

    b) What would you include in the cool-down and why?   **3 marks**

16) During a match a player received a severe tackle to the lower leg. How can a first aider assess the nature and severity of the injury?   **8 marks**

17) Screening is a key part of the professional sportspersons daily life. How can it be used in injury prevention?   **4 marks**

18) Rapid recovery from injury is vital for elite performers and they now use a wide range of injury recovery techniques. For each of the following methods describe the treatment and its purpose.
    a) Cryotherapy.   **3 marks**

    b) Proprioceptive retraining.   **3 marks**

    c) Therapeutic massage.   **3 marks**

19) Explain how the use of an ice bath can help to reduce the 'delayed onset of muscle soreness' (DOMS).   **4 marks**

20) Surgery is used in the treatments of sports injuries. Using examples of sporting injuries, discuss the advantages and disadvantages of keyhole surgery against open, invasive surgical techniques.   **10 marks**

Answers link: http://www.jroscoe.co.uk/downloads/a2_revise_pe_ocr/OCRA2_ch3_answers.pdf

BIOMECHANICS

CHAPTER 4: *Linear motion and angular motion*

Linear motion

Linear means in a straight line. Chapter 4 attempts to put into perspective concepts involving movement in a single direction such as speed, velocity, acceleration and force (through Newton's Second Law of Motion).

STUDENT NOTE

Newton's first, second and third laws of motion are discussed in detail in AS/A1 Revise PE for OCR, ISBN 9781901424911, Part 3 page 108 onwards.

Linear motion (linear accelerated motion) is produced by the action of forces on a body (by Newton's second law). Forces that act have to be added together to produce a resultant force using the laws of vector addition below.

To produce linear motion (as opposed to rotational, spinning or angular motion), this resultant force must act through the centre of mass of the body on which the force acts (centre of mass is discussed on page 114 of part 3 of AS/A1 Revise PE for OCR, ISBN 9781901424911).

This action is looked at in figure 4.1 in which a person taking a basketball jump shot wanrts to land on his feet after the jump - and not rotate and land on his front or back. Hence the net or resultant force acts through his center of mass.

figure 4.1 – resultant force act through the centre of mass of jumper

Scalars and vectors

The ideas behind **scalars** and **vectors** are used extensively in maths and physics.

Scalar

A **scalar** is a quantity which has size or value only. Quantities like mass, speed, energy, power, and length have a value only. For example, a person could have a mass of 60 kg, or 1000 joules of energy are used up when performing an exercise.

No directional angle is required when talking about these quantities.

Energy is a scalar which has a value only, and the value of energy consumed daily by a Tour de France cyclist is 6,000 kilocalories - which has no direction.

Speed (measured in metres per second - ms^{-1}), distance and time are scalars which are linked by a simple equation.

   Speed = distance travelled per second (ms^{-1})

   Speed = <u>distance travelled in metres (m)</u>
                  time taken to travel in seconds (s)

Vector

A **vector** is a quantity which has **size** (called magnitude) and **direction**. By quantity we mean something like weight, displacement, velocity, acceleration, force, and momentum, all of which are vectors, and therefore have to have a direction connected to them as well as value or size. For example, a force could be 100 newtons downward (the downward specifies the direction), an acceleration could be 10 metres per second squared forwards (the forwards specifies the direction).

Usually in maths, the direction is specified by the angle θ (measured in an anticlockwise direction to the x-axis) in a graph of an arrow drawn on the graph, with the size (magnitude) represented by the length of the arrow (figure 4.2).

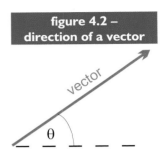

figure 4.2 – direction of a vector

Force as a vector

Force is a vector and therefore has a direction (shown as angle θ to the horizontal in figure 5.1) as well as a size or value. This point is very important to anyone thinking about what happens when forces are applied, because it enables a force in one direction to cancel out completely an equal force in the opposite direction so that, in spite of very large forces being involved in a given situation, forces cancel out to give a **zero** (or very small) net or **resultant force**.

A **resultant vector** is **two or more vectors added together**, taking into account their directions.

For example, consider the weight lifter in figure 4.3. As he pulls upwards on the bar, he exerts a force of 1000 newtons (N) upwards on the bar and gravity exerts a force of 980 newtons downwards on the bar.

The resultant or net force acting on the actual bar is therefore only about 20 N upwards, just enough to accelerate the bar off the floor.

The idea that net force causes acceleration is linked with **Newton's First** and **Second Laws** of Motion and is a fundamental property of force.

Also, it is possible for many forces acting in all sorts of different directions to cancel one another out. When this happens, from Newton's First Law we know that the object (or sportsperson) on which the forces act will either be stationary or moving at constant velocity (in a straight line). This situation is called **equilibrium**: where the object is stationary this is static equilibrium and where it is moving at constant velocity this is dynamic equilibrium.

figure 4.3 – forces acting on a bar

Pull on bar
1000 N

Weight of bar
980 N

Net Force

The point of this is that when more than one vector has to be taken into account, then they must be added together taking note of the direction of each vector.

In figure 4.4 for example, two forces of 500 newtons are acting, the green force acts upwards, and the red force acts downwards. Because they are acting in opposite directions, they add up to nil, in other words they exactly cancel out to give zero net force. Note that this gymnast is also in unstable equilibrium.

figure 4.4 – vectors cancel out

Net Force

- In figure 4.5, the **vertical forces** acting on the sprinter are the weight (W = force due to gravity) acting downwards, and the ground reaction force (R) acting upwards. These two forces are identical in value but opposite in direction and therefore cancel out exactly to give zero net force vertically.

- The **horizontal forces** are the friction force (F) acting forwards, and the **air resistance** or **drag** (A) acting backwards. These two forces are equal in value but opposite in direction, and hence cancel out to give zero net force acting horizontally.

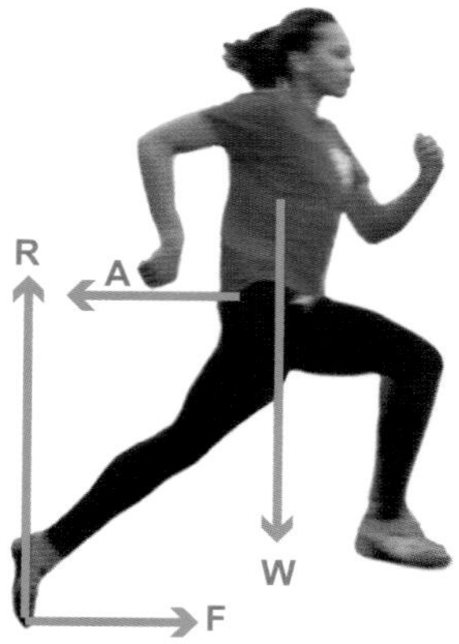

- Hence relatively large forces can act, but they can cancel out because of their direction. Note that zero net force does not mean that the sprinter is stationary, (from Newton's first law of motion).

- Equally, when the forces are added up and there is an unbalanced **resultant** (the forces **do not cancel out**), then there is a **net force** acting. The body on which this force is acting will then accelerate in the **direction** of this net force as specified by Newton's second law .

figure 4.5 – forces cancel out

Further notes on vectors

There are specific mathematical rules that enable you to add together vectors that are not in the same direction. You may notice from figures 4.6 and 4.7 that the resultant of two forces at an angle has been drawn by completing a **parallelogram** (in figure 4.6) or a **rectangle** (in figure 4.7, where the forces are at right angles). The resultant then lies along the diagonal of the parallelogram.

In figure 4.6, the resultant of the forces in the wires (T₁ and T₂) supporting the gymnast upwards **cancels out** exactly his/her weight (W) downwards (static equilibrium).

figure 4.6 – forces balance

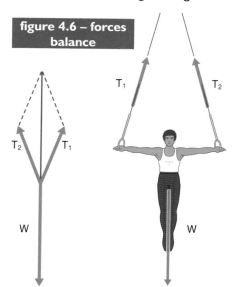

In figure 4.7, again, the **resultant** of the normal reaction force (R) and the combined friction forces (air resistance and friction with the ground) exactly cancels out the weight of the skier – note the geometric vector diagram (dynamic equilibrium).

figure 4.7 – forces balance

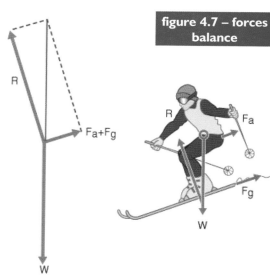

Figure 4.8 shows **resultants of forces** acting on a swimmer. His weight (W) is balanced by the upthrust of the water (U) and the forward thrust (T) cancels out the backward drag (D) of the water (again dynamic equilibrium).

figure 4.8 – forces balance

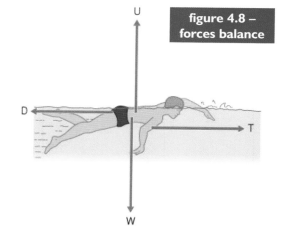

Resultants

It is also possible to calculate the size and direction of resultant vectors using trigonometry. Looking at figure 4.9 (page 83), in which R (the reaction force) and F (the total friction force) are at right angles, we note that angle α lies between F and the resultant X of the two vectors as drawn. Therefore using Pythagoras theorem on figure 4.9, page 83:

$$X^2 = R^2 + F^2 \text{ and}$$
$$X = \sqrt{(R^2 + F^2)}$$
$$= \text{the magnitude of the resultant } (\sqrt{} = \text{'square root of'}).$$

Net Force

Also:

$$\tan \alpha = \frac{R}{F}$$

and α = the angle between X and R, which gives the direction of the resultant.

Hence, looking at figure 4.9, the normal reaction force on the sprinter's foot has the value 700 N and the forward friction force 200 N, so that the resultant total reaction force on his/her foot, X, has the magnitude:

$$X \quad = \sqrt{(700^2 + 200^2)} \quad = \quad \sqrt{(530\,000)} \quad = \quad 728 \text{ N}$$

The angle α between X and the 700 N force will be:

$\alpha \qquad = \tan^{-1} \left(\dfrac{R}{F}\right) \quad$ = the angle between X and R which gives the **direction** of R.

$\qquad = \tan^{-1} \left(\dfrac{700}{200}\right) = \tan^{-1} 3.5 \qquad = 74.06°$

Hence the resultant force has a **value** of 728 N acting at an **angle** of 74.06° to the 200 N force (horizontal). Note that this force X passes through the centre of mass of the runner and therefore would cause no toppling or rotation of his/her body during the running action.

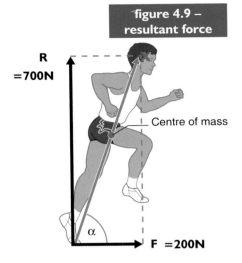

figure 4.9 – resultant force

R =700N

Centre of mass

F =200N

Distance, position and displacement

Speed (a **scalar**) and **velocity** (a **vector**) are ideas that involve a body or object changing its position. For example, if an athlete starts a race – the stopwatch or electronic timer starts also – and he runs 10 m in 2 seconds, his position has changed by 10 m from the start line, the distance moved is 10 m and the average speed over this distance is 5 metres per second.

The same idea could be used in a game situation but now the position of the centre-forward might be 20 m out from the opposing goal, on a line 10 m to the left of the left-hand post. At this point he might shoot for goal and the ball travels 25m – the distance from the striker to the net at the back of the goal – in 0.5 seconds. In this case the speed of the ball would be 50 metres per second.

So, you can see that distance is usually measured from one point to another point and the position of the points tells us where they are in space (or on a pitch or court). This distinction becomes important in races or games where starts and finishes are fixed.

The **displacement** of a sportsperson from the start of an event may also be important in some cases. For example, a triathlete may swim, cycle and run huge distances but he/she may only be displaced at most 2km from the start position. So the displacement of the triathlete is the distance (as the crow flies) between the start position and the position of the triathlete – usually the direction is also taken into account.

Speed and velocity

The difference between these two apparently similar concepts, is that velocity has direction and is therefore a vector, whereas speed is a scalar and has size only.

Both are expressed as metres per second and are defined by the same formula: (**v = distance/time**), velocity is a vector and has value and direction whereas speed is a scalar and has value only.

Sometimes, it doesn't actually make any difference whether we use speed or velocity to describe the motion of a sportsperson or object, because he, she or it always moves in the same direction. But once the direction changes, it is important to use velocity to describe the motion.

Speed, velocity and acceleration

Acceleration is the change of **velocity** per second or:

$$\text{acceleration} = \frac{\text{final velocity - starting velocity}}{\text{time taken to change}} \quad (ms^{-2})$$

Here, the velocity includes its direction, so we could have the velocity having the same value (magnitude), but just changing its direction. This happens for an object following a circular path (like the head of a hammer in the hammer throw).

This means that the velocity is changing and therefore there is an acceleration towards the centre of the circular path. This also means that there will be a force (by Newton's Second Law) towards the centre of the circular path.

Deceleration is the term which represents the **slowing down** of an object, so the starting velocity is bigger than the final velocity, and the result of the acceleration equation above is negative. Hence deceleration is **negative** acceleration

Graphs and curves of motion

Graphs of distance against time

The following graphs of **distance against time** will show the progress of an object as it moves along. In graph 4.10A, the distance remains the same as time goes along - which means that the object remains in the same place, there is **no movement**, the object is stationary, with speed zero.

In graph 4.10B, the distance changes with time - meaning that the object is **moving forward**, and eventually it comes to a halt with zero speed, so it **slows down** as the speed reduces to zero.

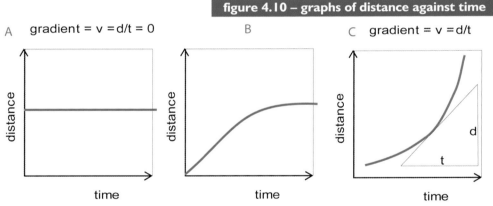

figure 4.10 – graphs of distance against time

A   gradient = v = d/t = 0   B   C   gradient = v = d/t

What changes is the **gradient** of the graph, and this is explained in graph 4.10C. The gradient is defined as the rate of change of speed with time and this is the gradient as shown in the graph.

$$\text{speed} = \frac{d}{t}$$

So the steeper the gradient or **slope** of the graph, the faster the movement and the greater the speed or velocity.

Graphs of speed/velocity against time

Graphs of **velocity against time** show how velocity changes with time and here, the gradient is the acceleration of the moving object

acceleration = change of velocity / time taken to change

In graph 4.11A, the velocity **remains the same**, the gradient of the graph is **zero**, therefore the body's acceleration is zero. This body has **constant velocity** and is subject to Newton's first law.

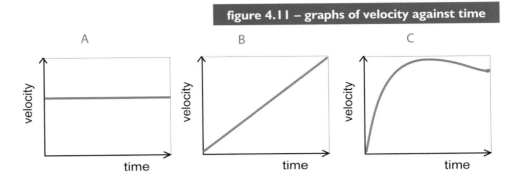

figure 4.11 – graphs of velocity against time

In graph 4.11B, the velocity changes continuously with time, and the gradient of the graph is constant, and therefore the **acceleration is constant**.

In graph 4.11C, the moving object is a 100 metre sprinter, whose **acceleration is largest** at the begining of the race, who reaches **maximum speed** at about half of the race, and who slows down slightly (**negative acceleration** or deceleration) before the end of the race.

This can be linked via **Newton's second law of motion** to the forces applied to the sprinter during the race.

The sprinter

figure 4.12 – start, middle and end of a sprint

- At the **start of the race** (figure 4.12A), there is a steep upwards slope on her velocity time graph (figure 4.11C) which means a large acceleration. This corresponds with a large forward net force applied at the start when friction is a large forward force acting on the foot of the runner. From figure 4.12A you will see that the vertical forces cancel out, and the friction force forward is much larger than the air resistance drag force backward. This produces a large net (resultant) force forward (marked in black on figure 4.12A). This force provides forward acceleration from Newton's second law.

- During the **middle of the run** (figure 4.12B), the velocity time graph is almost level, which means that acceleration is almost zero, therefore forces cancel out.

- At the **end of the run** (figure 4.12C), the velocity time graph has a small negative slope, showing that the sprinter decelerates, and that therefore there must be a net force backwards (shown in black) causing this deceleration.

Angular motion

Angle

Angle is a familiar concept to most people, so it is readily understood what is meant by 30°, 90°, 180° and 360°. In scientific terms, an angle is measured in radians. The radian as a unit of angle is defined as '**the angle subtended at the centre of a circle by an arc length of one radius**'. Suffice it to say at this point that one radian is approximately 60°.

Angular displacement

Angular displacement is defined similarly to displacement for linear systems and is the **relative angle** compared to some fixed position or line in space. For example, if a golfer starts his/her drive from the presentation position (i.e. with club just touching the ball) and backswings to the fully extended position with the club behind his/her back, the club shaft would have an angular displacement equal to the angle between the starting position and the fully extended position of the backswing. This would be a measure of the fluency and range of the swing and could be anywhere from 180° to 290° (or 3.142 to 5.06 radians).

Angular velocity

figure 4.13 – a high jumper turning

Angular velocity is the same thing as rate of spinning or twisting, and is defined as:

$$\text{angular velocity } (\omega) = \frac{\text{angle turned (in radians)}}{\text{time taken to turn}}$$

This is a similar definition to that for linear velocity, except distance is replaced by angle in the formula.

Angular acceleration

Again in a similar way to linear systems, it is possible to define angular acceleration as:

$$\text{angular acceleration} = \frac{\text{change of angular velocity}}{\text{time taken to change}}$$

This concept applies to situations in which the rate of spin **changes with time**. Examples of this would be the hammer throw (in which the rate of spin increases throughout the movement up to the release of the hammer) and the tumbler, gymnast or diver (who speeds up the rate of rotation or slows it down by changing his/her body shape).

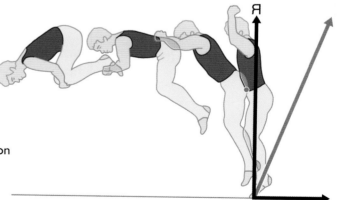

Torque and eccentric force

figure 4.14 – a gymnast tumbling

Torque is the twisting force which you could apply to a body to cause it to turn or spin. It is defined as the force applied to the body multiplied by the perpendicular distance to the axis of rotation (the moment of force about the turning axis).

This definition means that the bigger the force and the distance from the axis of turning, the bigger the turning effect.

Torque is therefore provided by an eccentric force - eccentric in that it is applied to one side of the centre of mass or axis of rotation and therefore causes turning or spinning.

For example, in figure 4.13, the upward resultant force acting on the take off foot of the high jumper acts to the left of his centre of mass thereby causing clockwise turning to the jumper's body.

In figure 4.14, the upward reaction force acting on both take-off feet of the gymnast acts to the right of his **centre of mass** (red dot) which initiates the foward anticlockwise somersault or tumble.

Axes and planes of the body

When sportspeople **spin, turn or twist, they do so about axes** as defined in figure 4.15. The twists, tumbles and turns involved in sports movements can all be described in this way.

Three imaginary axes of rotation

An axis of rotation is defined as '**an imaginary line about which the body rotates or spins, at right angles to the plane**' – as in figure 4.15, axes labelled A, B and C.

- **Longitudinal axis**
  - Axis A on figure 4.15.
  - This axis runs vertically from the top of the head to a point between the feet.
  - Movements in the **transverse plane** about the longitudinal axis are rotational movements.
  - Examples of sporting movements would be the spinning skater and the hammer throw (figure 4.16).

- **Transverse axis**
  - Axis B on figure 4.15. This axis runs horizontally from side to side across the body between opposite hips at right angles to the sagittal plane.
  - Movements within the **sagittal plane** about the transverse axis are flexion, extension, hyperextension, dorsiflexion and plantarflexion.
  - Sports movements about this axis include sit ups, and the high jump Fosbury Flop flight phase, and somersaults (figure 4.17).

- **Frontal axis (also** called **the sagittal axis)**
  - Axis C on figure 4.15.
  - This axis runs horizontally from front to back between belly button and lumbar spine.
  - Movements in the **frontal plane** about the frontal axis include abduction, adduction and spinal lateral flexion.
  - Examples of sports movements about this axis are a cartwheel (figure 4.18), and the bowling action in cricket.

Planes of the body

The term **body plane** is defined as '**an imaginary flat surface running through the centre of gravity of the body**', and is used to assist in the understanding of movement of body segments with respect to one another. Within each plane the turning axis can be identified as in figure 4.15.

It should be noted that the human body is capable of many complicated twisting or turning movements which could be in a combination of planes and around combinations of axes defined in this way.

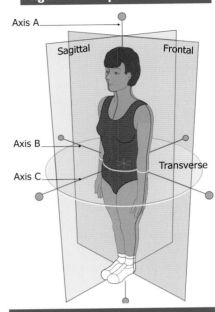

figure 4.15 – planes and axes

Axis A
Sagittal
Frontal
Axis B
Transverse
Axis C

figure 4.16 – a hammer thrower turning around longitudinal axis

figure 4.17 – a gymnast tumbling around the transverse axis

figure 4.18 – a cartwheel rotating about the frontal axis

Moment of inertia (MI)

This is the equivalent of mass (**inertia**) in the linear system, and is defined as:

    moment of inertia   = **sum of [(mass of body part) x
(distance of body part from the axis of rotation) squared]
over all parts of the rotating body.**

Mathematically: MI   = $\Sigma\, m\, r^2$

Objects rotating with large MI require large moments of force (torque) to change their angular velocity, and objects with small MI require small moments of force (torque) to change their angular velocity or ω.

Moment of inertia

The formula above means that moment of inertia depends on the spread of mass away from the axis of spin, so as the body shape changes, the moment of inertia of the shape changes. The more spread out the mass, the bigger the MI.

The unit of MI is kilogramme metre squared - kgm^2.

figure 4.19 – moments of inertia of different shapes

- Bodies with **arms held out wide** have large MI, the further the mass is away from the axis of rotation increases the MI dramatically.
- Sportspeople use this to control all spinning or turning movements.
- Pikes and tucks are good examples of use of MI, both reduce MI.

Values of moment of inertia

In figure 4.19, I is the MI for the left most pin man and has a value of about 1.0 kgm^2 for an average male person. From this diagram you can see how control of the arms will make a big difference to the value of MI, and that a tuck or pike can also **change MI** dramatically.

Angular momentum

Angular momentum is a quantity used to describe what happens when bodies spin and turn, it is defined as:

    angular momentum   = **moment of inertia** x **angular velocity**
                           = **rotational inertia** x **rate of spin**
        H   =   **I**   x ω

Conservation of angular momentum

The **law of conservation of angular momentum** is a law of the universe which says that angular momentum of a spinning body remains the same (provided no external forces act)

- This means that a body which is spinning, twisting or tumbling will keep its value of **H** once the movement has started.

- Therefore if moment of inertia (**I**) changes by changing body shape, then angular velocity (ω) must also change to keep angular momentum (**H**) the same.

- So, if MI (**I**) **increases** (body spread out more) then ω must **decrease** (rate of spin gets less).

- And conversely, if MI (**I**) **decreases** (body tucked in more) then ω must **increase** (rate of spin gets bigger).

Conservation of angular momentum

- Strictly, this is only exactly true if the body has no contact with its surroundings, as for example a high diver doing piked or tucked somersaults in the air, but it is almost true for the spinning skater.

Sporting examples of conservation of angular momentum

- **The spinning skater**. If the arms are wide, the MI is large and the skater spins slowly. If the arms are brought in, MI is small and the skater will spin more quickly (figure 4.20).

- The third (lower) skater in figure 4.20 has contrived to have both arms and legs spread as far form the axis of rotation as possible, which will bring about the slowest possible rate of spin.

figure 4.20 – a spinning skater

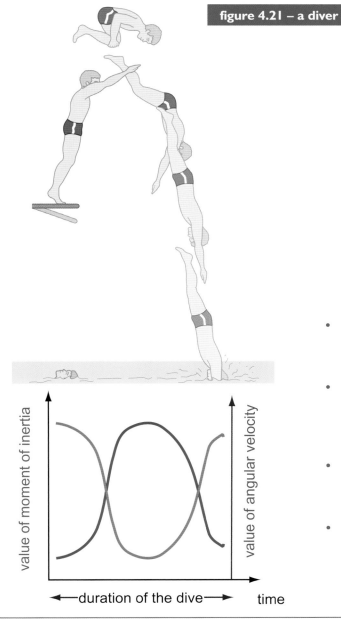

figure 4.21 – a diver

- **The diver.** (figure 4.21). As the diver takes off, his body is almost straight, with maximum moment of inertis, and minimum angular velocity, as reflected in the graph below.

- As he moves toward the apex of the dive, he forms his body into a tucked position, which therefore has minimum moment of inertia. This leads to a maximum angular velocity (rate of spin) portrayed by the green line in the graph below.

- Next, as he begins the fall, he straightens out thereby increasing his moment of inertia (red line in the graph), and reducing his rate of spin.

- He has conserved (kept constant) his angular momentum throughout the dive, but is enabled to change his rate of spin (angular velocity) by changing his moment of inertia.

Sporting examples of conservation of angular momentum

figure 4.22 – a tumbling gymnast

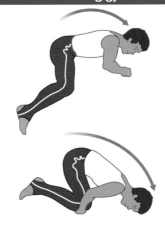

- **The tumbling gymnast** (figure 4.22). With the body position open, the MI is large and the gymnast (or diver or trampolinist) will spin slowly. When he or she creates a tucked body position, the MI is small and he or she will spin more quickly.

- **The dancer doing a spin jump** (figure 4.23). The movement is initiated with arms held wide which would therefore have the highest possible MI. Immediately he or she has taken off, the angular momentum is conserved, and so by tucking the arms across the chest, this will create the lowest possible MI. This then means that he or she will acquire the highest possible rate of spin, so that more spins can be completed before landing.

- **The slalom skier**. The slalom skier crouches on approach to the gate and therefore will have a large turning MI. As he or she passes the gate, he or she stands straight up (reducing MI). This enables the person to turn rapidly past the gate, then he or she crouches again (figure 4.24) - increasing MI which will resume a slow turn between the gates.

- **The discus thrower** (figure 4.25). The discus thrower kicks his right leg wide at the start of the turn, thereby giving his lower body angular momentum with a large MI. As he moves to the centre of the circle he brings his right leg closer to the body (and therefore closer to the turning axis), reducing his MI. This increases the rate of spin of the lower body so that it moves ahead of the upper body in the movement.

Newton's laws of angular motion

The laws of angular motion are similar to Newton's laws of linear motion except that they apply to turning, spinning, or twisting system or bodies. They are:

- **Newton's first law of angular motion** states that a spinning or rotating body will continue with a constant angular momentum except when acted upon by an external force or torque.

- **Newton's second law of angular motion** states that the rate of change of angular momentum of the body will be proportional to the torque acting on it, and in the same direction (of spin) as the torque.

- **Newton's third law of angular motion** states that when a torque is applied to one body by another body, an equal but opposite in direction torque will be applied by the second body to the first body.

figure 4.23 – a spinning dancer

figure 4.24 – a slalom skier

figure 4.25 – a discus thrower

Practice questions

1) Which of the following pairs of quantities is not a vector/scalar pair?
   a. weight/mass.
   b. reaction force/centre of mass.
   c. velocity/speed.
   d. energy/power.

2) Which of the following is a vector?
   a. gravitational field strength.
   b. centripetal force.
   c. the ratio of force to acceleration for a moving body.
   d. rate of change of speed.

3) Angle in radians is defined as:
   a. rate of turning.
   b. arc length subtending the angle divided by radius of the circle.
   c. radius of a circle divided by arc length subtending the angle.
   d. moment of inertia divided by angular velocity.

4) Angular velocity is defined as:
   a. angular acceleration divided by time taken to turn through an angle.
   b. distance moved per second in a certain direction.
   c. angle turned through in radians divided by time taken to turn.
   d. moment of inertia divided by angular momentum.

5) A dancer spinning with arms out wide will spin slower than when he crosses his arms across his chest during a jump because:
   a. angular momentum is bigger with his arms out wide.
   b. angular momentum is smaller with his arms across his chest.
   c. moment of inertia of his body with his arms out wide is bigger.
   d. angular momentum is conserved during the flight of the dancer.

6) Define what is meant by a scalar and a vector quantity.   2 marks

7) A sprinter uses her calf muscles to push on the blocks at the start of a run.
   Sketch a pin man diagram of the forces acting and use this to explain
   how this produces a forward force on her.   3 marks

8) Explain the nature of the reaction force which provides forwards impulsion for a cyclist.   4 marks

9) A weight lifter exerts an upward force of 2000 N on a barbell of 170 kg.
   What is the vertical acceleration?   2 marks

Practice questions

10) Table 4.1 shows the speed of a 19 year-old male sprinter during a 200 metres race.

Table 4.1

speed (ms^{-1})	time (seconds)
0.0	0
6.0	1
7.5	2
8.2	3
8.4	4
8.5	5
8.5	7
8.4	8
8.3	10
8.2	13
8.1	18
8.0	22

a) Plot a graph of speed against time during this race.
    When does he reach maximum speed and what happens to his speed between 8 and 22 seconds?   7 marks

b) Acceleration is the change of speed per second. Use the graph to establish his speed at 0.5 seconds
    and 1.5 seconds and calculate the average acceleration between 0.5 and 1.5 seconds.   3 marks

c) Successful games players are often able to change their velocity rapidly in the game situation.
    Explain the biomechanics behind this ability using examples from a game of your choice.   6 marks

11) a) What characterises a vector quantity?   2 marks

b) Figure 4.26 shows the forces acting on a runner at the start of a race.
    Use a vector diagram to show how you could work out the resultant
    force acting.   3 marks

c) Sketch a pin man drawing of a person standing still showing all the forces
    acting on him.   2 marks

d) Sketch a second diagram showing the vertical forces acting on a basketballer
    just before take-off while performing a jump shot. Represent the relative
    sizes of any forces you show by the length of the force arrows on your
    diagram.   2 marks

e) Use this second diagram and your understanding of Newton's laws of motion
    to explain why the basketballer is able to take off. If the vertical upward
    ground reaction force on him is 2000 N, and his weight is 800 N, estimate
    the net upward force acting on him.   4 marks

figure 4.26 – forces acting on a runner

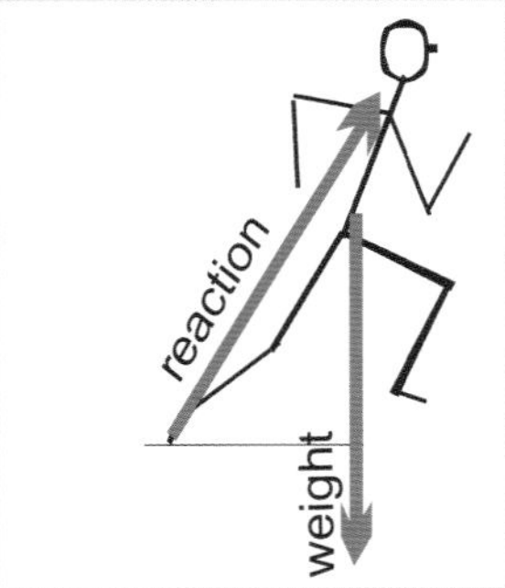

Practice questions

12) Tennis players have to change direction quickly during a match to recover to the centre of the court.
Figure 4.27 shows a tennis player just after hitting a forehand and then starting to recover to the centre of the court in the direction shown.

a) Draw a pin diagram of the tennis player as he pushes off the court surface to recover to the centre of the court, showing all forces acting on the tennis player at this point. All forces must be clearly identified.   3 marks

b) Explain the factors that affect the horizontal force at this point. Apply Newton's second law of motion to explain the effect of this force on the player.   4 marks

figure 4.27 – a tennis player moves between strokes

13) Figure 4.28 shows the distance/time graph for a 100 metres sprint.

a) Describe the motion of the sprinter in sections A and B.   2 marks

b) Calculate the speed at points C and D and the average acceleration between the points.   3 marks

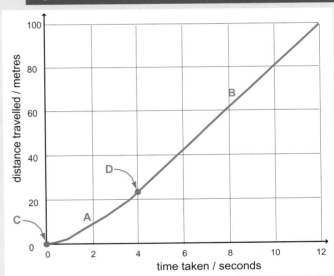

figure 4.28 – distance time graph for 100m sprint

14) Define the term angular velocity.   2 marks

15) Using sporting examples, explain the difference between planes of movement and axes of rotation.   4 marks

Practice questions

16) a) A diver can make a number of different shapes in the air. Table 4.2 shows three of these. Explain the meaning of moment of inertia (MI) in this context. **4 marks**

Table 4.2 – **data for shapes of diver during flight**

phase of dive	shape of diver		time during flight	MI of shape kgm^2
1	Z		0.0 - 0.5s	18
2	Y		0.5 - 0.7s	9
3	X		0.7 - 1.0s	3
4	Z		1.0 - 1.1s	18
entry	axis of rotation = ●		1.1s	

b) During a dive a diver goes through the shapes shown in table 4.1. Explain how the rate of spinning (angular velocity) would change through the dive. **5 marks**

c) Sketch a graph of this rate of spinning against time. Your sketch need only be approximate. **4 marks**

d) State the relationship between angular momentum, moment of inertia and angular velocity. **2 marks**

e) Name the law of conservation which accounts for these variations in rate of spin. **1 mark**

f) Explain and sketch the arc described by the diver as he or she falls. **3 marks**

17) a) Describe in detail the body shape and movement within a chosen sporting situation where rates of spin are affected by body shape. **6 marks**

b) How would you stop the spinning in this situation? **2 marks**

c) Figure 4.29 shows a sportsperson's leg in two different positions. The values quoted are the moment of inertia of the leg as it rotates about the hip joint (shown as a red dot on each diagram). Explain the implications of these data for the efficiency of running style in a sprinter and long distance runner. **7 marks**

figure 4.29 – shape of leg

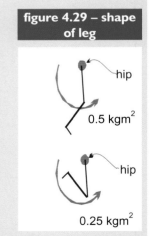

hip

0.5 kgm^2

hip

0.25 kgm^2

Practice questions

18) a)   Figure 4.30 shows a gymnast undertaking a forward somersault following a run up.
Sketch three traces on a single graph to represent any changes in angular momentum,
moment of inertia and angular velocity for the period of activity between positions 2 and 9.   **3 marks**

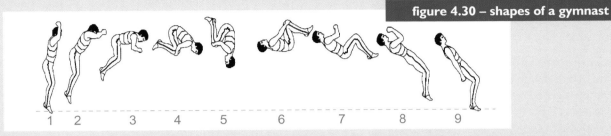

figure 4.30 – shapes of a gymnast

    1   2   3   4   5   6   7   8   9

b)   Explain the shapes of the traces on the sketch graph that you
have drawn.   **6 marks**

c)   Table 4.3 sets out measurements of angular velocities
(rates of spin) of the gymnast at successive frames from
the start of the somersault.

    Estimate from this table the ratio of angular velocities at
times **X** and **Y**.   **1 mark**

d)   If the moment of inertia of the gymnast is 8 kgm² at time **X**,
estimate the moment of inertia at time **Y**, using data
from table 4.3.   **2 marks**

Table 4.3 – **data for angular velocity of gymnast**

	frame	angular velocity (degrees s⁻¹)
	1	650
X	2	750
	3	850
	4	1100
	5	1400
Y	6	1500
	7	1000
	8	850
	9	650

19) a)   Figure 4.31 shows a spinning skater in various
positions. Under each diagram is an approximate value
for the moment of inertia of the skater spinning about
his or her central vertical axis.

    The angular velocity of the skater in position **W** is
2.0 revolutions per second. What is the formula
for calculating the skater's angular velocity?

    Calculate the angular velocity for the skater in
position **Z**.   **2 marks**

b)   Sketch a figure showing a possible position which could
cause the skater to attain an angular velocity of 3.0
revolutions per second and calculate what the moment
of inertia of this shape must be.   **2 marks**

figure 4.31 – shapes of a skater

    W   X   Y   Z

MI=1.0 kgm² MI=2.0 kgm² MI=4.5 kgm² MI=6.0 kgm²

c)   Principles of angular momentum can be used to improve performance in a variety of sports.
With the use of diagrams explain how a slalom skier turns through the gates at maximum speed.   **4 marks**

d)   Explain with the use of diagrams how a dancer manages to complete a triple spin in the air
before touching the ground.   **4 marks**

Answers link: http://www.jroscoe.co.uk/downloads/a2_revise_pe_ocr/OCRA2_ch4_answers.pdf

CHAPTER 5: *Fluid mechanics and projectile motion*

Fluid mechanics

Fluid friction force depends on the shape and size of the moving object, the speed of the moving object, and the streamlining effect (summarised in figure 5.1).

Drag and air resistance

In order to minimise drag, the following developments affect sport:
- The body position and shape for a swimmer.
- The shape of helmets for cyclists.
- The use of lycra clothing.
- The shape of sports vehicles (cars or bikes).

Low values of fluid friction

This discussion concerns **low values of drag** compared with other forces. Examples are:
- Any sprinter or game player for whom air resistance is usually much less than friction effects and weight. Therefore streamlining is seen as less important.
- A shot or hammer in flight, in which air resistance would be much less than the weight, and therefore the angle of release should be around 45°.

High values of fluid friction

High values of drag will occur for any sportsperson or boat moving through water, and hence fluid friction is the critical factor governing swimming speed.

- Body shape or cross section, and clothing (surface material to assist laminar flow), are adjusted to minimise fluid friction.

A cyclist (figure 5.2) travels much faster than a runner and therefore has **high fluid friction**:
- He or she crouches low to reduce the forward cross sectional area.
- The helmet is designed to minimise turbulent flow.
- Clothing and wheel profiles are designed to assist streamlining.

Cross sectional area is the area of the moving object as viewed from the front. The smaller the better to reduce drag, hence cyclists crouch down, and keep their elbows in.

Laminar flow and drag

Fluid friction (or drag) depends on **laminar** flow, the smooth flowing of air or water past an object. Laminar means flowing in layers, and streamlining assists laminar flow. Figure 5.3 shows images of a streamlined helmet, and a non-streamlined helmet. The point of the streamlined shape is that the air moves past it in layers which minimises the drag or fluid friction.

Vortex or turbulent flow

In the case of the non-streamlined helmet, vortices are formed where the fluid does not flow smoothly. When this happens bits of fluid are flung randomly sideways (turbulence) which causes drag.

The **drag** is caused by bits of fluid being dragged along with the moving object (the cycle helmet).

Some clothing (for example lycra running suits and shark suits in swimming) will minimise turbulent vortex creation (depending on the speed of movement) and maximise the laminar flow of the air or water past the body.

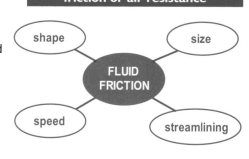

figure 5.1 – factors affecting fluid friction or air resistance

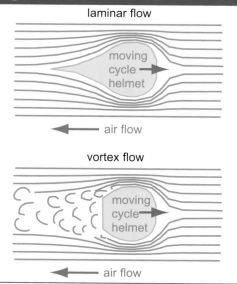

figure 5.2 – a cyclist needs good streamlining

fluid friction (drag) depends on forward cross section and streamlining

figure 5.3 – laminar flow and vortex flow

laminar flow

moving cycle helmet

air flow

vortex flow

moving cycle helmet

air flow

Drag and its consequences

So here we have briefly discussed how laminar flow and vortex flow influence the drag on the human body in sprinting and swimming, and how clothing or helmets (cycling) can influence this drag.

Technologies such as wind tunnels and flumes (fast moving water) can determine the patterns of fluid laminar flow and how these patterns affect the drag force. The forces are measured in the tunnel or flume and shapes are chosen which minimise the drag force measured

figure 5.4 – bike design in the wind tunnel

Wind tunnels

Wind tunnels are increasingly being used to assess the aerodynamics (improved flow of fluid - air or water - reducing drag or fluid friction) of bikes (figure 5.4), cycle helmets, and cyclist overall profile. This is done by blasting air past the stationary object in a tunnel, and using smoke to illustrate the layers of flow of the air. The task is to avoid vortex generation in the air flow, since a smooth (laminar) flow reduces drag, and the turbulence of vortex creation increases drag.

Factors investigated include:
- Wheel spokes and profiles.
- Width of handlebars.
- Riding posture, and hand position on the bars.
- Type of cloth and design of clothing.
- Forward cross-sectional area of frame and brackets.

Technology and drag

The computer programmes which simulate drag show how adjustments to shape can be made **before** construction, reducing expense and making more systematic the shape-making process. In addition to the cycling applications above, this is for:
- Kayaking and rowing.
- Bobsleigh, luge and skeleton.
- Speed skating (helmets, costumes and body angles).

Further application of the same technology is used to **increase the drag effect** in order to improve propulsion in water based activities.
This applies to:
- Improved patterns of pulling (hand and foot/leg positions and activity) in swimming.
- Shape of blades in rowing and canoeing.

Sports boats

The drag on the hulls of yachts, sailing dingies, canoes and rowing shells depend on the surface area in contact with the water. If this can be reduced then the potential maximum speed which could be achieved can be markedly increased.

The main application of these ideas are in the military (cavitation, which creates a bubble of gas around the craft and is used in torpedoes, attack boats, underwater bullets and so on).

In a hovercraft, the body of the boat is suspended on a cushion of air, thereby reducing fluid friction almost to zero. The main reason why such craft are less popular now, is the potential for lack of control during bad weather, a factor which also affects use of hydrofoil craft (which lifts the body of the boat off the surface of the water. The boat sits on special fins or wings).

Sports boats

Hydroplaning in sports boats (in which the hulls of speedboats are lifted off the surface to sit on a shaped bar at the rear of the boat) enable them to travel at speeds above 100 mph (figure 5.5).

The latest speedboats have shaped hulls which reduce drag, the shaping being determined in a **flume** (a tank containing fast flowing water, and force measuring devices which can be attached to the boat shape body), in a similar manner to the shaping of a formula one racing car (as well as other more commercial vehicles) in a wind tunnel.

figure 5.5 – sports boats at 100 mph

Projectile motion

Factors affecting horizontal displacement of projectiles

This section looks at the **motion of objects in flight**, such as human bodies (during the flight phase of a jump), throwing implements (shot, discus, javelin or hammer), and soccer, rugby, cricket, tennis and golf balls.

Flight of objects

The flight is governed by the forces acting, the weight, air resistance, Magnus effect (page 101), aerodynamic lift, and the direction of motion. If weight were the only force acting, the flight path would be **parabolic** in shape, and some flight paths are similar to this (shot or hammer, the human body in jumps or tumbles or dives as in figures 5.6, 5.7, and 5.8 (page 99) where weight is the predominant force acting).

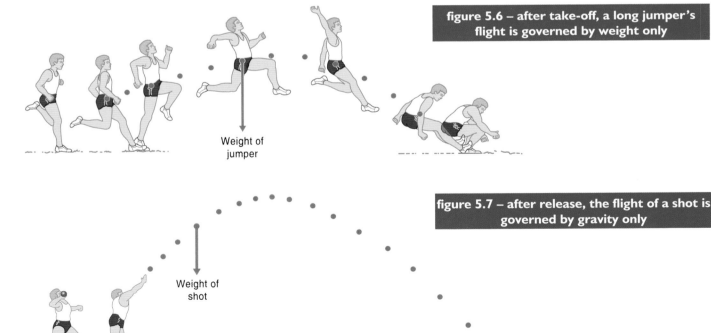

figure 5.6 – after take-off, a long jumper's flight is governed by weight only

Weight of jumper

figure 5.7 – after release, the flight of a shot is governed by gravity only

Weight of shot

Flight of objects

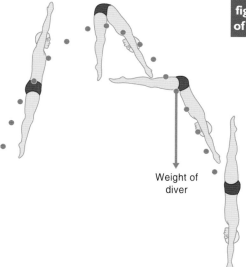

figure 5.8 – after leaving the board, the flight of a diver is governed by gravity (weight) only

Weight of
diver

Factors affecting horizontal displacement of projectiles

Figure 5.9 summarises the factors which influence the distance travelled, the **angle of release**, the **speed of release**, and the **height of release**.

The optimum distance moved before landing is acheived at 45° release angle.

If the height of release is about 2 metres off the ground, as in the shot put (figure 5.9), then the optimum angle of release (to achieve maximum distance) will be less than 45°, probably approximately 42°.

But if the landing of the object thrown is higher than the point of release (as in the case of a basketball shot), then the optimum angle of release will be greater than 45°.

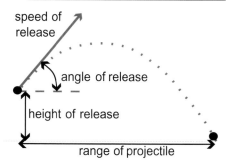

figure 5.9 – factors affecting distance travelled

speed of release

angle of release

height of release

range of projectile

The relative size of forces during flight

The forces acting during flight are: the weight of the object, the air resistance or drag, (the faster the projectile travels the greater will be the air resistance or drag), **aerodynamic lift** (page 100), and the **Magnus effect** or **Bernoulli effect** (page 101).

If the shapes of the flight path differ from a parabola then some combination of these forces must be relatively large compared with the weight (remembering that a flight of an object with only weight force acting would be a parabola).

For example, the badminton shuttle

For a badminton shuttle **struck hard** (figure 5.10a), the air resistance is very large compared with the weight, because the shuttle is moving quickly. The resultant force will therefore be very close to the air resistance. This would make the shuttle slow down rapidly over the **first part of the flight**.

Later in the flight of the badminton shuttle (figure 5.10b), when the shuttle is moving much more slowly, the air resistance is much less and comparable with the weight. This pattern of the resultant force changing markedly during the flight predicts a pronounced asymmetric path.

Figure 5.11 shows a badminton shuttle's flight path, which is markedly non-parabolic and asymmetric, because of the change of predominant force during the flight.

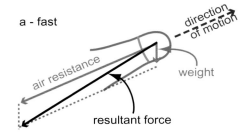

figure 5.10 – forces on a badminton shuttle

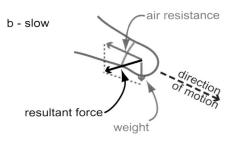

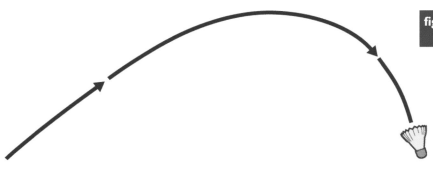

figure 5.11 – asymmetric flight of a badminton shuttle

Lift force

Aerodynamic lift (upward force) can be caused by the movement of the body. As the body moves forward, the angle presented by the lower surface of the body to the direction of motion (called the angle of attack) can cause the air molecules through which the object is moving to be deflected downward and hence would cause a downward force on the air through which the object passes (figure 5.12).

This **downward force on the air** would cause an **upward force on the moving object** in **reaction** to the downward force on the air (by Newton's third law). This is the lift.

Such a force can explain the flight of a discus.

A discus is a symmetrical object, which would therefore not be subject to the Bernoulli force which explains the flight of a wing moving horizontally through air. The **angle of attack** of the discus is such as to present its lower surface to the air flow (similar to the ski jumper and the javelin) which causes the lift as explained above.

There is a distinction between a force caused as a reaction to air (or water) thrown up or sideways to the direction of motion of for example a downhill skier or a cyclist, and the Bernoulli effect. **Air thrown upwards** by the body posture of a track cyclist would cause a **downward reaction force** on the cyclist, enabling **greater adhesion** to the track, and cornering capability.

figure 5.12 – lift force on a discus

lift force on discus

direction of motion of discus

α = angle of attack

air layers forced downwards

The Bernoulli effect

The force which gives lift to aircraft wings, and down-pressure on racing car bodies (figure 5.13, enabling greater friction between wheels and the road, and hence faster cornering speeds) is called the **Bernoulli effect**.

This effect depends on the fact that fluids which move quickly across the surface of an object cause a reduced pressure when compared with slower moving air across another surface.

Hence, in figure 5.13, the laminar flow of air across the **lower** surface of the wing (or car body shaped like an inverted wing) is **quicker**, because the air has to travel **further** in the same time as the air moving a shorter distance across the upper surface of the wing. Hence the shape of the wing is crucial to create the Bernoulli lift (in aeroplanes) or down force (in racing cars, figure 5.14).

The **Bernoulli effect** has been built into racing cars to increase the down force (which would therefore increase the friction force between wheels and the ground).

So, formula 1 racing car manufacturers build this **shape into the whole car** (figure 5.14), not just the artificial wings sometimes attached to the car upper surfaces.

The Magnus effect

The **Magnus effect** is the Bernoulli principle applied to spinning balls.

As a **spinning ball** moves through the air (from left to right on figure 5.15), the air layers which flow round the ball are forced into the path shown in the diagram. Here you can see that the air flow is **further** round the top of the ball, and hence the air flow is **faster** over the top of the ball than the bottom. This means that the **air pressure** will be **less** over the top of the ball than the lower half of the ball (following from the Bernoulli effect), hence the ball will experience a force upwards in the view of figure 5.15.

Hence **top-spin** as shown in figure 5.16, would cause a dipping effect on the ball in flight, the force is downward in this figure. Most tennis players use the top spin effct to cause a ball to dip into the opponent's court after a very firm hit of the ball. Rafael Nadal is a prime exponent of this technique.

Similarly, **side-spin** will cause a swerve in the flight whose direction is in the same sense as the spin of the ball. Golfers cause a ball to fade to the right or hook to the left by imparting side-spin to the ball during the strike.

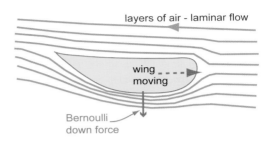

figure 5.13 – Bernoulli effect on an inverted wing

figure 5.14 – shape of a racing car body

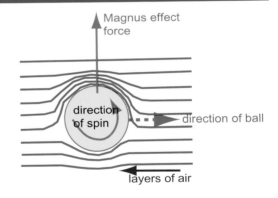

figure 5.15 – Magnus effect on a spinning ball

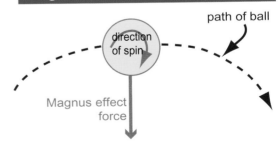

figure 5.16 – flight of a spinning ball

The Magnus effect

The diagrams in figure 5.17a show how side spin causes swerving sideways by golfers or soccer players, The sense of swerve is in the same direction as the spin on the ball.

The sports in which back spin (figure 5.17b) and top spin (figure 5.17c) are used to the maximum are racquet sports such as tennis and table tennis.

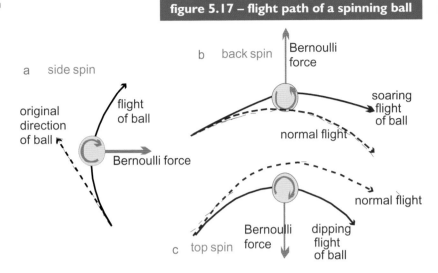

figure 5.17 – flight path of a spinning ball

Applying spin to a ball

figure 5.18 – golfers can control ball spin to place the ball on the green

Applying spin to a ball requires the ball player to apply an eccentric force out of line with the ball's centre of mass.

Golfers at the top level can apply hook and slice (under control) to place their ball on the fairway or the green.

A **slice** is a curving shot with a lot of **sidespin** which sends the ball **left to right** rather than straight. The clubface will be open several degrees in relation to the path, which applies a force to the ball to the left of the ball's centre of mass.

The **hook** is the opposite of a slice, sending the ball right to left rather than straight. The clubface is closed more than a few degrees relative to the path, which applies a force to the right of the ball's centre of mass.

Tennis players apply spin to a struck ball using exaggerated racket movements, but all of which apply force out of line with the centre of mass of the ball.

The sideways Magnus force that is produced when perfect sidespin in football, or topspin to produce a dipping flight, can take the ball beyond a goalkeeper's diving reach.

figure 5.19 – top-spin on a soccer ball

Note that in figure 5.19, the line of action of the force applied by the kicker's foot to the ball, passes above the ball's centre of mass. This eccentric force will result in the ball acquiring top-spin after the kick, and hence the ball will dip as described above.

If he applies a force which is to the side of the centre of mass, then a **side spin** will occur, which will cause the ball to swerve **sideways** via the Magnus effect (as illustrated in figure 5.17).

Practice questions

1) Which sentence best explains the flight of a projectile?
   a. the projectile travels further if air resistance is large compared with its weight.
   b. a projectile ejected at 45° to the horizontal will travel the furthest.
   c. the flight path of a projectile falls from its initial direction caused by gravity only.
   d. weight and fluid friction are the only forces acting on a projectile.

2) The Bernoulli effect causes a sideways force on an object moving through a fluid because:
   a. fluids flow in a laminar pattern past a moving object.
   b. the pressure exerted by a fast moving fluid is less than that exerted by a slow moving fluid.
   c. the pressure exerted by a fast moving fluid is greater than that exerted by a slow moving fluid.
   d. an unstreamlined object will cause fluid flow to break into vortices.

3) If every particle of fluid has irregular flow, then flow is said to be:
   a. laminar flow.
   b. turbulent flow.
   c. fluid flow.
   d. both a and b.

4) A racing car has a body with:
   a. laminated design.
   b. turbulent design.
   c. flat design.
   d. streamlined design.

5) Which of the following reasons explains why the best take-off angle for an elite long jumper
   is much closer to 22 degrees than to the predicted optimum angle from projectile
   motion theory of about 42 degrees?
   a. the jumper needs to generate rotation.
   b. achieving a take-off angle close to the theoretical value would drastically reduce take-off speed.
   c. the theory ignores air resistance.
   d. the jumper does not understand projectile motion theory.

6) a)   Using examples, explain how the shape of an object can alter its flight path.   4 marks

   b)   Explain the effect of air resistance on the flight of two badminton shuttles,
        one of which has been struck hard and the other gently.   10 marks

   c)   Briefly explain why the flight path of a shot in athletics is so different from
        the flight of a badminton shuttle.   4 marks

7) a)   Identify three physical factors (not skill factors) which govern a swimmer's
        speed and explain how one of these occurs.   3 marks

   b)   Describe the factors which determine the amount of fluid friction acting on a swimmer.   4 marks

   c)   Explain how you would minimise turbulent flow (high drag) of the water past the swimmer's body.   2 marks

   d)   Give three examples, each from a different sporting context,
        to show how fluid friction affects the sportsperson.   3 marks

   e)   How would you attempt to reduce fluid friction?   3 marks

   f)   Look at figure 5.20 showing the vertical forces acting on a swimmer
        during a stroke. Explain why it is difficult for a swimmer to keep
        a horizontal floating position.   4 marks

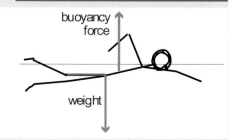

figure 5.20 – forces acting on a swimmer

Practice questions

8) a) Fluid friction is a force which acts on a bobsleigh once it is moving. Identify the nature of the
fluid friction in this case and explain how this might limit the maximum speed of the bob.   3 marks

   b) Explain the term 'turbulent flow', and how the bobsleigh is used to minimise this factor.   3 marks

9) a) Sketch a diagram to show the flight path of the shot from the moment it leaves
the putter's hand to the moment it lands.   2 marks

   b) State and briefly explain three factors (excluding air effects) which should be used by
the putter to optimise the distance thrown.   6 marks

   c) Explain why the turn in a discus throw produces greater horizontal range than the standing throw.   3 marks

10) a) The Magnus effect (the Bernoulli effect applied to spinning balls) states that a faster flowing
liquid or gas exerts less pressure than a slower moving liquid or gas.
Using figure 5.21, show how the Magnus effect explains the swerve of a spinning ball.   4 marks

    b) Use diagrams to show how your explanation relates to the flight of a table tennis ball
with side, back and top spin.   3 marks

    c) Sketch a vector diagram of all forces acting on a table tennis ball in
flight with back spin, and explain how the resultant force on the ball
predicts the actual acceleration of the ball.   4 marks

    d) Identify one sport other than a ball game, in which the Bernoulli effect
plays a part.   1 mark

**figure 5.21 – Magnus effect on
a spinning ball**

direction of air flow

11) What do you understand by the Magnus effect?
Explain how a knowledge of Magnus forces can assist a tennis player to
execute different types of spins.   10 marks

12) Compare and contrast the use of side spin in football, and the hook in golf.   4 marks

13) a) Describe how a lift force is generated by a discus in flight.   4 marks

    b) Explain how a high angle of attack will affect the distance travelled by a discus.   3 marks

Answers link: http://www.jroscoe.co.uk/downloads/a2_revise_pe_ocr/OCRA2_ch5_answers.pdf

PART
4

SKILL ACQUISITION

CHAPTER 6
MEMORY MODELS

CHAPTER 6: Memory models

The memory system

Memory plays a critical part in the overall learning process. The **central nervous system** (CNS) consists of the brain and the spinal cord. When the brain receives sensory information from the spinal cord and other sensory organs (eyes and ears) and a decision needs to be made, memory hepls facilitate the decision making process.

All the senses feed a vast amount of information into the CNS. The senses (figure 6.1) used to collect information are collectively known as the **receptor systems**.

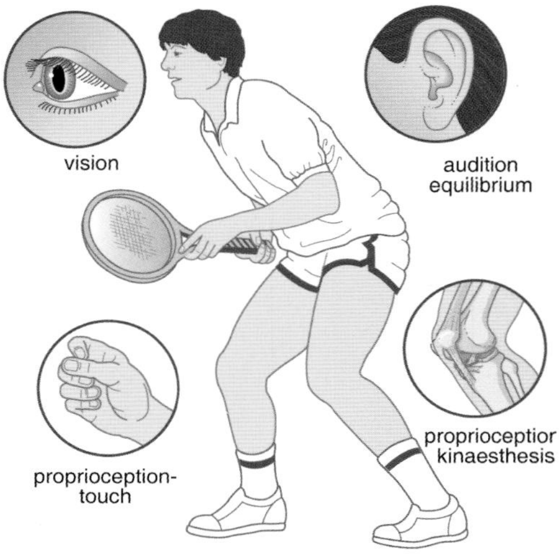

When we are doing any physical activity we are aware of our surroundings. We use all our senses to locate ourselves in space and decide on the requirements of the task, whether it is to pass a ball or perform a gymnastic or dance movement.

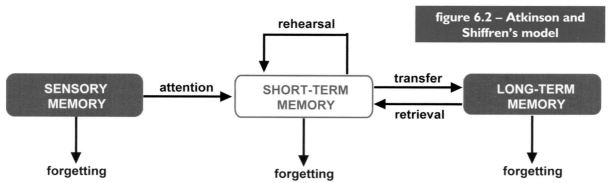

figure 6.1 – sensory input

vision

audition equilibrium

proprioception-touch

proprioceptior kinaesthesis

Atkinson and Shiffren's multi-store memory model

Now we move on to a model which simplifies and provides more structure to the basic memory model of human memory.

The brain is viewed as **changing** and **organising** elements of information as opposed to just **storing** it.
Parts of the brain will **encode** information into **visual**, **auditory** or **semantic** (according to meaning) codes. Then **relevant** information is **selected**, which is then **stored** and made available for **retrieval** ready for action.

The Atkinson and Shiffren model (figure 6.2, sometimes also called the modal model) is a linear three part model in which information is passed from one memory store element to the next, with each having an input, process and output.

The three elements to this model are:
- The **sensory memory**, in which information enters the memory via the **senses** (figure 6.1).
- The **short-term memory**, also called the **working memory**.
- The **long-term memory** in which **rehearsed** information is stored **indefinitely**.

figure 6.2 – Atkinson and Shiffren's model

rehearsal

| SENSORY MEMORY | → attention → | SHORT-TERM MEMORY | → transfer → ← retrieval ← | LONG-TERM MEMORY |

forgetting

forgetting

forgetting

The sensory memory

When a stimulus from the environment via the senses is detected (by the person involved), the content and or meaning of the stimulus is briefly retained in the sensory memory. The sensory memory does not process the information carried by the stimulus, but rather detects and holds the information for use later in the short-term memory. This is termed a **buffer function**, which prevents a very large amount of information from overwhelming later cognitive processes.

The point is that the sensory memory only holds the information for between 0.25 and 1.00 seconds, during which the process of **selective attention** sorts out the relevant activities to be forwarded to the short-term memory.

Perception (figure 6.3)

The first part of the process is known as perception which is identified as **stimulus identification**.

As information is received from the environment, the performer needs to **make sense** of it, to **interpret** it and to **identify** the elements which are **relevant** and **important**. Perception consists of three elements:

- **Detection**: the performer needs to be aware that something notable is going on around him or her. In a field game situation, this could be where the ball is, where the other players from both sides are in relation to the pitch dimensions, and what the goalkeeper is doing.

- **Comparison**: in which the performer will compare what is happening with his or her past experiences of similar situations, where are the players in comparison with set plays rehearsed in a training situation?

- **Recognition**: in which the performer realises that what is happening requires an activity in response, for example, what is the response to the rehearsed set play in the field game?

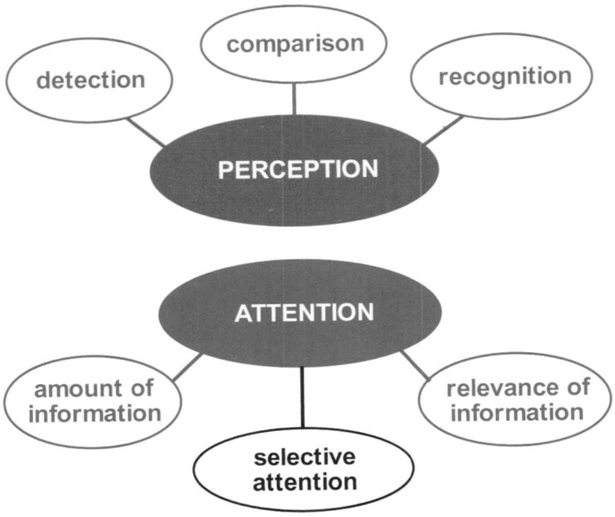

Attention (figure 6.3)

A games player can **switch attention** from the opponent to the ball to the grip on the bat very quickly (figure 6.4).

He is able to do this because all the information that enters the sensory system is held for a **very short time** in the sensory memory (which has a very large capacity for information but a minimal storage time), compared with all the information held in the long-term memory for identification or recognition purposes.

This **filters out irrelevant information** so the system is **not overloaded**.

If the **perceptual mechanism** decides that the stimulus is not **relevant** or important, the information held in the sensory memory fades and is lost and **forgotten**. All this happens before we are conscious of it.

figure 6.3 – perception and attention

detection · comparison · recognition

PERCEPTION

ATTENTION

amount of information · relevance of information

selective attention

figure 6.4 – switching attention

Selective attention

This is the process of sorting out **relevant** bits of information from the many which are received.

The process of **selective attention** then passes the information to the **short-term memory** which gives time for **conscious analysis**. This is discussed in the context of psychological skills training in chapter 8.

Developing selective attention

- Lots of **relevant** practice.
- Increase the **intensity** of the stimulus.
- Use **verbal** or **kinaesthetic** cues to focus on important information. For example, 'keep your eye on the ball' or a swimmer might selectively attend on the feel of the hand pulling through the water.
- Use **visualisation** or mental rehearsal techniques without movement.
- Watch performer's **video replays** to refine technique.
- **Observe and copy** the behaviour of a player who plays in the same position as the subject.
- The coach needs to direct attention and give appropriate **feedback** to improve performer's motivation and alertness.

- Use **concentration** exercises, such as players scanning the field of play, followed by correct pass, alongside distracting background sounds or different instructions that may simulate the presence of noisy spectators that could distract players (figure 6.5).

- Develop **performance rituals** that automatically trigger focused attention that leads to good performance. Continue to **evaluate** and **reappraise** methods to ensure refinement and adjustments to selective attention techniques are an ongoing process.

figure 6.5 – distraction?

Benefits of selective attention

- Directs performer's attention on particular aspects of performance thereby **avoiding distractions**.
- Gives performer a better chance of making the correct **decision**.
- Improves performer's **reaction time** significantly.
- Helps performer to make **quicker** decisions.
- Helps **regulate** performer's **arousal** and **anxiety** levels.
- Reduces performer's potential **memory overload**.

Short-term memory

This is sometimes called the **working memory** because this zone of the memory system is where it is decided what is to be done in response to the stimulus identified by the selective attention process outlined above.

This memory zone will retain information for up to 30 seconds, which could be extended by rehearsal (of the information) or repetition of a relevant activity, or using chunking or chaining.

Chunking

- More information can be held in STM if information is **lumped together** (this is called chunking).
- There appears to be a maximum number of 7 ± 2 'chunks' which can be remembered and stored.

Chaining or association

- **Link new** information **with old** already learnt information.
- Multiple links can form a chain.

The **rehearsal process** could be via **mental rehearsal** (page 133), **imagery** or by **self-talk**, and not necessarily actual practice of a physical task such as a discus throw (figure 6.6) repeated 10,000 times.

Hence, if information is considered important enough it would then be transferred to the long-term memory, called **encoding** the information.

Information not considered important enough - through lack of rehearsal for example - is then lost from the short-term memory or **forgotten**.

figure 6.6 – discus throwers need lots of rehearsal

Long-term memory

Long-term memory is almost limitless in capacity, and will hold information almost indefinitely. Meaningless information will be forgotten, and the remainder is **encoded** and **stored** by chaining or association with other encoded information.

This is why it is sometimes difficult to remember unfamiliar names (of either people or objects). Such unfamiliar or unusual names may need to be rehearsed many more times than common and familiar names in order to be retained in the long-term memory.

Motor programmes which specify a physical skill such as throwing a discus or hammer wil need to be **practiced** (**rehearsed**) many times until the skill becomes almost **automatic** and hence recalled in its entirity from long-term memory.

Also, **continuous rehearsal** of a skill (for example, riding a bicycle or horse) over a long period of time will lead to such a skill being more likely to be remembered. So bike riding, horse riding or swimming are never totally forgotten.

Retrieval

When the situation arises, memories in the long-term memory can be **retrieved** by the short-term memory for action (for example, the action of throwing the discus in a competition which draws on long-term memories made from years of training, figure 6.6).

Note that memories can deteriorate, as the associations or links between well-learnt skills are **forgotten**. Rehearsal of the correct skill model will restore the memory to its function.

Craik and Lockhart's levels of processing memory model

This model (figure 6.7) developed by the authors in 1972, looks at how the **depth of meaning** of a piece of information can affect its **capacity** to be stored in the memory.

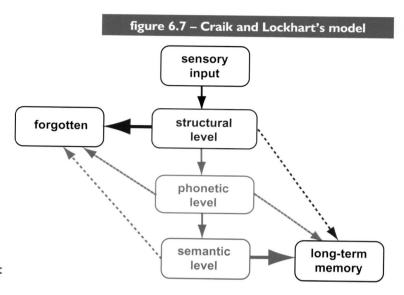

figure 6.7 – Craik and Lockhart's model

In other words, the more meaning the information has, the deeper the **processing level** which will be utilised, and the more likely it will be remembered, and the deeper the level of understanding or analysis. Hence the more elaborate, longer lasting and stronger the memory trace.

They identified **three** levels of memory trace type relating to the processing of verbal information.

The structural level

The **structural level** in which attention is given to what a word looks like as opposed to its meaning (if any).

The phonetic level

This level processes words according to the **sound** of the word.

The semantic level

The semantic level considers the actual **meaning** (**meaningfulness** is the relevance of specific information to an individual's needs) of a word. This is the deepest level of processing and which therefore is the most likely to be remembered and acted upon.

- In this model, the memory recall of stimuli is a function of the **depth** of mental processing, and the depth of processing falls within a **shallow to deep** continuum.
- **Shallow** processing (based on information at the structural level) leads to a **fragile** memory trace susceptible to **rapid decay** or forgetting.
- **Deep** (semantic) processing based on the **meaning** of the information to be processed, results in a more **durable** memory trace - it will be more likely to be remembered.

Example of use of the levels of processing approach

When coaching a physical skill, such as throwing the hammer, it will be important to explain the reasons for certain postures or movements (for example, the fact that the radius of the hammer movement should be as big as possible to increase its path length during the throw) so that this fact has more meaning and is therefore more likely to be remembered. Hence the thrower can see and remember that keeping her arms straight during the movement would be important and remembered at all phases of skill development.

Advantages and disadvantages of the Atkinson & Shiffren model (page 106)

Table 6.1 - **Atkinson and Shiffren model**

advantages	disadvantages
simple and straightforward model which helps understanding	too simple, does not take into account the real complexity
research has shown that people with brain damage do have separate regions of the brain corresponding to the model	does not explain why an athlete remembers some activities but not others depending on the context
also those with amnesia appear to distinguish between short-term and long-term memory	does not explain effectively the difference or interaction between short-term and long-term memory

Advantages and disadvantages of the Craik and Lockhart model

Table 6.2 - **Craik and Lockhart model**

advantages	disadvantages
explains why we might remember meaningful information rather than random information	research has shown that the longer the time taken to process information does not necessarily produce a stronger memory
understanding complex information is the key to memory	it is difficult to explain what is meant by depth of processing
explains why the longer we consider information, the more likely it will be remembered	does not take into account individual differences, since some people might forget a basic skill in spite of strenuous efforts to remember it or people who have not deeply processed a skill are sometimes able to repeat complicated tasks without prompting
	participants spend a longer time processing difficult/deeper tasks

General strategies to improve the memory model

Retention of information and facts in the memory (figure 6.8) can be improved by:

Input

- **Educate** the performer about the details of a skill.
- **Explain** what to do and how to do it.
- Ensure that input is **clear** and **uncluttered**,
- Keep advice or instruction **simple** and **clear.**
- **KISS** - keep it simple stupid.
- Carefully **separate** similar skills to enable the performer to distinguish between them
- Organise the process of skill learning to ensure the information is **meaningful**.
- Be **brief** and do **not overload** the short-term memory which can only hold small amounts of data.

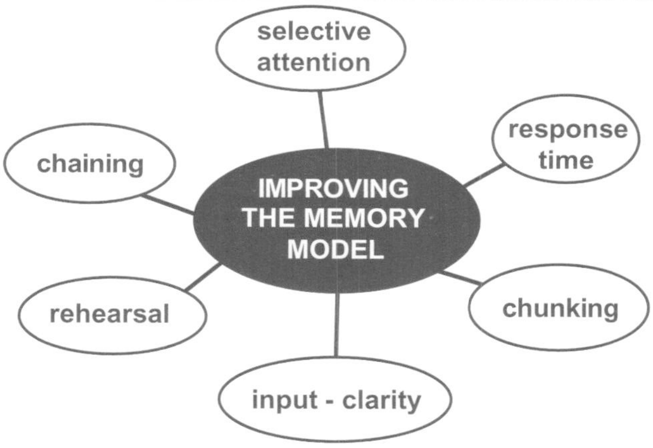

Chunking

- More information can be held in STM if information is **lumped together** (this is called chunking). See page 109 for further information.

Chaining or association

- **Link new** information **with old** already learnt information.
- Multiple links can form a chain.

Rehearsal

- **Practice makes perfect** (figure 6.9).
- The more **practice** that can be done to a **correct technical model,** the better the **skill** will be formed and the better the immediate performance.
- Perfect practice makes a skill perfect.
- **Repetition** of any information or skill will enable it to be remembered better.
- Make use of mental imagery or rehearsal (page 109).

figure 6.8 – improving retention

selective attention

response time

chaining

IMPROVING THE MEMORY MODEL

chunking

rehearsal

input - clarity

figure 6.9 – practice makes perfect

Response time

- A coach will teach performers to **anticipate** and so reduce the time they take to respond to a stimulus. For example, the tennis player who anticipates the type of serve the opponent will use (spatial or event anticipation). In this case, the player has learnt to detect **certain cues** early in the serving sequence that predicts the potential type of serve. This means that players can start to position themselves for the return earlier in the sequence than usual and thus give them more time to play the shot when the ball arrives.

- Another example of trying to reduce response time is in a sprint start, getting the performer to focus on the starter's voice and the sound of the gun and separating this from background crowd noise and negative thoughts.

- **Decision making**: working on set pieces and game situations provides opportunities to focus on different aspects of the game. For example, drills that switch quickly from concentration on the opponent to concentration on the field of play in invasion games.

- Ensure performers **warm-up** adequately so that the sense organs and the nervous system are ready to transmit information and the muscles to act upon it.

Practice questions

1) Which of the following sequences reflects the order in which the human brain processes inputs from the suroundings?
   a. sensory memory, short-term sensory store, long-term memory.
   b. sensory memory, long-term memory, short-term memory.
   c. sensory memory, short-term memory, long-term memory.
   d. long-term memory, short-term memory, sensory memory.

2) Selective attention is best described as:
   a. many bits of information are received.
   b. focusing on at least five bits of information.
   c. disregarding undesirable bits of information.
   d. focus on the relevant bits of information from the many which are received.

3) Which one of the following does not help in retaining memories?
   a. chunking.
   b. chaining.
   c. practice.
   d. overload.

4) Which of the following is not a description of elements of the Atkinson and Shiffren multi-store memory model?
   a. information enters the memory system via the senses.
   b. the long-term memory quickly forgets memories after a short period.
   c. the short-term memory is intermediate between the sensory memory and the long-term memory.
   d. the sensory memory forgets most of its input except for those memories to which it has attention.

5) Which one of the following is the correct order of depth within Craik and Lockhart's levels of processing memory model?
   a. phonetic level, semantic level, structural level, long-term memory.
   b. semantic level, phonetic level, structural level, long-term memory.
   c. long-term memory, phonetic level, semantic level, structural level.
   d. structural level, phonetic level, semantic level, long-term memory.

6) Identify the three main receptor systems used by a performer in sport.   3 marks

Practice questions

7) Identify and describe the three elements of perception.   3 mark

8) How can information be retained in the long-term memory?   4 marks

9) a) Using the example of a table tennis player receiving a serve, what information would be
held in the sensory memory and for how long?   4 marks

   b) Name and describe the purpose of the process by which information is transferred
from the sensory memory to the short-term memory.   4 marks

   c) What factors could affect response time in any game or sport?   4 marks

10) a) Define and explain with examples the process of selective attention. 3 marks

    b) Explain, using a sporting example, how the use of selective attention depends on
an athletes' level of ability.   3 marks

    c) How can a coach improve an athlete's selective attention?   3 marks

11) During sporting situations it may be necessary to process
information using memory systems.

What are the features and functions of the working memory?

What strategies could the players in figure 6.10 use to improve
their memory systems?   10 marks

figure 6.10 – soccer player's attack

12) Outline the main features of Craik and Lockhart's levels of
processing memory model.   8 marks

13) Outline the main features of Atkinson and Shiffren's multi-store memory model.
Use sporting examples to illustrate your answer.   10 marks

14) Compare the advantages and disadvantages of the usage of the Atkinson Shiffren
and Craik Lochart memory models, paying attention to the sporting applications.   .   10 marks

Answers link: http://www.jroscoe.co.uk/downloads/a2_revise_pe_ocr/OCRA2_ch6_answers.pdf

SPORT PSYCHOLOGY

CHAPTER 7: *Attribution theory, confidence and self-efficacy*

Attribution

Attribution is the process of giving **reasons** for behaviour and ascribing **causes** for events. For example, the player played badly today because the weather was poor.

Weiner's model

Weiner's model has four attributions, **ability**, **effort**, **task difficulty** and **luck** (see figure 7.1).

As in figure 7.1, these attributions are arranged in two dimensions, **locus of causality** and **stability** (with a possible third dimension, **controllability**).

figure 7.1 – Weiner's model of sports attribution

		LOCUS OF CAUSALITY	
		INTERNAL	EXTERNAL
STABILITY	STABLE	ability 'we were more skilful'	task difficulty 'the opposition are world champions'
	UNSTABLE	effort 'we tried hard'	luck 'the court was slippy'

Locus of causality dimension

Locus of causality is the performance outcome caused by:
- **Internal factors** under the control of the performer such as ability and effort.
  - **Ability** is the extent of the performer's capacity to cope with a sporting task.
  - **Effort** refers to the amount of mental and physical effort the performer gives to the task.

- **External factors** beyond the control of the performer such as task difficulty and luck.
  - **Task difficulty** is the term describing the extent of the problems posed by the task including the strength of the opposition.
  - **Luck** describes factors attributable to chance, such as the weather or the state of the pitch.

Locus of stability dimension

Stability refers to the performance outcome caused by stable or unstable factors:

- **Stable** factors are fixed factors which don't change with time such as **ability** or **task difficulty**.
- In a closed skill, such as pole vaulting (figure 7.2), the vaulter has learnt the specific movement patterns needed to create a stable technique. This is provided by a motor programme that contains all the information required to complete the skill.
- Hence, although the pole vault is a difficult skill, the performance of it will be **habitual**, the **dominant habit** being stable.

- **Unstable** factors are factors which can vary with time such as **effort** or **luck**.
- If the pole vaulter **tries too hard**, the learned skill might break down (the inverted U hypothesis) and performance failure will occur. This is then unstable, and effort is a negative.

In attribution theory, **success** is explained by internal attributions, and **failure** is explained by external attributions. **Future expectations** are related to stability. If we attribute success to stable factors, or if we attribute failure to stable factors, then we expect the same next time.

figure 7.2 – a pole vaulter

Relationship to sports achievement

- **High achievers** (such as Andy Murray, figure 7.3) tend to attribute **success** to internal factors (such as Andy's incredible state of fitness), and attribute **failure** to external factors (such as the high temperature or strong wind during the match).
- **Low achievers** tend to attribute success to external factors (such as a favourable wind), and attribute failure to internal factors (such as lack of fitness or ability).

- The process of changing attributions is called **attribution retraining**. The point of this is to change a person's tendency to ascribe reasons for success or failure so that it is more like that of a successful performer rather than an unsuccessful performer.
- Attributions affect a sportsperson's **pride**, **satisfaction**, and **expectancy of success**. Some people exhibit **avoidance** tendencies when faced with a sporting situation (they try to avoid participating), and this is called **learned helplessness**.

Locus of controllability, the third dimension

The **locus of controllability** covers attributions under the control of the performer (and sometimes not under the control of the performer). The locus of control dimension relates to the intensity of a performer's feelings of **pride** and **satisfaction**, **shame** and **guilt**.

- **Pride** and **satisfaction** are maximised if success is attributed to internal controllable factors like ability and effort, therefore motivation would be enhanced.
- If **success** were attributed to **external** and **uncontrollable** factors such as luck or the fact that the task was very easy, then satisfaction would be less intense and there would be less motivation.
- If **failure** is attributed to internal controllable factors such as **lack of ability** and **lack of effort**, then the overpowering emotion would be dissatisfaction and motivation would be reduced.

The self-serving bias

- This idea crops up because **successful performers** tend to take credit for success. They do this by **attributing success** to their own overwhelmingly outstanding **qualities** (natural ability, **ability** to respond to the competitive situation), thereby enhancing their feelings of pride, self-worth, and **self-esteem**. They also tend to **blame external factors** for failure.

- Failure is automatically attributed to **avoid internal** controllable and stable factors (even if such factors may be true). This is the **self-serving bias**, people tend to give attributions to **protect their self-esteem** rather than look for true attributions which would reflect the reality of the situation.

- **Unsuccessful performers** do not always attribute failure to external factors and therefore do not protect their self-esteem. This tends to reduce motivation.

Figure 7.4 summarises the **attribution process**.

figure 7.3 – Andy Murray - high achiever

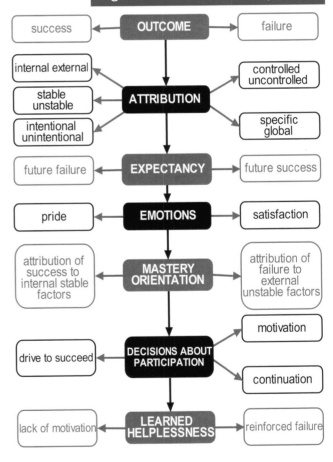

figure 7.4 – the attribution process

The link between motivation, attribution and task persistence

Table 7.1 – motivation, attribution and task choice and persistence

	high achiever	low achiever
motivation	high motive to achieve success low motive to avoid failure focuses on pride and on success	low motive to achieve success high motive to avoid failure focuses on shame and worry about failure
attributions	ascribes success to stable internal controllable factors ascribes failure to unstable external uncontrollable factors	ascribes success to unstable external uncontrollable factors ascribes failure to stable internal controllable factors
goals adopted	adopts task oriented goals	adopts outcome oriented goals
task choice and persistence	seeks challenging tasks and competitive situations and stays with them	avoids challenge, seeks very difficult or very easy tasks or competition and easily gives up
performance	performs well in front of evaluative audiences	performs badly in front of evaluative audiences

Learned helplessness (LH)

Repeated failure (or lack of success) can lead to a state known as **learned helplessness**.

This is explained as a **belief** acquired over time that one has no control over events and that failure is inevitable (for example, if a batsman repeatedly gets a duck, he may feel that he no longer has the skill to succeed at sport). It is characterised by a feeling of **hopelessness** in which a person with the physical potential to achieve highly at sport no longer feels that it is possible for him or her to do so (figure 7.5).

This is what is behind the common belief that if you fall off a bike, you must get back on straight away, otherwise you may never do so.

figure 7.5 – get back on the bike straight away

General and specific learned helplessness

- **General (global) learned helplessness** occurs when a person attributes failure to internal and stable factors, and this feeling of failure is applied to all sports. For example, the comment 'I am useless at all sports'.

- **Specific learned helplessness** occurs when a person attributes difficulties to internal and stable factors, and this feeling is applied to one specific sport. For example, the comment 'I am good at soccer but useless at racquet games'.

Attribution retraining strategies

Figure 7.6 summarises the process which must be undertaken if learned helplessness is to be avoided or recovered from. Following failure, low achievers need to learn to attribute success and failure to the same reasons as high achievers, namely:

- Success should be attributed to stable internal factors.
- Failure should be attributed to unstable external factors.

This would raise the **self-efficacy** (page 122) of the performer for his or her sport.

Hence attribution retraining will influence how the performer deals with a situation. During this process, the coach can provide encouraging feedback and set realistic achievable goals.

The positive and negative applications of attribution theory on performance and sustaining a balanced, active lifestyle is summarised in table 7.1.

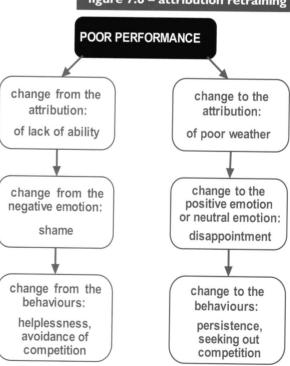

figure 7.6 – attribution retraining

POOR PERFORMANCE

change from the attribution: of lack of ability

change to the attribution: of poor weather

change from the negative emotion: shame

change to the positive emotion or neutral emotion: disappointment

change from the behaviours: helplessness, avoidance of competition

change to the behaviours: persistence, seeking out competition

Mastery orientation

Mastery orientation is at the opposite end of the attribution scale to learned helplessness. Here, instead of the sportsperson believing that he or she is hopeless at a certain sport or activity, he or she will continuously search for new skills and exposure to new and more demanding situations (such as playing in cup finals, or competing in national events as opposed to local club events).

Such an attitude attributes failure to internal, controllable and unstable factors, such as effort - which can be improved with determination and the will to succeed. So he or she will have mastery orientation, a situation for which every good coach will strive.

figure 7.7 – failure needs retraining

figure 7.8 – a confident save

Confidence and self-efficacy

Confidence

Confidence is an element of mental preparation for sports performance, as outlined in figure 7.9.

Confidence arouses positive emotions which allow the athlete to:
- Remain **calm** under pressure.
- Be **assertive** when required.
- **Concentrate** easily.
- **Focus** on the important aspects of a task.
- Set challenging but realistic **goals**.
- Increase **effort**.
- Devise effective game **strategies**.
- Keep psychological **momentum**.

Confidence affects us by:
- Arousing **positive** emotions.
- Facilitating **concentration**.
- Enabling **focus** on the important aspects of a task.

figure 7.9 – confidence

calm • assertive • positive • concentration • playing to win • CONFIDENCE • focus • taking risks • realistic goals • never give up • effort

Self-confidence

Self-confidence is a feature of a sportsperson's attitude to his or her sporting activity which boosts personal self-worth and self-belief as outlined in figure 7.10. This belief centres around the notion that he or she can win or perform well.

Self-esteem

The term **self-esteem** is component of the umbrella idea of **self-concept**. Self-concept is a general term used to refer to how someone thinks about, evaluates or perceives himself or herself. To be aware of oneself is to have a concept of oneself.

Carl Rogers (1959) believes that the self-concept has three different components:
*   The view you have of yourself (**self-image**).
*   What you wish you were really like (**ideal-self**).
*   How much value you place on yourself (**self-esteem** or **self-worth**).

figure 7.10 – self-confidence and self-efficacy

belief that one can succeed

an attitude

SELF-CONFIDENCE

an aspect of self-esteem

perception of ability to perform a particular sporting task successfully

SELF-EFFICACY

a situation-specific form of self-confidence

Self-image
This does not necessarily have to reflect reality.
*   For example, a person with anorexia who is thin may have a self-image in which the person believes he or she is fat.
*   A person's self-image is affected by many factors, such parental influences, friends, the media etc.

Ideal-self
This concept revolves around what you **would like to be**.
If there is a **mismatch** between how you see yourself (for example, your self-image) and what you'd like to be (for example, your ideal-self) then this is likely to affect how much you value yourself.

The coach, who should merely serve as a guide and not an authoritative figure, should demonstrate **empathy**, **understanding**, and **memories** of what it was like to be an athlete.

This relationship should be **athlete-centred** and **focus** on the athlete developing **self-awareness**, **growth**, and **development**.

Self-esteem
Self-esteem is the **regard** you hold for yourself. Everyone has a concept of his or her person (**self-concept**). If you like your self-concept (who you think you are), then you have self-esteem. Self-esteem is not the same as self-confidence.

Self-esteem should be based on **who you are as a person** instead of how well you can perform in your sport or how high you go in a sporting career. Think about this: if you take away the part of you who is an athlete, how would you describe yourself? What are your **personal characteristics** that describe you? This is what self-esteem should be based on.

If you feel like you struggle with self-esteem, have hope, since this is a **learned capability** and it can change with practice, and the will to improve.

High self-esteem i.e. we have a **positive** view of ourselves. This tends to lead to:
*   **Confidence** in our own **abilities**.
*   **Self-acceptance**.
*   Not worrying about what others think.
*   **Optimism**.

Self-esteem

Low self-esteem i.e. we have a **negative** view of ourselves. This tends to lead to:

- **Lack** of confidence.
- Want to be/look like **someone else**.
- Always worrying what **others might think**.
- **Pessimism**.

Self-confidence is the **belief in your ability** to perform a task - it is not a judgment.

You can have self-confidence, but not self-esteem, and vice versa. Optimally, you want both high self-confidence in your abilities and self-esteem.

figure 7.11 – Jessica Ennis wins in London 2012, she had great self-confidence

Vealey's model of sport-confidence

A confident player plays to win even if it means **taking risks**, will take each point or play at a time, and **never gives up** even when defeat is imminent.

Vealey's **sport-confidence** is the level of belief a person has in his or her ability to be successful at sport.

- Success in sport could be related to winning (**outcome orientation**), or performing well (**performance orientation**).

- Different performers have different ways of enhancing sport confidence. Their **competitive orientations** can be varied according to the situation and whether a performer is motivated towards a performance goal or an outcome goal.

Table 7.2 – **sport-confidence**

factors influencing sport-confidence	definition and example
trait sport-confidence	the level of sport confidence a person usually has example, a discus thrower is generally confident about making a throw (figure 7.12, page 122)
competitive orientation	the perceived opportunity to achieve a performance or outcome goal example, the discus thrower is motivated by a challenging competition to throw well
state sport-confidence	the level of sport confidence a performer has in a specific sport situation example, the discus thrower feels confident because the wind is in the right direction
subjective perceptions of outcome	after performance, performer will be pleased or disappointed by outcome this then affects confidence and competitiveness in future performances
objective sporting situation	the performance takes into account the situation in which performance occurs example, the discus thrower competes well in the World Championships

Relationship of confidence to attribution

A performer's attribution of success or failure will relate to sport confidence. Attributing success to factors like ability and effort will increase a performer's sport confidence, by increasing his or her future expectancy of success.

Results of research

*   **Males** (in the general population) have a higher sport-confidence than **females**.

*   **Elite performers** have high sport-confidence.

*   Elite sporting females have the **same level** of sport-confidence as elite sporting males.

*   Therefore elite sporting females are **less affected** by **traditional female stereotyping** and roles.

*   Elite performers are more **performance oriented**, which means that their feelings of confidence are based more on how well they perform than whether they win or lose.

Self-efficacy

Self-efficacy is a situational form of self-confidence. It is specific to the sport or activity which a person is undertaking.

Bandura's self-efficacy

Bandura's self-efficacy model (figure 7.13) outlines **four** factors relevant to the self-efficacy of a sports performer.

Performance accomplishments

*   **Performance accomplishments** consist of **past experiences**, for example, a previously performed skill at dribbling a soccer ball.

*   If this is successful, then this leads to greater self-efficacy at this particular task in the future.

Vicarious experiences

*   **Vicarious experiences** consist of what has **been observed in others** performing a similar skill (the sports performer experiences the same feelings of mastery and competence by watching another person perform a skill as if he or she has performed the skill himself or herself.

*   For example, observing another player in your team dribbling a soccer ball. This is most effective if the model is of similar age or ability and is successful. This may lead to greater self-efficacy.

Verbal persuasion

*   **Verbal encouragement** can lead to greater self-efficacy if the person giving encouragement is of **high status** compared with the performer.

Emotional arousal

*   If **arousal** is too high, then **state anxiety** (anxiety produced by the specific situation of an activity - otherwise known as **A-state**) can be too high.

*   This could lead to low self-efficacy. Mental rehearsal or physical relaxation techniques could lead to greater confidence and a calmer approach - this also contributes to greater self-efficacy.

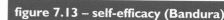

figure 7.13 – self-efficacy (Bandura)

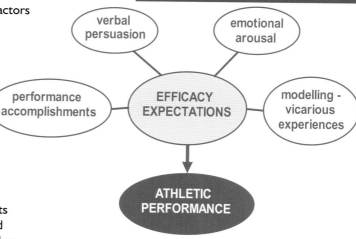

Lack of confidence

Lack of confidence can cause **stress** under pressure. What tends to happen is that attention and concentration tend to focus on outside stressors such as mistakes (falling during an ice-skating or gymnastics programme), or spectators (shouted comments or applause on a neighbouring court).

- What also tends to happen is the setting of **goals** which are either **too easy** or **too hard**.

- Lack of confidence also causes the athlete to try to **avoid mistakes** (fear of failure or tendency to avoid failure).

- Non-confident athletes find it difficult to reverse negative psychological momentum, so that once things start to go wrong it is difficult to think positively.

Over-confidence or false confidence

Over-confidence is dangerous because it can lead to inadequate preparation (the athlete thinks he or she is better prepared than is actually the case, figure 7.14).

Low motivation and low arousal can occur, which are difficult to correct when competition is under way.

figure 7.14 – over-confidence can lead to injury

Strategies for the coach in building self-efficacy

Coaches can raise a performer's self-efficacy, resulting in a more positive and successful performance, as suggested in Bandura's self-efficacy theory (page 122):

- Build upon **successful experiences** by reminding performer of past successes. A previous performance is the strongest factor affecting self-efficacy and there is no reason why it cannot be repeated.

- Observe a **good demonstration** from a performer who shares the same characteristics, such as ability, gender and age, as the young performer. For example, a gymnast of similar age and standard, performs a forward roll on the beam. This performer will feel 'If she can do it, so can I'. Such a demonstration reduces worry and develops confidence.

figure 7.15 – Johanna Konta

- Use **role models** (figure 7.15) to inspire and motivate performer of potential long-term goals.

- Use **specific positive feedback**, such as words of encouragement and support, that may be related to a previous performance. The aim would be to convince the athlete of his or her ability to accomplish the task. Therefore, saying 'You can do it!' is not as effective as saying 'You successfully long jumped 4 metres, you can do 4.2 metres.' This positive talk or persuasion will elevate self-belief.

- **Break down complex skills** (whole-part-whole learning) into smaller specific components that challenge the performer but are within his or her current ability level, thus allowing the performer to have successful experiences which will over time increase the performer's self-efficacy.

- Use **mental rehearsal** or **imagery** techniques to reinforce skill learning.

- Control of **arousal levels** of the performer's internal feelings and physiological state, for example, increased heart rate and sweating. This may include **cognitive** and **somatic** strategies.

Practice questions

1) Weiner's model of attribution refers to:
   a.   stable factors, such as efforts and luck.
   b.   unstable factors, such as ability or task difficulty.
   c.   future expectations are related to unstable factors.
   d.   success is best explained by internal attributions.

2) Bandura's model of self-efficacy does not include:
   a.   performance accomplishments.
   b.   excitement-arousal.
   c.   vicarious experiences.
   d.   verbal persuasion.

3) Vealey's model of sport confidence includes:
   a.   competitive orientation.
   b.   a nurtured personality.
   c.   confidence at all sports.
   d.   a subjective outcome.

4) A thrower prepares for a qualifying competition, but suffers from
   stress and tries too hard and so performs badly. Which theory explains this behaviour?
   a.   catastrophe theory.
   b.   multi-dimensional anxiety theory.
   c.   inverted U theory.
   d.   drive theory.

5) Over-confidence is dangeraous to the athlete because:
   a.   it can lead to inadequate preparation for a major event.
   b.   it can lead to over arousal in the competition siuation.
   c.   it might lead to an increase in motivation to continue with the sport.
   d.   it might be too easy to correct faults which occur.

6) a)   Figure 7.16 partly illustrates Weiner's model of attribution.
         Explain the term attribution using a sporting situation.   2 marks

   b)   Explain the terms locus of causality and stability when applied to
         attribution theory.   4 marks

   c)   Redraw the model and place on it relevant attributions for each of
         the four boxes.   4 marks

   d)   What attributions would you encourage if your team were playing
         well but often losing?   5 marks

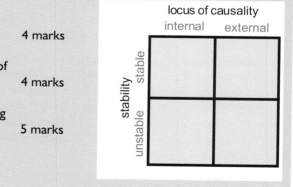

figure 7.16 – Weiner's model of attribution

7) a)   Many young people claim to be hopeless at gymnastics. Suggest three reasons why these
         youngsters might have a negative attitude to gymnastics.   3 marks

   b)   What is meant by learned helplessness (LH) and how is it caused?   3 marks

   c)   How would you attempt to attract beginners to a gymnastics class, and then change
         any negative attitudes?   4 marks

Practice questions

8) Those who achieve little in sport often attribute their failure to factors outside their control and learned helplessness can result.
Using examples from sport, explain what is meant by learned helplessness and identify how self-motivational techniques may help to limit the effects of learned helplessness.

6 marks

9) a) What is meant by the term self-efficacy when applied to sports psychology?

1 mark

   b) Bandura suggested that self-efficacy is influenced by four factors. Identify and apply these factors to a sport of your choice.

8 marks

   c) As a coach of a sports team, how would you raise an individual's level of self-efficacy?

4 marks

10) Drawing on your knowledge and understanding of sports psychology, examine the theories and methods that you might use to raise the levels of confidence of a sports performer. Illustrate your answer with practical examples.

20 marks

11) How can self-concept affect performance in a sporting situation?

6 marks

12) a) How does self-efficacy explain performance?

4 marks

   b) Describe each of the sections of self-efficacy theory.

8 marks

   c) Provide a sport-based example of self-efficacy theory.

3 marks

Answers link: http://www.jroscoe.co.uk/downloads/a2_revise_pe_ocr/OCRA2_ch7_answers.pdf

CHAPTER 8: Leadership and stress management

Leadership in sport

Leaders play an important role influencing groups and individuals as well as setting goals. In terms of sport, leaders include team captains, coaches, managers and teachers. Successful teams have strong leaders.

A leader can influence the behaviour of others towards required and desired goals and will influence effective team cohesion. He or she will also help fulfil the expectations of a team, and will develop an environment in which a group is motivated, rewarded and helped towards its common goals. Recognised characteristics of successful leaders are summarised in figure 8.1.

Carron suggested that leaders emerge in two ways:

- **Emergent leaders** come from within a group because of their skill and abilities or through nomination or election.

- **Prescribed leaders** are appointed by a governing body or agency outside the group.

figure 8.1 – leadership characteristics

The Chelladurai continuum

The **Chelladurai continuum** theory covers the notion that there are three types of leader, and that an actual leader may adopt all three of the types in different situations depending on the circumstances. These three types of leader are:

- The **autocratic authoritarian** leader who makes all the decisions.

- The **democratic** leader who shares the decisions (with members of a group or team), and seeks advice from the group itself. He or she will be prepared to change his or her mind based on this advice.

- The **laissez-faire** leader who lets others make decisions and is prepared to go along with whatever they decide.

Effective leadership

Table 8.1 - **effective leadership**

	autocratic style	democratic style	laissez-faire style
what is it?	the leader commands, and other team members have no input	team members discuss with leader what to do	leader has the same role as rest of the team, he or she is passive, but provides support where necessary
characteristics	leader makes all decisions leader tells them all what to do	team members give input social development encouraged	team members take responsibility for decisions lleader has very little input
when is it effective?	dangerous situations team performing badly team members not familiar with tactics or skills	small groups team members are highly skilled team members are all capable of being leaders	most people think this does not work but may function for very experienced team members

Theories of leadership

figure 8.2 – Kate Richardson-Walsh

These theories centre around the **nature** or **nurture** debate.

The 'great man' or trait theory

This is the '**nature**' theory, that leaders are born not made, and have relevant innate personality qualities.

Social learning theory

This is the '**nurture**' theory, in which leaders learn their skills through watching and imitating other people (models). This theory says that leaders are formed throughout life by social or environmental influences.

According to this idea, learning to be a leader starts by observation of a model, then continues by imitation or copying of the behaviour of the model. The effectiveness of this process would depend on the model having high status.

Kate Richardson-Walsh (figure 8.2) was the inspirational captain of the women's hockey team which won gold at the Rio Olympics 2016. She had 375 caps for her country and was captain for 13 years. She is an example of a highly successful leader.

Interactionist theory

Interactionist theories are those which assert that a combination of trait and a person's situation or environment builds up a person's leadership qualities, and that traits determine behaviour but can be modified by situations. **Lewin** was the theorist who stated that behaviour is a function of both the person (personality P) and the environment (E), and put this in the mathematical form:

$$B = f(P, E)$$

This is identical to the interactionist approach for **personality** covered in year 1 of this course.

Example of the interactionist theory approach

A coach or team captain may not show leadership qualities in normal life siuations, but be an outstanding leader on the sports field or pitch. In this situation, assertiveness and man management and communication skills can be produced when required.

Fiedler's contingency theory

Fiedler's theory states that there is a continuum between:

- **Task-centred leadership**, which would be best for the most favourable or least favourable situations.
- **Person** (or relationship) **centred leadership** which would be best for moderately favourable situations.

Whether or not the task-centred or person-centred approach should be used depends on whether relationships are warm, if the task has a clear structure, or if the leader is powerful and people will do exactly what he or she says.

There would also be the pressure of time which might affect the choice of leadership style.

Factors affecting leader effectiveness

Fiedler's ideas are summarised in figure 8.3 which outlines the three broad groups of factors affecting the effectiveness of a leader with any given group or team.

Leader characteristics

The following **leadership qualities** will determine a leader's effectiveness (this is expanded in figure 8.3):

- Ability to communicate.
- Respect for group members.
- Enthusiasm.
- High ability.
- Deep knowledge of the sport and techniques or tactics.
- Charisma.
- The leader will empathise with athlete problems and be sympathetic to individual difficulties.

Situational factors within leadership

- If things are going **well** for the team, or things are going **badly** (for example there are poor facilities or no support), then a leader needs to be **task-oriented**.

- On the other hand, if things are going **moderately well**, then a leader needs to be **person-centred**.

- In **team sports**, a leader should be **directive** (task-oriented) and would organise and structure group tasks according to a plan (tactics or game strategy).

- In **individual sports**, however, we would look for a person-oriented leader, who would empathise with athlete problems, and be sympathetic to individual difficulties.

- The **size of the group** will affect leadership style, since the more members in a group, the less likely individual needs will be taken into account.

- If a **decision needs to be made quickly** (for example in a dangerous rock climbing situation), then an **autocratic** style of leader would be essential to ensure that the correct action is taken immediately (people will need to be told what to do to avoid danger).

- **Tradition** can sometimes play a part in which style of leadership should be used, since within some groups, group members might tend to resent change. Sometimes change is essential, and it would be necessary to be **autocratic** and **task-centred** to implement change (the leader would not try and explain why change is needed, just that it needs to be done for the good of the team).

Members' characteristics within leadership

A good leader will adapt to the expectations, knowledge and experience of group members.

- If members of a group are **hostile**, then a leader would adopt an **autocratic** style.
- If members of a group are **friendly**, then the leader would adopt a more **democratic** and **person-centred** style.

Problems arise if the strategies for preparation used by a leader do not match group expectations (for example, if members of a team do not feel that the proposed strategy will achieve a win in the next match against a particular opposing team).

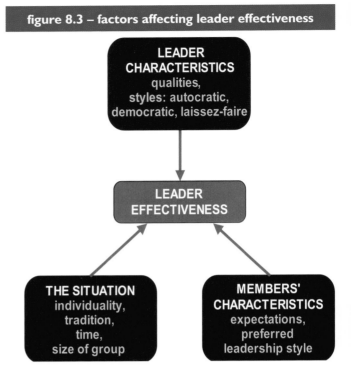

figure 8.3 – factors affecting leader effectiveness

LEADER CHARACTERISTICS
qualities,
styles: autocratic, democratic, laissez-faire

LEADER EFFECTIVENESS

THE SITUATION
individuality,
tradition,
time,
size of group

MEMBERS' CHARACTERISTICS
expectations,
preferred leadership style

Chelladurai's multidimensional model

Chelladurai set out the model in figure 8.4, which sets out the links between **leader**, **situation** and **member** characteristics, and **required**, **actual** and **preferred** leader behaviour.

All these factors will affect the eventual performance of a team or group, and the satisfaction gained or perceived by both group members and the leader him or herself.

The point made by the model is that all the factors discussed above are linked in a real situation.

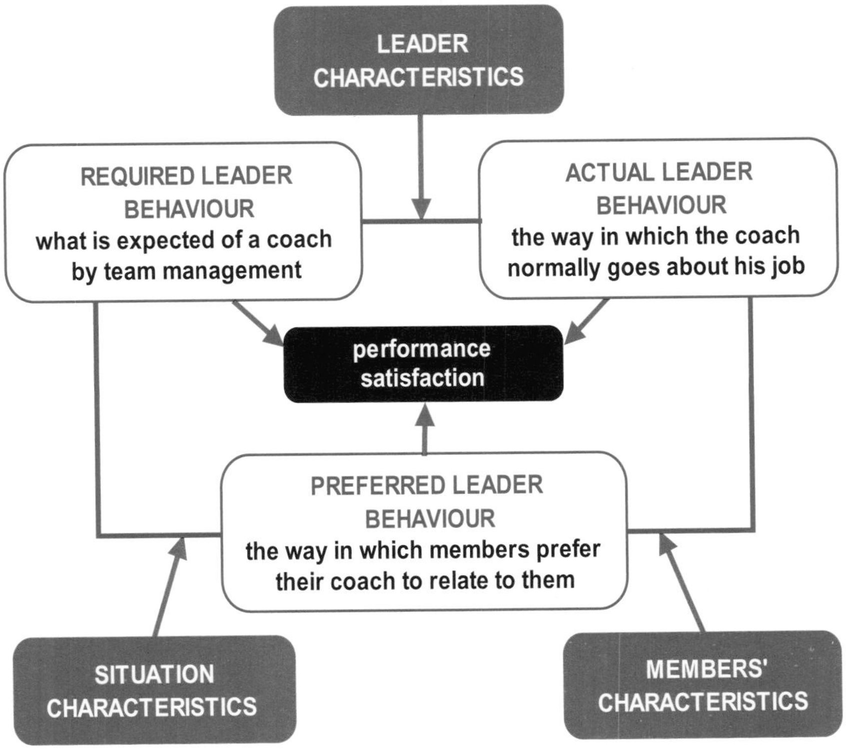

Chelladurai's five types of leader behaviour

Training and instruction behaviour

This behaviour is aimed at improving performance. This type of leader behaviour is strong on **technical** and **tactical** aspects.

Democratic behaviour

This approach is one in which the leader allows decisions to be made **collectively**.

Autocratic behaviour

This approach is one in which a leader uses his or her **personal authority**.

This type would be least preferred if the leader or coach **does not show** that he or she is aware of sportspeople's needs and preferences.

Social support behaviour

This approach is one in which concern is shown for the **well-being of others**.

This might be preferred by youngsters.

Rewards behaviour

A leader uses **positive reinforcement** to gain the **authority** of leadership.

figure 8.4– Chelladurai's multidimensional model

LEADER CHARACTERISTICS

REQUIRED LEADER BEHAVIOUR
what is expected of a coach by team management

ACTUAL LEADER BEHAVIOUR
the way in which the coach normally goes about his job

performance satisfaction

PREFERRED LEADER BEHAVIOUR
the way in which members prefer their coach to relate to them

SITUATION CHARACTERISTICS

MEMBERS' CHARACTERISTICS

figure 8.5 – what type of leadership is shown here?

Stress management to optimise performance

figure 8.6 – stress and stressors

Stress can be used positively in sport, but at the same time it can result in a **bad experience**.

Stress and **anxiety** are closely linked, with stress being a major cause of health issues in our society. Figure 8.6 outlines the main factors associated with stress and stressors.

Stress is a response of the body to any demands made on it. The symptoms of stress are **physiological**, **psychological** or **behavioural** (see table 8.2 for details).

Stress and stressors

Stressors are the causes of stress and are:

- **Social**, including the disapproval of parents or peers, the effects of an audience, a 'win-at-all-costs' attitude, excessive expectations from pre-match pep talks.
- **Chemical** or **biochemical**, in which damage is inflicted by ingestion of harmful substances.
- **Bacterial**, which would be an illness caused by micro-organisms.
- **Physical**, in which a person would suffer injury, pain or exhaustion.
- **Climatic**, in which extremes of weather are experienced, such as hot weather for endurance activities, or rain and cold on bare skin.
- **Psychological** or **cognitive**, in which there is a mismatch between the perception of the demands of a task and the ability of a person to cope with these demands.
- **Physiological** or **somatic**, which produces a physiological response such as increased heart rate.

Symptoms of stress

Table 8.2 – **symptoms of stress**

physiological symptoms	psychological symptoms	behavioural symptoms
increased heart rate	worry	rapid talking
increased blood pressure	feeling overwhelmed	nail biting
increased sweating	inability to make decisions	pacing
increased breathing rate	inability to concentrate	scowling
decreased flow of blood to the skin	inability to direct attention appropriately	yawning
increased oxygen uptake	narrowing of attention	trembling
dry mouth	feeling out of control	raised voice pitch
cold clammy hands	negative self-talk	frequent urination
constantly feeling sick	apprehension	dazed look in eyes

Control of stress and anxiety

Stress and anxiety management techniques become important for sports performers when performances fall, or failure is experienced.

Cognitive and somatic relaxation techniques

Cognitive relaxation techniques use the power of **thought** to redirect attention away from failure or perceived failure. A performer will take **control** of emotions and thought processes, will **eliminate negative feelings**, and will develop **self-confidence** and **self-efficacy**, pages 120 to 123.

Somatic relaxation techniques are used to control the **physiological** symptoms of stress and anxiety.

Cognitive relaxation techniques

Psychological skills training

Psychological skills training (PST), refers to the total experience of training at the following various techniques for improving cognitive relaxation. The point is that such activities have to be repeated (**trained**) if they are to be effective. Most top sports clubs and national teams employ sports psychologists to supervise and direct this training.

Attention

Attention relates to:

*   **Amount of information** we can cope with. Since the amount of information we can attend to **is limited**, we therefore have limited **attentional capacity**.

*   **Relevance of the information**. The performer must therefore attend to only **relevant information**, and **disregard irrelevant** information. This is called **selective attention**.

Selective attention

This is the process of sorting out **relevant** bits of information from the many which are received. Attention passes the information to the **short-term memory** which gives time for **conscious analysis**. This is mentioned in the context of the memory model in chapter 6.

figure 8.7– selective attention

A good performer can **focus totally** on an important aspect of his or her skill which **can exclude other elements** which may also be desirable. Sometimes a performer may desire to concentrate on several different things at once.

When some parts of a performance become **automatic**, the information relevant to those parts does not require attention, and this gives the performer **spare attentional capacity**. This allows the performer to attend to new elements of a skill such as tactics or anticipating the moves of an opponent.

The coach will therefore need to help performers to make best use of their spare attentional capacity, and will also need to **direct the attention** (figure 8.7) of performers to enable them to **concentrate** and reduce the chance of **attentional switching** to irrelevant information or distractions.

Concentration

Concentration is **a state of mind in which attention is directed towards a specific aim or activity**. Concentration and **attentional focus (control of attention** towards a task) are essential components of a sportsperson's armoury of mental techniques to assist performance.

Use of cognitive techniques to assist concentration

Cognitive techniques such as imagery and mental rehearsal or relaxation can be used to direct the sportsperson's mind towards a specific task (page 133). These techniques can be used to manage the stress of the situation, or to manage anxiety in a productive way.

Attentional narrowing

Attentional narrowing (figure 8.8) occurs when some parts of a performance become automatic. The information relevant to those parts then does not require attention, which gives the performer spare attentional capacity. This **spare capacity** will allow the performer to attend to **new elements** of a skill, for example as tactics or anticipating the moves of an opponent.

The **coach** will need to help the performer to make best use of spare attentional capacity, and direct the attention of the performer to enable him or her to concentrate. This would reduce the chance of **attentional switching** to irrelevant information or distractions.

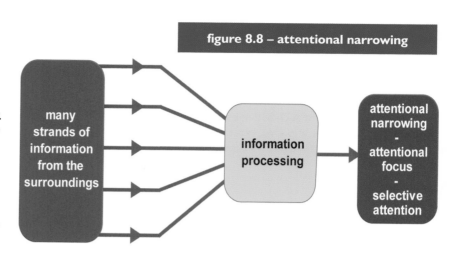
figure 8.8 – attentional narrowing

Attentional control training (ACT)

Attentional control training is a personalised programme which targets a performer's specific concentration problems. It assesses the demands of the sport, the situation, and the personality of the performer.

Nideffer's attentional styles

On the chart in figure 8.9, the axes represent attentional styles that are narrow to broad and internal to external, and a particular event or sports activity will have a mixture of all four styles.

The following attentional styles are highlighted:
- **Narrow (A)**, in which a player concentrates on one aspect of the game, for example the goalkeeper who has predominantly closed skills.
- **Broad (B)**, in which a player concentrates on the whole game, with all players' positions and movements. This applies to open skills of this type.
- **Internal (C)**, in which a player decides to concentrate on his own technique.
- **External (D)**, in which a player focuses on the position or technique or ability of his opposite number.

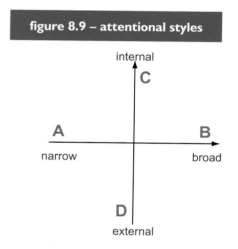
figure 8.9 – attentional styles

Cue utilisation

Cue utilisation (Easterbrook's theory) describes a situation in which cues can be used by the sportsperson to direct attention, and to trigger appropriate arousal responses.

This would enable attentional focus at a relevant moment. Sometimes, **narrowing of attentional focus** by an aroused player will cause lack of awareness of broader play issues.

Positive self-talk

- **Positive self-talk** is a procedure where a person will talk through the process of a competitive situation, talking positively and building self-confidence.
- It creates a **positive** message tied to a belief.
- It can also reduce **cognitive state anxiety**.
- It is crucial for **concentration**.

Negative thought stopping

Thought stopping is an intervention technique that is used when negative thoughts or worry (about failure) begin. At that point, a performer should immediately think '**stop**', and substitute a **positive thought**.

Rational thinking

Successful sportspeople tend to use this process in the attempt to limit the stress encountered in a specific situation.

Rational thinking is about limiting the damage caused by stress, and rationally explaining the causes and outcomes of the stress. The fact of engaging in this process will produce a reduction in the impact of the stress.

For example, the pain produced by training (particularly extreme training) can be perceived as the normal outcome experienced by the majority of elite athletes and which is something to be coped with, without damage to muscles or joints. This is a rational explanation of the situation and hopefully will reduce the stress of training, and allow the person to make progress with training goals.

Mental rehearsal

Mental rehearsal (figure 8.10) or practice describes the mental or cognitive rehearsal of a skill by a performer without actual physical movement. The performer will consciously imagine a performance, sometimes whlie being prompted by a coach, with attention to technical or tactical issues.

This process helps **concentration**, and helps the performer to focus on strengths and weaknesses. This technique is used by most top level sportsmen, and is often prompted by video or talk from a coach.

The point of this in stress or anxiety control is that it brings an activity away from the actual performance, and therefore away from any anxieties associated with the performance itself. Figure 8.10 outlines the main features of this process.

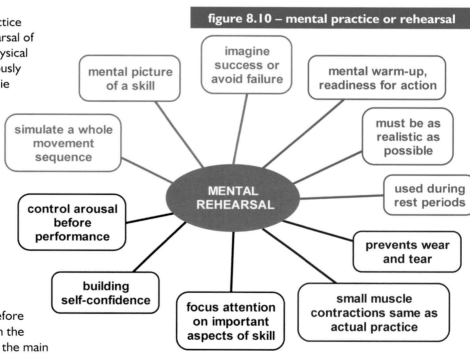

figure 8.10 – mental practice or rehearsal

- mental picture of a skill
- imagine success or avoid failure
- mental warm-up, readiness for action
- simulate a whole movement sequence
- must be as realistic as possible
- used during rest periods
- MENTAL REHEARSAL
- control arousal before performance
- prevents wear and tear
- building self-confidence
- focus attention on important aspects of skill
- small muscle contractions same as actual practice

Visualisation

figure 8.11 – visualisation

The process of visualisation asks a performer to rerun a past experience, or an experience in training in a simlar way to mental rehearsal (figure 8.11). This will continue with a preview of hoped-for success in a future performance.

Again, this activity can be prompted by a coach and will intend to remove the stress and anxiety associated with the actual performance, particularly without the stress of a negative audience or aggression from other players The intention will then be to rebuild a new performance without such features.

Imagery relaxation

Imagery relaxation, in which a performer will think of a place with associations of warmth and relaxation, then imagine the activity or technique.

This process involves practice in non-stressful situations, and will be used prior to competition.

Goal setting

Goal setting is discussed in the year 1 book in this series on page 161.

The process of goal setting can be an important tool in the management of stressful sporting situations. The setting of realistic and acheivable goals - and then acheiving them in spite of the stress is a consequence of this idea, and will also improve confidence and motivation.

For example, the goal of running a 400 metres in 48 seconds. This would be achieved after 5 racing attempts, agreed by both performer and coach, assessed at an 80% success rate, providing an exciting challenge, with a record of training and racing times. Hence the stress of acheiving the goal is staged into several steps, each of which is achievable.

Goals (figure 8.12) should be:
- **Easily** attained initially and therefore **realistic**.
- **Incremental**, a little bit at a time.
- **Challenging** but **achievable**.
- **Progressively** more difficult.
- **Training goals** should be planned around **overall goals**.

Goals are either:
- **Outcome oriented**:
    Towards the end result of the sporting activity. For example to win a race.

- **Performance oriented**:
    Judged against other performances, and related to improvement and enhancing the performer's current standard. For example to beat his or her best time.

- **Process oriented**:
    To obtain an improvement in technique.

Effective goal setting

Goals (figure 8.13) should be:
- Stated **positively**.
- **Specific** to the situation and performer.
- **Time phased**, to be achieved in one week or two months for example.
- **Challenging and aspirational**.
- **Achievable and realistic**.
- **Measurable**, so that you can actually say exactly whether or not a goal has been achieved.
- **Negotiated** between sportsperson and coach.
- **Progressive**, from short-term to long-term.
- **Performance oriented** rather than outcome oriented.

figure 8.12 – goals should be?

figure 8.13 – effective goals

Effective goal setting

Goals should be:
- **Written** down.
- **Reviewed** regularly (with downward adjustment if necessary - in the case of injury).

Failure to achieve goals should be followed by the resetting of goals to maintain the performer's **self-esteem**.

Goal setting and performance

- Give the performer an aim or **focus**.
- Increase **motivation** when the goal is accomplished.
- Increase **confidence** levels.
- Control **arousal**, **stresss** or anxiety levels.
- Focus **efforts in training** on game or competitive situations.

Mindfulness

Athletes in many sports are turning to this technique to cope with the high stress of elite performance in their sport.

This involves meditation, awareness of the environment, and the performer's relationship with others. This should be adjusted to recover from moody responses to irrational behaviour in others.

Somatic relaxation techniques

Progressive muscle relaxation

Progressive muscle relaxation (also known as PMR), sometimes called **self-directed muscle relaxation training**, enables a performer to focus on each of the major muscle groups in turn, then to allow breathing to become slow and easy. The athlete will visualise the tension flowing out of a muscle group until it is completely relaxed. Eventually a sportsperson will be able to combine muscle groups, and achieve total relaxation quickly.

Biofeedback

- **Biofeedback** is the process of monitoring skin temperature (cold if stressed, warm if unstressed), and the galvanic skin response in which the electrical conductivity of skin increases when moist (tense muscle causes sweating).

- A further measurement is made by electromyography, in which electrodes are taped to specific muscles which can detect electrical activity and hence tension in muscle.

- The point is that these measures are perceived by the sportsperson during a performance, and he or she can then alter his or her behaviour to reduce the symptoms of stress or anxiety.

Centring

- **Centring** involves the control of physiological symptoms of stress by focusing on control of the diaphragm and deep breathing.

- The famous John McEnroe (famous for throwing tantrums on court and shouting at the umpire 'you can't be serious', then going on to win Wimbledon titles, figure 8.14), used centring to bring himself down from a major row with a court official to playing the perfect serve or shot - within 10 seconds!

figure 8.14 – John McEnroe used centring

Breathing control

- The way a person breathes affects the **whole body**. Those things which happen when an individual is stressed, such as increased **heart rate**, increased **breathing rate** and **high blood pressure**, all decrease when the individual breathes deeply to relax.

- During such a process, on relaxation, messages are **sent to the brain** which therefore closely links breathing control with somatic performance.

- **Deep controlled breathing** can be achieved using a variety of techniques (such as **belly breathing** - using the diaphragm to initiate air intake), and this will direct attention away from a stressful situation, and enable redirection of attention to a desired one.

Practice questions

1) Which one of the following is not an aspect of the trait theory of leadership?
   a.   leaders are born not made.
   b.   people have innate leadership qualities.
   c.   people's leadership qualities can be nurtured.
   d.   people's leadership qualities are enduring.

2) What is meant by emergent leaders?
   a.   they are appointed by a governing body.
   b.   they are appointed by the national coach.
   c.   they are elected by the team.
   d.   they are motivated by internal desires to do well.

3) The social learning theory of leadership is best described as:
   a.   leaders learn their skills by watching others.
   b.   leaders are formed throughout life by social or environmental influences.
   c.   the high status of a sporting model will influence a leader most.
   d.   people have innate leadership qualities.

4) Which one of the following is not a type of leader according to Chelladurai?
   a.   a task centred leader.
   b.   an autocratic or authoritarian leader.
   c.   a laissez-faire leader.
   d.   the democratic leader.

5) Which one of the following is the best example of a stressor?
   a.   bacterial infections.
   b.   disapproval by parents or peers.
   c.   injury suffered during a game.
   d.   extremes of weather.

6) A somatic relaxation technique does not involve:
   a.   progressive muscle relaxation.
   b.   centring.
   c.   deep breathing.
   d.   mental rehearsal.

7) a)   What is meant by a leader and what sort of qualities would you expect to see in a leader within the context of sport?

4 marks

   b)   Using psychological theories describe how an individual becomes a leader.

4 marks

Practice questions

8) a) Name three leadership styles.   3 marks

   b) What factors should be taken into consideration when deciding upon
       which leadership style to adopt?   6 marks

9) Fiedler's Contingency Model suggests that the effectiveness of a leader can
   change depending on the situation.
   Use sporting examples to explain this theory.   4 marks

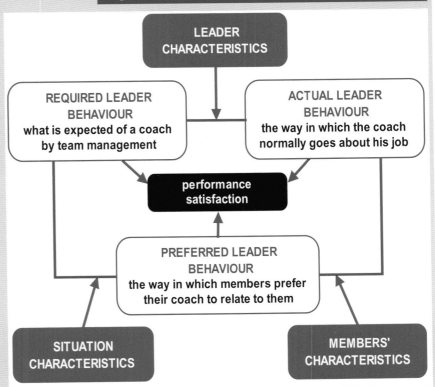

figure 8.15 – Chelladurai's multidimensional model

10) Look at figure 8.15 of Chelladurai's
    multidimensional model of leadership.

    a) Explain each part of the model using
        examples from sport.   5 marks

    b) Behaviour of the group associated
        with leadership can be viewed from
        three perspectives. Briefly name and
        explain each of these perspectives.
                                    5 marks

    c) Discuss the statement 'Good leaders
        are born not made', and explain
        whether you agree or disagree in the
        light of psychological theory. 5 marks

11) With reference to sporting performance, explain how cognitive and somatic stress differ.   5 marks

12) a) Discuss the possible relationships between stress and performance in sporting activities.   7 marks

    b) High levels of arousal have often been linked with stress.
        Sketch a graph showing the relationship between the performance of a
        complex skill and level of arousal.   2 marks

    c) Add a second curve to your graph showing how the performance of a
        simple skill might be affected by arousal.   2 marks

Practice questions

13) a)   What is meant by the term stress?   2 marks

   b)   Explain two psychological symptoms of stress.   2 marks

   c)   Identify three main stressors in the context of sport.   3 marks

   d)   What is the difference between state and trait anxiety?   2 marks

   e)   What coping strategies should the anxious performer draw upon?   5 marks

14) Give examples of positive self-talk and explain why it is important.   4 marks

15) Describe the main physiological signs associated with increased levels of stress and
    explain what the technique of imagery involves and how it can help stress management.
    How can a coach and performer ensure that imagery is effective?   20 marks

   Answers link: http://www.jroscoe.co.uk/downloads/a2_revise_pe_ocr/OCRA2_ch8_answers.pdf

CONTEMPORARY ISSUES IN PHYSICAL EDUCATION AND SPORT

CHAPTER 9: *Ethics and deviance in sport*

Ethics in sport

Ethics describes the **code**, **rules** or **guidelines** that reflect **morality** and are intended to direct behaviour. For example, the ethical codes governing the use of violence in sport reflect wider social practices and traditions.

Baron Pierre de Coubertin was instrumental in establishing many of the Olympic traditions. One of his most famous quotes was: '**the important thing in the Olympic Games is not winning but taking part. Just as in life, the aim is not to conquer but to struggle well**.'

Competing, not winning, was the objective of most amateur elite athletes for the first few decades of the twentieth century as epitomised in the **Olympic Oath** of **sportsmanship** and **fair play**.

Today, many elite sports performers are professional and the spirit in which sports are played has changed to become based on a '**win-at-all-costs**' ethic, alongside the gradual erosion of the principles of sportsmanship and fair play and increased evidence of gamesmanship,

Gamesmanship is right on the margins of fair game, strictly speaking legal, with the intention to compete to the limit of the rules and beyond if you can get away with it. It is a form of behaviour designed to gain an **unfair advantage**. Gamesmanship is often driven by a 'win-at-all-costs' attitude and shows no regard for the well-being of the opponent. For example, a soccer player diving without having been fouled in an attempt to get a free kick.

Deviance

The term **deviance** describes behaviour in which people find a way around the rules, however they are framed and can be institutional, group specific, or individual.

Deviant behaviour could be one of three possibilities:
*   **Voluntary**: the performer decides to take drugs.
*   **Cooperative**: the performer decides to take drugs, because all his friends are.
*   **Enforced**: an East German swimmer took drugs provided by her coach.

Deviance in sport concerns the **intention to cheat** as part of deviant behaviour, and includes **aggression** and **violence** among competitors and spectators, as well as the issue of **doping**.

In **sociological terms**, deviance means the variation of behaviour from the norm (what is normal). This can be upwards (positive) or downwards (negative) deviance. Positive deviance is when someone will over-conform to norms with no intention to harm or break the rules.

figure 9.1 – player violence

Negative deviance

Negative deviance involves behaviour that fails to meet accepted norms and has a detrimental effect on individuals and on society in general.

Examples of negative deviance include using performance enhancing drugs (PEDs), cheating within a contest, using bribes to influence the outcome of a match, fan violence or hooliganism, illegal betting on the outcome of a contest, financial irregularities in the transferring of players and player violence (figure 9.1).

Positive deviance

Examples of positive deviance include training through injury, adopting a 'no pain, no gain' attitude which implies an 'over' commitment to sport. For example, it used to be a common occurrence within rugby union, to continue 'playing through' an injury in the interests of the team as a whole. This behaviour has largely disappeared with the advent of substitutions, but used to be the major reason for the ending of a promising career in the sport.

Causes of deviant behaviour

- NGBs may **feel less able** to punish players due to their commercial interests.
- Fear of the offending player taking them to **court**.
- Deviant behaviour may have become more **socially acceptable**.
- Individuals lack **moral restraint** to maintain an acceptable code of conduct.
- The **fact of winning** may have more value than the loss of respect or punishment that may occur.
- **Rewards** are great and so individuals may be prepared to take **risks**, particularly true of positive deviance.

Legal supplements versus illegal drugs and doping

An **ergogenic aid** is any substance or method which enhances performance. This includes any method used in training which has this effect including training equipment, nutrition, medication as well as doping and dietary supplementation.

Ergogenic aids fall under two categories, **legal** and **illegal**. The line between legal and illegal supplements/drugs has long been debated, since they give the consumer an advantage over the non-consumer.

STUDENT NOTE

Refer to AS/A1 Revise PE for OCR, ISBN 9781901424911, Part 2, Chapter 4 to refresh your memory on nutritional supplements used in sport and their advantages and disadvantages.

Dietary supplements are products used alongside a **normal diet** and are perceived to improve general health and wellbeing or enhance sporting performance.

figure 9.2 – whey protein

They can include supplements such as sports drinks, vitamin tablets, creatine monohydrate, bicarbonate loading, caffeine and whey protein (figure 9.2). These dietary supplements claim to help with building muscle, increasing endurance, weight gain or loss, improving suppleness, rehydrating, aiding recovery or overcoming a mineral deficiency. Dietary supplements can be found in pill, tablet, capsule, powder or liquid form.

Pain killers and **anti-inflammatory drugs** are often used by elite athletes, particularly in contact sports such as rugby.

They may help to improve training performance because they can reduce recovery time after a hard session, but they do have negative effects on body tissues, maybe irreversible effects.

Why are dietary supplements such a high risk for the elite performer?

Elite athletes and the sporting individual need to be aware that the use of supplements can present a risk to athletes for several reasons:

* Some supplements contain banned substances.
* Some supplements can be contaminated during the manufacturing process.
* Some supplements will list ingredients on the label differently to how they would appear on the WADA Prohibited List.
* Risk of counterfeit (fake) supplements, especially when purchased online.

Is it worth the risk?

* Such supplements may produce short-term gains, but may also have long-term health risks.
* For example, the high sugar content in hypertonic sports drinks may be a contributory factor to the development of type 2 diabetes or tooth decay.

* Many of these supplements have long-term effects on organs such as the liver and kidneys.
* For example, whey protein (figure 9.2) has been described by nutritionists as 'expensive poo' and excess protein can cause liver and kidney damage due to eliminating all the waste products of protein metabolism.

* Many **dietary supplements** are responsible for stomach problems such as cramping, vomiting and bloating as is the case with bicarbonate loading.

* In an example of a recent case of contamination, nano traces of anabolic steroids were found in the Mountain Fuel Extreme Energy product, which led to the ban of two international Welsh athletes in 2014.
* The consequences of a positive drug test for inadvertent doping is a 2-year ban.

If an athlete has made a decision to use a supplement, it is better to be taking one that has been subjected to credible testing and appropriate manufacturing controls. The best way to avoid such risks is to have a well-balanced nutritional diet (without supplements) that meets the sporting needs of the individual.

Performance enhancing drugs (PEDs)

The use of performance-enhancing substances or techniques to augment an athlete's ability to succeed in competitive sports is a pertinent topic for athletes and coaches. The use of these agents or methods, whether legal or illegal, can occur at all levels of sport.

At the professional and Olympic level, each athlete is responsible for the drugs they consume and should know if any of these substances are on the **World Anti-Doping Code Prohibited List**, which is published yearly.

STUDENT NOTE

Refer to AS/A1 Revise PE for OCR, ISBN 9781901424911, Part 2, Chapter 4 to refresh your memory on illegal ergogenic aids used in sport and their effects and known health risks.

WADA prohibited list

Typically, a substance or method will be considered for the **WADA Prohibited List** if the substance or method meets any two of the following three criteria:

* It has the **potential to enhance** or enhances sport performance.
* It represents an actual or potential **health risk** to the athlete.
* It **violates the spirit** of sport.

Broken down by categories, the WADA Prohibited List identifies which substances and methods are prohibited **in-competition**, **out-of-competition**, as well as in some cases, by **specific sports**.

WADA prohibited list

WADA banned category substance list 2017 includes:

- Anabolic steroids.
- Erythropoietin.
- Human growth hormone.
- Insulin like growth factor.
- Blood doping.
- Diuretic and masking agents and similar substances and methods.
- Alcohol and beta blockers are prohibited in sports such as air sports, archery, darts and golf.

Banned methods include:

- Manipulation of blood and blood components, for example **blood banking** and **reinfusion**.
- Chemical and physical manipulation, such as **tampering** with a sample to alter integrity and validity of sample collection during doping control.
- **Gene doping** including the use of genetically modified cells, for example, insulin-like growth factor I (IGF-I) a protein used to promote the growth of skeletal muscle.

The reasons people take drugs

The reason sportspeople take PEDs or other nutritional ergogenic aids, is to attempt to gain an advantage over other competitors or players.

Some drugs are **against the law** and others against sporting regulations, but young people can be attracted to these unethical and dangerous substances because their heroes and role models are presumed to have taken them.

- Thus taking drugs ceases to be only a personal decision.
- This is part of the win ethic, the willingness to win-at-all-costs, or simply a desire to excel in something as an unbridled ambition.
- The International Olympic Committee and International Sports Authorities view drug taking as **cheating**, and it is deemed totally unacceptable for the unscrupulous to be allowed to take unfair advantage. Let's not forget the Olympic oath sworn on behalf of all participant States.

Sociological, **psychological** and **physiological**, informed analyses of drugs abuse in sport requires an understanding the reasons why deviant drug abuse is prevalent on a global scale.

Elite athletes are full-time professionals and every part of their training and competitive life is geared up to enhancing his or her performance so that he or she can win. Yet some of these enhancements are banned.

Figure 9.3 provides an overview of the reasons why sportspeople should not take these substances, along with the reasons why people take these drugs.

figure 9.3 – performance enhancing drugs

Social reasons to aid performance

A major social reason for drug taking is the belief that **everyone else is doing it**. This belief makes drug taking acceptable and reinforces the **win-at-all-costs** attitude that success cannot be achieved without drugs and that the benefits of winning are greater that the risk of being found out.

Whilst the need for the athlete to win and their potential use of drugs is a personal affair, it has become a public issue because the use of PEDs has been banned. The importance of national pride, (as was the case with the GDR national programme State Plan 14.25) and the overriding need to win, impact on the decision of the individual athlete in relation to the use of PEDs.

The commercialisation of sport means that **profit** becomes the overriding **motivation**, **eclipsing** ideals of **fair play** and **sportsmanship**. Victory has become the ultimate goal of sporting clubs, coaches, and athletes and the **rewards** of winning are considerable.

Athletes must try and win and so are highly motivated, otherwise they will not get **government** support, sponsorships and endorsement contracts. **Tangible rewards** override moral values. If PEDs can offer that competitive edge (as observed in table 9.1, page 148) it is not surprising that contemporary athletes will use them at the expense of their known health risks.

Contemporary opinion **undermines** the ideals of **fair play** and **health** when it comes to sporting endeavours as today's sport is neither fair nor healthy.

Modern sociologists believe that **commercialisation** and **commodification** of sport has fundamentally changed sport. The pressures on young potential athletes with such a short playing career can only encourage the use of anything that might give them an advantage and lengthen their career. With the UK Pathway programmes, such as **Long-Term Athlete Development programmes** (LTAD, page 176) it is hoped that such schemes can overcome these social pressures.

Athletes are vulnerable and socially influenced by:

- **Media coverage**: in their attempt to sell newspapers the media tend to give extensive coverage to **doping scandals** within sport.
- This may give the athlete a misleading impression of the extent to which PEDs are used in sport.

- **Peer pressure**: athletes may directly observe or hear of the practices of fellow athletes who use PEDs and may be offered drugs by their fellow competitors or team members.
- There is a perceived suspicion that rivals are using something (PEDs?) that assists them in meeting the physical demands of intense training and competition.

- **Support team pressure**: family members and coaches may instil additional pressure on athletes to improve performance by any means available.
- It has been suggested that governing bodies 'turn a blind eye' to some drug takers in order to benefit from the commercial benefits that result from success.

- **Deterrence**: there are few deterrents that discourage an athlete from taking illegal drugs as drugs are readily available in gyms, over the counter and on the Internet.
- **Fame, salaries and sponsorship deals** which also tempt athletes to **cheat**. But when found out, professional sports careers can be shattered as was the case for Maria Sharapova (figure 9.4) after failing a drug's test in 2016 followed by a two year ban. In 2017, Maria was able to resume her professional career.
- Nike and Tag Heuer cut ties with Maria Sharapova. Up until that point Maria was the world's highest paid female athlete.

figure 9.4 – Maria Sharapova, ups and downs

Psychological reasons why people take drugs to aid performance

- **Beta blockers** help to decrease anxiety and steady the nerves.
- **Anabolic steroids** increase arousal and aggressive tendencies, traits that are needed in sports such as weightlifting and contact team sports, such as rugby.
- **Stimulants**, such as amphetamines, increase mental alertness, concentration, motivation and confidence.
- **Perception of pain** is dulled, thus enabling an athlete to work harder and longer.
- There is the fear of '**not making it**'.
- **Motivation**: athletes are driven to succeed as a result of **internal** and **external** motivation.

- **External rewards** are central to competitive sports and are immense, where athletes receive publicity, awards, money and sponsorships for their sporting achievements.
- **Taking illegal drugs** is one way to achieve this success.

Positive and negative implications of drug taking to the sport and the performer

Athletes don't take drugs to level the playing field, they do it to get an **advantage**. A vicious cycle of upping dosages to get a **bigger advantage** happens.

figure 9.5 – regular injections to short-term success

- The pay-off is now **fame**, **image and money** and the long-term health consequences are minimised (figure 9.5).
- PEDs can cause **impotence**, **worsening acne**, **balding**, and '**steroid rage**'.
- **Females** acquire masculine traits such as a **deep voice**, **facial hair** and **breast reduction**.
- PEDs can also **stunt growth** in adolescents.
- More serious side effects include heart and **liver damage**, and an increased risk of blood clots.
- The risk of being caught is reducing. As **undetectable drugs** become more available, more athletes will choose to cheat.

Over the years there have been allegations of **doping in the Tour de France**. Lance Armstrong won seven Tour de France titles, because **blood doping** is the difference between being really, really good and being world class. When Armstrong finally admitted to blood doping, he actually said that he had to cheat just to be competitive at the top of the sport.

Other high profile drug cheats include the infamous sprinters Ben Johnson, Marion Jones and Dwayne Chambers.

figure 9.6 – Sir Bradley Wiggins

Positive and negative implications of drug taking

Athletes are allowed to use powerful drugs that deal with **health conditions**, such as asthma, providing they have a **therapeutic use exemption** (TUE) certificate.

Recently Sir Bradley Wiggins (figure 9.6) has come under sustained fire from the media for using a prescribed drug called **corticosteroid** to deal with his chronic asthma and allergies. He says that he does not obtain an unfair advantage over his rivals. However, this drug can rapidly reduce an athlete's weight whilst maintaining power.

Positive and negative implications

The dilemma here is that, on the one hand inclusive sports participation should be encouraged, but on the other hand this can facilitate drug abuse via the backdoor which is an unintended and undesirable consequence. As a result, WADA is considering a blanket ban on corticosteroids.

Drug cheats can often tarnish a **sports image** and call into question the **validity of results** in competition. **Public respect** for all sports professionals suffers if there are frequent drug scandals. It becomes **harder to believe** that all athletes aren't cheats. That may cause all victories to be viewed with suspicion. This is hardly fair on the honest athletes, and it's no fun for the spectators either.

Uncovered drug cheats risk losing their **reputation**, professional **earnings**, long-term **career prospects**, as well as negatively impacting on their **social and psychological well-being**.

The essence of sport exemplifies values such as fair play, honesty, health and excellence in sport. The challenge is for role models, parents and coaches to influence these positive values.

Strategies for elimination of performance-enhancing drugs in sport, WADA

The impact of illegal drug abuse in sport has led to the development of random drug testing programmes under the supervision of WADA (the **World Anti-Doping Agency**), set up in 1998 and tasked with enforcing the international regulations on doping or drug taking (figure 9.7).

- **WADA** aims to bring together governments, the IOC, international governing bodies and national governing bodies to sort out difficulties by athletes performing on the international stage.

- WADA is tasked to get all international governing bodies and national governing bodies to adopt and implement its **World Anti-Doping Code**.

- Under WADA's World Anti-Doping Code, athletes are required to state 3 months in advance their locations for one hour per day, 7 days a week. This is the time during which random testing could take place which is called the '**whereabouts rule**' - a system designed to support out-of-competition testing and regarded as a fundamental part of an anti-doping programme. This rule has evoked anger from tennis players including Andy Murray, Rafael Nadal and Roger Federer, who feel that the European Union privacy law has been breached.

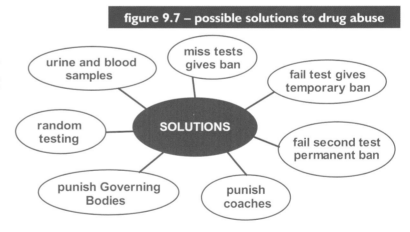

figure 9.7 – possible solutions to drug abuse

- **Random drug testing**, (particularly out of season) ensures that athletes are discouraged from cheating the system. This includes missing these random tests under the whereabouts rule.
- Christine Ohuruogu (Olympic and World 400m track champion) missed three random tests and in 2006 received an automatic one year ban. This was in spite of her passing many other tests during the period when this was happening.

- The major problem for WADA is to **police** the globe when some national governing bodies do not do out of season random testing.

Strategies for elimination of PEDs in sport, WADA

In 2016, WADA initiated a major **retesting programme** on global sport. The anti-doping laboratory in Lausanne holds stored urine and blood samples (up to 10 years) that can be retested with improved technology to catch drug cheats who escaped detection at the time. 31 unidentified athletes in six sports have been caught during retests from the 2008 Beijing Olympic Games.

UK Anti-Doping Organisation

UK Anti-Doping (UKAD) is the UK's National Anti-Doping Organisation and is an active participant in the global fight against doping and recognises the need to take an international approach with partners such as WADA.

It is responsible for ensuring sports bodies in the UK comply with the National Anti-Doping Policy. UKAD coordinates the UK's intelligence-led risk based testing programme across more than 40 sports and is responsible for the collection and transportation of samples to a WADA accredited laboratory (figure 9.8).

figure 9.8 – accredited laboratory

In season, testing normally takes place after competitions or matches.

UKAD aims to instil a culture of clean sport by ensuring that all athletes and athlete support personnel understand and practise the **values of clean sport** and the **dangers** of physical, psychological and moral issues associated with illegal drug usage.

Initiatives, such as **100% Me**, educate athletes throughout their careers by providing anti-doping advice and guidance that embrace key values such as hard work, determination, passion, respect and integrity, associated with clean, fair competition.

Drug testing, its pitfalls and benefits

Great care has to be taken when testing takes place. Britain's **Diane Modahl** (figure 9.9) failed a test in 1994 just prior to the Commonwealth Games of that year. It was later discovered that her urine sample had undergone changes while being stored in the testing laboratory and she was cleared of the doping offence. She then sued the British Athletic Federation (BAF) for their mishandling of the situation. This led to the eventual bankruptcy of BAF and the destruction of Diane's athletic career. Although she was reinstated, she was unable to regain the fitness and excellence needed to compete at elite level.

figure 9.9 – Diane Modahl

In the news (in 2017) is the FBIs investigation into Mo Farah's coach, Alberto Salazar, who is alleged to have abused medicines and used prohibited infusions to boost the testosterone levels of his athletes. Mo Farah (double double Olympic Champion) denies breaking anti-doping rules.

There are several **benefits** that come out of law-enforcement involvement:
- It can force people to talk.
- If people don't talk, this can give the impression that they are not a good people.
- It can dig deep into personal information, for example, uncovering illicit bank accounts.

What are the consequences of drug use?

Currently each case of drug use is considered individually. There are rules and regulations that guide the punishments for drug use, but as in the legal system, each case gets a different consequence depending on the circumstances. Often the consequences include **suspension** or **expulsion** from the sport, **fines** and **stripping** of awards and titles won and **repayment** of earnings.

Table 9.1 - **summary of arguments for and against drug testing and drug taking**

For drug testing and eliminating drug taking	Against drug testing, and allowing drug taking
athletes are role models and young people seek to emulate sports stars	strict more expensive tests have been introduced that may not be affordable for third world countries to use
testing protects athletes reputations and produces positive role models	a strict test returns more false positives (a test result that seems to detect a drug which isn't there)
drugs are not natural	the labelling of some supplements may not be complete or accurate, and some safe supplements may contain traces of prohibited substances athletes can protest that these secondary chemicals may be the products of another bodily process
creates a deterrent for athletes who may consider using drugs to cheat in sport	drug testing does not always catch athletes, and is often having to develop new testing methods for the new drugs being released retesting of stored samples is a very expensive process
anti-doping programmes seek to preserve what is intrinsically valuable about sport (values such as fair play and equity) often referred to as 'the spirit of sport' and the essence of Olympism	the whereabouts rule is time consuming and is perceived as an infringement of human rights
drug taking is illegal, a form of cheating, is unethical and immoral	public respect for all sports professionals suffers if there are frequent drug scandals it becomes harder to believe that all athletes aren't cheats and may cause all victories to be viewed with suspicion
discredits negative role models and reinforces the message to stay clean	false accusations can have an adverse effect on an athlete's career - even if she or he is later proven innocent the loss of earnings is usually significant
promotes health and safety and avoidance of the physical side-effects associated with taking PEDs	drug taking is a short-cut to realising potential, even if athletes risk their health and their athletic careers
the detection methods are accurate and reliable	a stricter test returns more false positives (a test result that seems to detect a drug which isn't there)
TUE certificates protect athletes who suffer from general illnesses/allergies and injury rehabilitation	regulated scientific research in producing safer PEDs, could reduce health risks and recovery it is hard to identify those athletes who are awarded TUE certificates who inadvertently physically benefit from such prescriptions
rewards athletes for their ability, training and efforts, and preserves what is intrinsically valuable about sport	elite athletes gain unfair advantage from training methods such as altitude training and the use of hypobaric chambers, so why not include PEDs?
alternative legal methods can enhance athletic performance, such as altitude training and nutritional supplements, for example, creatine	testing is made more difficult because some drugs are broken down quickly inside the body to produce secondary substrates
public perception could be that PEDs reduce the role of skill and replaces it by chemically induced brute strength and endurance, and as a result may lose interest in the sports in which it is used the harm would be primarily financial	false positives, if leaked to the media, are bad publicity it is sometimes hard to prove one way or another could lead to the demise of professional leagues
drugs are bad for business and commercial organisations do not donate their money out of the goodness of their hearts they do it to attract further business	if everyone took PEDs, spectator entertainment and standards in performance would increase and with it a level playing field and more income

Limitations of drug testing

The use of drug testing in sport does have limitations in its use, which some people use to debate its place in sport. These include:

- Not all drugs can be tested for. **New drugs** are created all the time, and until they are created, tests cannot be developed for them.
- During testing, the athlete is **exposed** (nudity) before the tester - athletes have to be **observed** where urine samples are taken.
- This stringent procedure was enforced after two male winners in the Athens Olympic Games were found using prosthetic **(false) genitals** and a hidden storage bag for production of their samples.
- **New prohibited lists** are developed each year, which athletes need to know and follow as they are currently held responsible.
- Testing is **expensive**.

Arguments for and against drug taking and testing

The positive and negative implications to the sport and the performer regarding drug taking have been discussed throughout this chapter. Table 9.1 (page 148) summarises the arguments for and against drug taking and drug testing.

Anti-doping rules often lead to complicated and costly administrative and medical follow-ups to ascertain whether drugs taken by athletes are legitimate therapeutic agents or substances which violate the definitive WADA rules and are not allowed.

In the meantime, clean athletes, who are upgraded to podium medal status as result of cheats who have been stripped of their titles, could wait many years before this process is completed.

Violence in sport

Player violence

This issue arises when **acceptable aggression** (assertion) in sport becomes **violence**.

Violence is normally where aggression goes beyond the agreed codification in that game or activity. There is an additional dimension, in that **acceptable aggression** in the activity may not match up with the **laws of the land** and so players can misunderstand their legal position.

Figure 9.10 summarises the issues affecting player violence.

Physical aggression and an unacceptable level of verbal abuse may be identified as part of player violence:

- The presence of **spectators** can **increase player arousal**.
- Many games require players to be **hyped-up** to perform at their best, making aggression and outbreaks of violence more likely.
- More recently, the use of **drugs** may have increased this tendency.
- On the other hand, some sports require **calmness** and **focus**.
- For example, darts, snooker, dance and gymnastics, and players in these sports are less likely to be violent.
- **Gamesmanship**, aimed at putting an opponent off, can be equally unacceptable.

Aggression by sports performers is a part of their sporting life. The need to be **competitive** and the **frustration** felt at failure can lead sportspeople to be violent as an extreme expression of this aggression. The level at which aggression becomes violence varies according to the activity.

figure 9.10 – aggression and violence in sport

Player violence

For example, **boxing** involves punching an opponent, which would be violence in any other sport. In this case, it is argued that the essence of boxing is 'the art of self-defence' and that boxing has its own code of acceptable behaviour with a referee to see that this is observed, as well as the safety precaution of gloves. There is also a difference here between amateur and professional boxing, and between junior and senior competitors.

This rules difference also is relevant to a variety of other activities and games, such as tag rugby with young children.

Causes of player violence in sport

The **causes of violence** among players are summarised in figure 9.11.

- The **crowd** response to player activity (chanting, booing, name calling) can affect player tendency to violence.
- The **confrontational nature** of most top professional games (the gladiatorial influence) can increase the tendency to violence.
- The **popular** nature of some sports can lead to **player expectation of violence** as part of the game **culture**.
- The presence of a **large number of spectators** and the significance of victory can increase the **emotion** of a sporting occasion, and again make violence more likely.
- The **failure** of sports administrators to adequately **punish** players who are persistently violent can cause players to cynically commit further violent offences on the field.
- Stadium design may create a confrontational environment for both players and spectators, for example, a stadium in which spectators from opposite sides are allowed to mix.

figure 9.11 – causes of player violence in sport

crowd — administration — players — **CAUSES of VIOLENCE in SPORT** — facilities — popular — gladiatorial — emotionally charged

Strategies for preventing violence between players

The solutions lie in the **code of behaviour** being part of the **tradition** of the activity from school onwards and the quality of **control by officials** during a game, and the efficiency of the administration of sanctions by NGBs on offending players.

Officials
- Officials should include an **explanation** of their action (figure 9.12).
- The use of the **television match official** (TMO - fourth official) during the match, advising the on-field referee, on close calls and post match video evidence, such as the Rugby League '**on report system**' that can be used by referees to review controversial play.
- The use of deterrents, such as **sin bins**.

Managers and captains
- Establish a clear **code of conduct** and expectation.
- Understand individual player's level of arousal and train players to **manage their own arousal** levels.
- Where possible ensure that **players**, who have a low flash point, are kept away from **high stress** situations.
- **Avoid** an attitude of **winning-at-all-costs**.
- Discuss **stress appropriate behaviour** during team talks.

NGBs
- **Punishments** by controlling bodies should be seen to be **fair** and **consistent**, and should therefore fit the offence.
- Recognise players with a good disciplinary record as **role models**.
- The use of **educational campaigns** and awards, such as the **Fair Play Awards** that reward clubs with good disciplinary records.

figure 9.12 – is it worth arguing with the referee?

NGBs

- Train officials in **player management**, such as how to defuse situations between players.
- NGBs like to deal with violence themselves, but increasingly are getting more involved with the **legal system**.

But the most essential element is the **attitude** of each player.

Spectator violence

Spectators get very **emotionally involved**, desperately wanting their side to win.

figure 9.13 – Russian and England supporters brawling during Soccer Euro16

A crucial feature of football followers is their **identity** with the team they follow. They refer to members of their team as 'us' and 'we', and members of the opposition as 'them and 'they'. This leads to the **emotional attachment** which can often be directed at opposition players on the pitch, and also at opposition supporters.

This can lead to **violence in the stadia** and on the streets, but can also involve **extreme verbal abuse**. In such instances the law is probably being broken, but access by the stewards and the police is not possible because of the crowd effect. The facilities of a stadium, in respect of the **mixing of the fans** of opposing teams, can be a cause of spectator violence particularly in **professional soccer**.

Hooliganism

The dominance of a youth culture, where gangs identify with a professional football club and are prepared to fight an opposition group in a chosen place, is a frightening extension of soccer hooliganism. **Hooliganism** is **anti-social** or **aggressive**, **violent** and **destructive** behaviour by troublemakers, typically in a gang.

Acts of hooliganism (figure 9.13) often overspill and impact local surroundings such as shops and bars, as witnessed between Russian and English football supporters in the 2016 European Championships in France. Although there is a strong working class peer group culture associated with soccer, this has, occasionally, involved middle class male groups.
The media can encourage confrontational situations by highlighting players' comments about opponents and giving these hooligan gangs publicity.

But spectators certainly need to recognise that no matter how much they get worked up, their violence is measured in legal terms.

Causes of spectator violence in sport

There are numerous causes in what is naturally an antagonistic and often frustrating situation. For example, the tendency towards violence by a supporter group is linked to whether or not their team is winning. Supporters of a winning team are more likely to be benevolent and good natured, whereas supporters of a losing team can be violent, particularly in 'derby games'.

Spectator violence has been explained as a form of **social deviance** and it is caused by:
- Being in a crowd, where there is **confinement** and poor crowd control.
- **High emotion**, **diminished responsibility** and the likelihood of **shared aggression**.
- Consumption of **alcohol** exacerbates these problems.
- There is also an element of **depersonalisation** that a crowd gives an individual, where it is 'easy to be lost in a crowd'.
- **Poor officiating**.

Causes of spectator violence in sport

In the case of hooliganism, the question arises as to whether these are **hooligans at football** or **football hooligans**.

In the case of the former, the solution lies in the **conditions and control** needed to prevent this anti-social behaviour. If, however, football makes them behave as hooligans, then one must look at the **behaviour of the players** and the causes of frustration.

Strategies for preventing spectator violence

Measures (figure 9.14) which have been taken to reduce the chances of spectator violence are:

*   **Segregation** of home and away supporters.
*   The introduction of **all-seater stadia** (outcome of the Taylor Report).
*   Increase the 'family' concept.
*   Increase the number of **stewards** and police.
*   Ensure that **alcohol** cannot be bought or brought into grounds.
*   More responsible **media** reporting.
*   Detect trouble by using **CCTV**.
*   In addition, campaigns like '**kick racism out of football**', sponsored by major soccer clubs, player and governing bodies, can defuse unacceptable racial aggression.
*   **Legal intervention** that punishes offenders.

figure 9.14 – preventing spectator violence

The impact of commercialism on the sportsmanship ethic and the growth of gamesmanship in the UK

The **commercialism of sport** is subject to the **market forces** of commerce. The rise of **professionalism** in sport has led to a rise in **commercialisation**.

*   Increased availability of **professional** contracts, sponsorship, player endorsements and prize money has allowed UK athletes to train and compete as full-time professional athletes.
*   **Lucrative commercial deals** put great **pressure** on athletes to do well.
*   Without the **moral values** as guides, some athletes may decide the financial benefits from **winning** significantly overshadow the likelihood of being **caught** and so winning becomes an obligation and gamesmanship becomes part of the winning strategy.
*   The commercial **rewards** for winning become so **significant** that a '**win-at-all-costs**' mentality has **eroded** away the concept of **sportsmanship** and increased the growth of **gamesmanship** within UK sport.
*   Today, the **win ethic** almost totally controls the professional sport scene within the UK.
*   Here, there is clear link to the impact of **Americanisation** of sport.
*   Americanisation of sport is the influence which **American culture** and business has on other countries. Within the sporting context, it represents the **copying** of **American values** in sport such as the win-at-all-costs or Lombardian ethic, and sports entertainment.
*   Within **gamesmanship**, the need to win is associated with financial rewards.
*   Increased level of **commercial finance** in sport will increase the need to win.
*   Winning can secure a **position in the team** and its status.
*   For example, a team winning a world cup creates global **superstars** and associated **wealth**, **fame**, **national pride**, **sponsorship** and player **endorsements**.
*   An outcome of the need to win is that athletes will find different ways to help them to win and gamesmanship is seen as a **more palatable way** of **bending the rules**, without infringement of the rules.
*   Some commercial sponsors may prefer to be associated with the more traditional clean image of sport. For example Andy Murray provides an impeccable image of sportsmanship for his sponsor Under Armour.

Gambling in sport

Gambling in sport is a **legal** activity of predicting sports results and placing a wager/bet through a bookmaker on the outcome of an event. Animal blood sport such as cock fighting and dog fighting, and human contests such as bare-knuckle fighting, date back in time as popular recreation over the centuries. The thrill of watching these contests was enhanced by **wagering** and money frequently changed hands among the spectators.

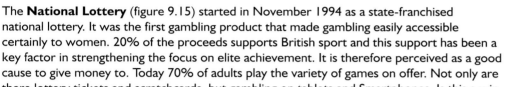

figure 9.15 – National Lottery logo

Today gambling in sport is a huge global business.

The **National Lottery** (figure 9.15) started in November 1994 as a state-franchised national lottery. It was the first gambling product that made gambling easily accessible certainly to women. 20% of the proceeds supports British sport and this support has been a key factor in strengthening the focus on elite achievement. It is therefore perceived as a good cause to give money to. Today 70% of adults play the variety of games on offer. Not only are there lottery tickets and scratchcards, but gambling on tablets and Smartphones. Is this a win-win situation or are gamblers aware of the dangers of **addiction**?

Many betting corporations are closely associated as sponsors of individual sports. For example, **BetFred** is the World Snooker Championship's main sponsor (figure 9.16).

figure 9.16 – BetFred sponsors snooker

The rise of the global sports betting industry is worth billions of pounds per year. The current estimations, which include both the illegal markets and the legal markets, suggest the sports match-betting industry is worth anywhere between $700bn and $1tn (£435bn to £625bn) a year.

About 70% of that trade has been estimated to come from trading on football. Much of this growth has been fuelled by the rapid increase of **online betting**.

Illegal betting industry

The illegal betting industry is growing not just in terms of revenue, but also in its reach due to effects of **globalisation**. Match fixing and illegal sports' betting are a threat to the integrity of global sport as attempts are made to exploit players, umpires and other officials to achieve various ends.

Bribery

Bribery is the act of taking or receiving something with the intention of **influencing** the recipient in some way favourable to the party providing the bribe. Recently there has been alleged corruption, bribery and vote-rigging relevant to the election of FIFA ex-president Sepp Blatter and the organisation's decision to award the 2018 and 2022 World Cups to Russia and Qatar. These allegations have lead to a legal prosecution in the USA and the increased popular cynicism about the fairness and honesty of the whole international process.

Bungs

A **bung** is an unauthorised and **undisclosed payment** to a club manager, or any other decision maker within a club, for example to a scout or club official to 'grease' a deal.
In other words, a **secret financial incentive** that makes a transfer happen.

The most common method would be an agent paying a club official, perhaps a manager, a '**backhander - bung**', or slice of his own cut, to persuade someone to do a deal. In some cases an agent might work in cahoots with a selling club. For example, a club wants to sell a player and values him at £1m. An agent hawks him around and sells him for £1.5m. The difference is then split between the agent and whoever he has 'bunged' at the buying club to make it happen.

Match fixing

In organised sports, **match fixing** occurs as a match is played to a completely or partially **pre-determined result**, violating the rules of the game and often the law.

For example, in December 2013, six people in Britain, including Blackburn forward DJ Campbell, were arrested for allegedly fixing football games. The arrests were made by the National Crime Agency after release of a report from FederBet, a Brussels-based gambling watchdog which is an organization created by the online bookmakers to watch the flow of bets across Europe.

The allegations of match-fixing across various sports have got sporting bodies and lawmakers across the globe worried and they are trying to find ways to counter the sector's growing might.

Sports Betting syndicates

figure 9.17 – gambling in sport is big business

Sports betting is the activity of **predicting sports results** and placing a **wager** on the outcome. A sports betting syndicate is a group of bettors that pool the various backgrounds in mathematics, professional gambling, and sport, and produce information that can be used by the syndicate to select the best betting option.

The successful sports-betting syndicates employ a powerful computer that crunches an enormous amount of data to determine the betting between one side and the other. This process is called **simulation**.

Simulation

Simulation is used as a betting methodology that relies on repeated **random sampling** to obtain **numerical outputs** when other mathematical approaches would prove to be too complicated. It takes some programming skills to set it up (though it can be done in a common programme like Excel) but it's a proven way to see what happens when you repeat a set of circumstances over and over again.

The more likely outcomes will occur most frequently, giving you a distribution of probabilities. Knowledge of how frequent the likely and less likely outcomes are to occur is really useful for model bettors. An example of a simulation service is the **Monte Carlo simulation** package.

There are commercially-based corporations whose aim is to make money by encouraging betting habits, in spite of claiming to encourage 'responsible gambing'.

What is the attraction of illegal betting?
*   In some countries, the most basic reason is a ban on sports betting.
*   In other countries some of the illegal betting syndicates offer better odds for a sporting event, making the payout more attractive in the case of a winning bet.

Most illegal syndicates operate in a very discrete manner, not least to protect their own identities and those of their consumers.

Practice questions

1) Which one of the following is not an example of sportsmanship-like behaviour?
   a. respect for an opponent.
   b. win-at-all-costs attitude.
   c. punish foul behaviour.
   d. use drug testing procedures to eliminate cheats.

2) An example of positive deviance is:
   a. using bribes to influence the outcome of a match.
   b. continue playing through an injury.
   c. using performance enhancing drugs.
   d. financial irregularities in the transferring of players.

3) Which one of the following is not a strategy for preventing player violence?
   a. officials should include an explanation of their action.
   b. the use of educational campaigns and awards, such as the Fair Play Awards.
   c. train officials in player management stress techniques.
   d. referee ignores a confrontational incident during the match.

4) Deciding which drugs are true performance aids and which drugs should be banned is often difficult because:
   a. medical researchers lack the technology to study the drugs that athletes use.
   b. athletes often use new substances before scientists have studied them.
   c. drug companies outlaw research on performance-enhancing substances.
   d. NGBs have abandoned all efforts to control drug use in sports.

5) Which one of the following statements does not describe how sports governing bodies perceive violence?
   a. it elicits strong feelings among fans.
   b. sports are conducive to violent behaviour and aggressive conduct.
   c. practically every sport that features contact or collision either tolerates or promotes violence.
   d. being a fan is a relatively safe experience.

6) Which one of the following strategies could be employed by officials to help reduce the likelihood of on-field aggression and violence amongst players?
   a. players could be made more aware of the concept of fair play.
   b. violent incidents could be ignored.
   c. use on-field aggression to increase the thrill and hostility amongst fans.
   d. avoid taking action due to the pressures of the media.

7) Critically evaluate the use of legal supplements versus illegal drugs and doping in sport. 10 marks

8) In 1998, the head of the IOC (Juan Antonio Samaranch) told a newspaper that 'substances that do not harm to an athlete's health should not be banned and should not be considered as a case of doping'. Discuss this statement. 20 marks

9) What social issues can encourage a performer to take drugs? 4 marks

10) Suggest three ways in which national governing bodies are attempting to discover, punish and prevent the use of performance enhancing drugs. 3 marks

Practice questions

11) Explain using one example, how each of the following people interact with the law in sport.
   a) Performers.   2 marks

   b) Officials.   2 marks

   c) Spectators.   2 marks

12) Explain the terms positive and negative deviance giving examples in a sporting context.   4 marks

13) Give reasons for spectator violence at professional association football matches.   5 marks

14) Hooliganism has affected football over the past 40 years.
   Define the term hooliganism and discuss the reasons why it might occur.
   What steps have been taken to reduce the incidents of hooliganism in Premiership soccer?   10 marks

Answers link: http://www.jroscoe.co.uk/downloads/a2_revise_pe_ocr/OCRA2_ch9_answers.pdf

CHAPTER 10: Commercialisation and the media

Factors leading to the commercialisation of contemporary physical activity and sport

Key definitions

* **Advertising** is a means of communication with the potential users of a product or service.
* **Commercialism** is the treating of sport as a commodity, involving the **buying** and **selling** of assets with the market place as the driving force behind sport.
* A **commodity** is something that is **useful**, has **value** and that can be turned to **commercial** or other advantage.
* An **endorsement** is a deal whereby a company will pay an individual for its brand to be associated with that individual.
* The **golden triangle** links and provides an overlap between the **media**, **commercialism**, and **sport** and its governing bodies.
* **Merchandising** refers to a variety of products available for sale and the display of those products in such a way that stimulates interest and entices customers to make a purchase.
* **Professionalism** is the practising of an activity, especially a sport, by professional rather than amateur players.
* **Social media** is the use of websites and applications that enable users to create and share content or to participate in social networking.
* **Spectatorship** is the act of **watching** an event, especially a sports contest.
* **Sponsorship** is when a person or organisation **pays** the cost of an activity or event.
* **Role model** is a person who someone admires and whose behaviour he or she tries to copy.

The historical and social context of commercialism

The **evolution** of commercialisation in sport has occurred through the past three centuries.

This began with tradesman **donating prizes** in kind at holy days to highly organised rural sports often sponsored by local publicans. Such **sponsorship** was supplemented in the eighteenth century with noble **patronage** or by a town or district that had **local government**.

This led to increased **gambling** and **spectatorism**, which in turn encouraged event organisers to seek further commercial development.

By 1900 the tradition had produced **folk heroes**, national **competition networks**, **international** championships and the popular interest of selling thousands of **newspapers** daily and bringing whole cities to a standstill.

Broken time payments

Opportunities for **working classes** to participate in sport were restricted by their long six-day working weeks and Sunday Sabbatarianism. In the UK, the Factory Act of 1844 gave working men half-a-day off, making the **opportunity** to take part in sport more widely available. Working class sportsmen found it hard to play top level sport due to their working hours.

On occasions, **cash prizes**, particularly in individual competitions, could make up the difference in loss of earnings, with some competitors also wagering on the outcomes of their matches. As professional teams developed, some clubs were willing to make '**broken time payments**' to players, i.e. to pay top sportsmen to take time off work.

Broken time payments

As attendances increased, it became feasible to pay men to concentrate on their sport **full-time**.

In the late 1880's, the industrial North of England had many working class men (mill workers and miners), who started to play rugby (figure 10.1). The **loss of earnings** that such a worker experienced whilst playing rugby on a Saturday was considerable and so became a major inhibitor. Some clubs began to make '**broken time payments**' as compensation for the loss of income.

Many in the RFU (North and South) simply refused to accept the concept of broken time payments.

A notable development was in 1893 when clubs in the industrial north of England put it to the Rugby Football Union that players who worked should be given 'broken time payments' to compensate them for pay lost while representing their club.

Many of the Northern administrators were ex-public school and strongly defended **amateurism**. The eventual outcome in 1895 was a split between twelve northern clubs who decided to break all links with the union and form the **Northern Rugby Football Union** (NRFU) on amateur lines, but with the acceptance of the principle of payment for broken time.

In the 1896/7 season the Northern Union introduced a challenge cup with all teams allowed to enter which caused great excitement. The final was held on May 1st 1897 between Batley and St. Helens at Headingley. Batley won 10-3 watched by between **13,000 to 14,000 fans** who paid £620 (gate money) between them.

It was not until late August 1995, that **professionalism** in the Union game was agreed. The IRB did not really have a choice, with a lot of money beginning to flow into the game from advertising and TV. It was considered to be a complete injustice (by the players) that the players themselves were not able to share in this bounty.

Spectatorism

A **spectator sport** is a sport that is characterised by the presence of spectators, or watchers, at its competitions (figure 10.1). A spectator is a person who **watches** an event.

Victorian Sport (1830-1901)
- **Mass spectator** sport began to take off.
- For the masses, **Saturday afternoon** free from work was the turning point, enabling them to play and spectate.
- For example, the **Heathens** (Newton Heath Football Club) - home ground at Belle-Vue Stadium Manchester (figure 10.2 shows large numbers of spectators surrounding the pitch).
- 'The Heathens' became a professional football team in 1885 and adopted its present name in 1902, **Manchester United FC**.

Edwardian sport (1901-1918)
- Organised sporting involvement expanded rapidly across all classes.
- **Male working class** influence increased, notable for football in England and rugby in Wales.
- **Working class women** were largely excluded from sporting involvement.
- Sport was increasingly a matter of **national** concern.
- **Commercialisation of sport** continued with large numbers of spectators and increased number of **professionals** in major sports.

Between the wars (1918-1940)

- **Commercialisation** of sport expanded rapidly, especially the provision of spectator sport.
- Sport as part of a **national culture**, now extended to the majority of the population.
- Most sports were still **class oriented**.
- **Football** continued to increase in popularity and by the 1930s was the most popular spectator sport.
- Most spectators at professional soccer games were **men** who were able to **spend** some money at the turnstiles to support their local teams.

1940-today

- An improved **standard of living** and working conditions has enabled **participation** and **spectatorism** for most social groups.
- **Amateur** administrators reluctantly allowed commercial forces to enter the world of sport.
- **Television** coverage increased in importance for sport, sponsors and spectators.

In the twenty first century the core audience of sports fans is a reliable **commodity** that can be profitably sold to advertisers. On occasions a much larger and less committed audience can be drawn in to take place in the general national and international spectacles which generate their own momentum through their sheer size. This was witnessed by the support the UK population gave to the Olympic and Paralympic Games in London 2012.

The promised sporting legacy of these games was to inspire a generation through sport and there is evidence that many sports have shown an upward trend. For example, cycling, gymnastics and track and field athletics (mainly driven by the weekly Parkrun intiative) have increased their participation levels.

The biggest live attendance at a global sporting event occurs at the FIFA World Cup. The 2010 FIFA World Cup attracted live audiences of 3,178,856 and this increased by 7.31% to 3,429,873 in 2014, with the competition reaching a global **in-home television audience of 3.2 billion** people. FIFA partners, such as Adidas, Coca Cola and Visa have direct advertising and promotional opportunities and preferential access to FIFA World Cup broadcast advertising and so are able to target live spectators and the in-home television audience.

Participation

A comparison of how many adults are taking part in sport at various frequencies in 2005-2006 (47.6 million) and 2015-2016 (54.2 million) is illustrated in figure 10.3 (the frequency of exercise is coded in the figure). Note that the exercise level base is 30 minutes of moderate exercise and the overall participation increase is **11.4%**.

figure 10.3 – participation figures

Number of adults taking part in sport at moderate intensity by frequency (30 minutes at moderate intensity)
At least once in last month   At least once a week   At least twice a week   At least three times a week

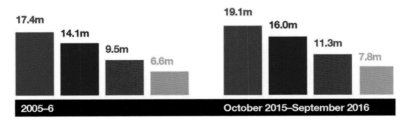

17.4m 14.1m 9.5m 6.6m
19.1m 16.0m 11.3m 7.8m

2005–6   October 2015–September 2016

Source: Active People Survey 1 and Active People Survey 10
(Sport England, April 2005–2006 and October 2015–September 2016)

Participation

Various trends account for the increase in these participation figures:
* More than 7.2 million women now play sport and do regular physical activity – 250,000 more than following the launch of **This Girl Can campaign** (figure 10.4) thus reducing the gender gap.

figure 10.4 – This Girl Can

* More disabled and black minority groups are taking part in sport.
* The number of people over 16 playing sport once a week has risen to over 15.6 million.
* There is evidence that participation and sports spectatorship are symbiotically linked. Spectating at live sporting events appears to have complementary effects on participation and vice versa.

Commercialism and commodities

Sport commercialism and British social history are intertwined as witnessed by:
* The commercialisation of leisure pursuits during the **eighteenth century**.
* The growth in the spread of organised sport and physical recreation during the nineteenth century.
* The spread of television and the media coverage of sport in the latter part of the twentieth century and into the twenty first century.

figure 10.5 – facilities as a heritage

The **growth of commercial activity** has increased participation and audience numbers, resulting in an improvement in sporting excellence (as witnessed by TeamGB's results since the 2004 Olympic Games) and improved sporting facilities (figure 10.5).

The fact that **governing bodies** clung onto the concept of **amateurism** for so long, has in turn forced athletes into the arms of commercialism.

Sport as a commodity

Sport and its audience are sold as **commodities** to **advertisers**.

The high price of the **advertising** slots during **major sport events** is based on the capacity of the sport to reach millions of potential **customers** for any number of products. The audience benefits from an increase in **televised** sport.

Sport is a **commodity** which simultaneously has evolved from **cultural** and **economic** activity.

Rules and codification

To become a commodity, sport not only has to be producible but also to be **reproducible** within a standard format, yet maintain **uniqueness** for each game, match or event. This requires that particular games within sport are played under identical and **stable rules** in both amateur and professional sports.

It requires the training of players to maintain the ethics of **sportsmanship** and the teaching of **fair play**, a basic underlying principle that underpins the **role** of sport in society.

STUDENT NOTE

For an introduction to this topic, refer to AS/A1 OCR ISBN 9781901424911, Part 6, Chapter 14.

The **codification** process was one of the first functions of early sports organisations and was important to **amateurs**.

Spectators

Spectators consume the sport commodity over a period of time, with different degrees of intensity of consumption and in a variety of ways:

• Attendance.
• Broadcast in TV or radio, but mostly TV.
• Print, in tabloid newspapers.
• Word of mouth.

Today, the **Olympic Games**, soccer's **World Cup** and **Formula 1** motor sport dominate all other sports competitions, attracting audiences in their millions.

Sports labour

Both professionalisation and rule changes push sports organisations into becoming involved in the **sport labour market** and the development of **elite sportspeople as commodities** within the global labour markets. Hence they have an economic value and players and coaches are under pressure from stakeholders to deliver.

Advertising

Advertisements are messages paid for by those who send them and are intended to inform or influence people who receive them.

The selling or **merchandising** of products associated with sport is a major media objective. For example, electronic billboarding around an arena is aimed at the cameras. Advertising breaks on TV (although usually coincide with a break in play) attract large sums of money from the products they advertise.

These types of adverts not only get the general public interested in specific sports, but interest is also directed towards the advertised product.

Merchandising

In the sports merchandising business, the property of value to a team is their name, logo and sports stars.

figure 10.6 – MU merchandise

Through sponsorship and merchandising agreements the licensee is able to manufacture goods with logos, trademarks and trade names of the team, for example Manchester United merchandise (figure 10.6). The licensees believe that with the goodwill of the fans, they will associate with their clubs' identity and buy the merchandise.

A **sponsor** will expect to promote its products by using a performer's image in return for financial support. A contract will be commercial and dependent on the star status of the sportsperson.

Advertising and merchandising are closely related concepts in the area of retail marketing and communications. Retailers use advertising to project a brand image and to drive traffic to retail **stores** or **websites**.

Merchandising is the strategic placement of products that attracts attention and contributes to sales once customers are in stores (figure 10.6 of the Man United shop).

Sponsorship

Sponsorship advertising is a type of advertising where a corporation pays to be associated with a specific event, for example, Virgin Money London Marathon (figure 10.7).

Sports with the best sponsorship deals are sports with a **high fan base** such as football, tennis and snooker. During televised football games, the **half-time** TV adverts tend to have a heavy sports orientation. Equally, many adverts are tennis based around the time of Wimbledon.

Sponsorship is varied and covers all aspects of the team sports and events/competitions, stadium and grounds:

- **Team sponsorship** is one of the most prominent forms of sports advertising. Many businesses of all sizes choose to sponsor a sports team as a way to **promote** their company.
- The brand name will be featured on the kits of the player, for example, Chelsea's £60m a season deal with **Nike**.
- Eclipsed by Manchester United's £75m a season deal with **Adidas**.

- Sponsoring a local team can generate lots of **revenue**, great publicity and create a huge amount of valuable goodwill for businesses of all sizes.

- Adidas has a long-standing relationship with Team GB (figure 10.8), which began 31 years ago at Los Angeles 1984 and extends to the 2024 Olympic Games.
- Adidas remains the British Olympic Association's (BOA) longest serving domestic sponsored partnership for team kit and footwear.

- Nowadays the **sponsorship of stadia** is a common occurrence and selling the stadium's naming rights can bring in massive revenue.
- For example, Stoke City FC announced (from the start of the 2016/17) the Britannia Stadium was to be known as the **bet365 Stadium** for the Premier League season.
- Stoke City Chief Executive Tony Scholes said: 'The Premier League is constantly evolving and to ensure that Stoke City remains as competitive as possible it's important we explore as many ways as possible of generating revenue'.

- **Event/competition sponsorship** ranges from local to national to international level.
- For example, **Aegon** have been investing in British tennis since 2009 and crosses all levels of the game,
- From **nurturing young talent** through our Aegon FutureStars programme, encouraging amateur participation through tournaments such as the Aegon County Cup.
- Helping professional players reach **further potential** through the platform of the Aegon GB Pro-Series.
- And **supporting top players** through our national Davis and Fed Cup Teams.

Endorsement

Sporting role models (figure 10.9) often gain the attention of a corporation who wish to use the athlete's popularity and reputation to help **promote** a service or product. The sponsoring corporation will therefore pay that individual for him or her to endorse its product.

The individual will be seen to be endorsing the product by **wearing** the brand name, appearing in advertising campaigns both on television and in the print media for that particular product. Legally endorsements will be created through an **endorsement agreement** between the individual sporting star and the brand which they are endorsing.

figure 10.7 – Virgin Money London Marathon

figure 10.8 – BOA Logo

TEAM GB

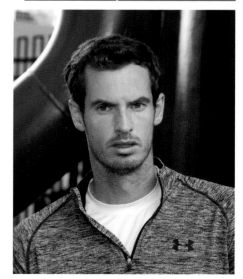
figure 10.9 – Andy Murray, now endorsed by UnderArmour

Advertising, sponsorship and endorsement deals and the sports star

Puma is Usain Bolt's largest sponsor (figure 10.10). In 2013, he signed an endorsement deal worth an estimated $10 million per year to remain with the company throughout his competitive sporting career.
He is expected to earn $4 million annually to stay on as a brand ambassador following his retirement.

Advertising, sponsorship and endorsements are packaged together when contracts are exchanged between corporations and celebrity sports stars.

Figure 10.11 lists how advertising affects the sports star.

However, the **motives** of the commercial media differ from sport motives, even though some products may be seen to help sport in other than financial ways.

The **sports performer** is helped by:
*   Provision of equipment.
*   Income.

The **sports governing body** or organiser is helped by:
*   Sport funding, which can be used to for example promote grass roots sport.
*   Positive associations between the product and the sport.
*   Greater exposure of the sport to the public via the media.

The **product** gains by:
*   Broadening the publicity given to the product.
*   Tax relief for the advertiser, since the exposure involves a cost which can be set against tax.

In the face of the recent recession, several companies have withdrawn sponsorship because **profit** is their central motive.

Drug scandals have also had an impact on player's earning, for example, Nike and TAG Heuer cancelled their sponsorship deals with Maria Sharapova after she failed a drugs test (page 144). The media have often sensationalised the lifestyle choices of a sports performer, and exert psychological pressure on high profile athletes through excessive media attention.

Sports have **marketing managers** and promoters to generate income and athletes have agents and managers to look after their finances.

figure 10.10 – Usain Bolt and Puma

figure 10.11 – advertising

sport exposure · sport funding · tax relief for advertiser · positive associations · ADVERTISING and the SPORTS STAR · equipment for performer · product exposure · endorsement for performer · income for performer

The golden triangle

The so-called '**golden triangle**' (figure 10.12) links and provides an overlap between the **media**, **commercialism**, and **sport** and governing bodies. Without one, the other two cannot survive and increased media attention has led to sports becoming more exciting, leading to greater commercial sponsorship and greater participation in sport.

This key concept has been developed throughout this chapter.

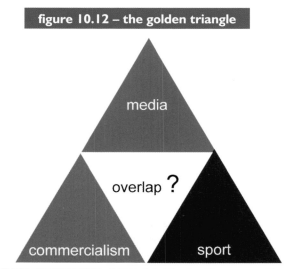
figure 10.12 – the golden triangle

media · overlap ? · commercialism · sport

Role of the media and sport since the 1980s

The roles of the media, in terms of sport, are **fourfold** (figure 10.13).

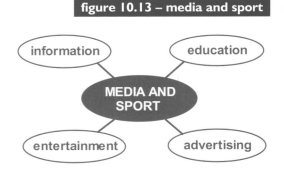

figure 10.13 – media and sport

- The basic function of the media has always been to give **information**. Radio and television give immediate **results, event descriptions** and **rankings**.

- **Education**: the media **inform**, **advise** and **critically analyse** issues through explanation, discussion and debate. Terrestrial and satellite TV have **documentaries** which give coaching advice, explain the risk of drug-taking, and give post-event discussions on games.

- **Entertainment**: a TV programme will give experience and pleasure to an armchair spectator almost equivalent to the live event. Attending live events is expensive, hence the popularity of screens in pubs, clubs or parks near to the venues, (Henman's Hill/Murray's Mound at Wimbledon for example).

- **Advertising**: the selling or merchandising of products associated with sport is a major media aim. An example of this is a tennis player wearing a certain make of headband, sports shoe or shirt. Each club in both rugby and soccer displays sponsors' names on its shirts. **Electronic billboarding** around an arena is aimed at the cameras. Advertising breaks on TV (although usually coincident with a break in play) attract large sums from the products being advertised.

The impact of the media on sport

The impact of the **media on sport** is extensive. They can **promote** balanced, active, healthy lifestyles and lifelong involvement in physical activity. This is via the people it presents, the way these people act and the messages they give. These messages could be given in children's programmes as well as in adult news and documentaries.

Hence the media's **selective** use of visual and written material can have a major influence. Most important is the **balance** of the message, not just the hero worship of sports stars, but help in recognising the **problems** as well as the pleasures of achievement. The media can give insight into the effort needed for success, and a belief in the ideal of fair play.

20th/21st century developments to ticket sales

Today media coverage of sport is widespread.
- By listening to **commentators**, **pundits** and **watching replays**, spectators, players and coaches improve their knowledge and understanding.
- **Participation** in sports covered by the **media** is always higher than for those that are not.
- Developments in the media are linked to **commercialisation** and **sport**.
- The **media** includes newspapers/magazines, radio and television broadcasting.

Newspapers

Today there are two types of press that are also available online:
- **Popular tabloids**, such as the Daily Mail, the Express, the Sun and the Mirror, focus on popular male dominated sports. Hence football, rugby and cricket are given great exposure.
- More **high-brow broadsheets**, such as the Telegraph and the Guardian, and tabloids the Independent (available online) and the i, cover a variety of sports and analyse sport in more depth.

Magazines are a distinctive media form in their close connection to the social lives of consumers, and cover specific sports enthusiasms, for example, Athletics Weekly.

Since 2014, in the newspaper industry there has been rapid **digital** growth, driven by readers. Digital newspapers and online versions of printed periodicals provide advertisers further opportunity to capitalise on a growing, smart, affluent, and digitally savvy audience.

Online sports media

Digital Sports Group is a UK digital network connecting sports fans and participants worldwide, featuring the latest news, expert opinions, results and fixtures and a variety of features. **sport.co.uk** is rapidly emerging as a major player in online sports media.

Radio

Since the 1980s there has been a rapid growth in radio audiences who have enjoyed the broadcasting of popular sporting events such as rugby and football matches, the major channel being **BBC Radio 5 Live Sports Extra**.

This national digital radio station is operated by the BBC, and specialises in extended additional sports coverage. **5 Live Sports Extra** broadcasts a variety of sports including test match special, Wimbledon tennis, and the National Hockey League's Stanley Cup Finals. The best bits from the BBC's sporting commentary are available as free **podcasts**.

The role of the BBC

Traditionally the BBC played a dominant role in televising sport, providing extensive high-quality advertisement-free coverage and free publicity in exchange for being granted broadcast rights for low fees.

Today (2017) the BBC showcases key global sport festivals, such as the Wimbledon fortnight (without commercial breaks) making it one of the UK's most prestigious, entertaining and much watched sporting events.

ITV broadcast a smaller portfolio of events, and **Channel 4** broadcast a few events from the 1980s, mainly horse races and so-called minority sports.

TV programmes can be accessed via a range of interactive computer devices and watched on multi-purpose screens which can vary from very small mobiles to large, flat, high definition screens. TV companies found sport fairly cheap entertainment compared with dramas or documentaries and so sport has been the beneficiary of media growth.

The influence of technology

Technological advances have revolutionised the way in which humans communicate. Communication satellites (figure 10.14) enable live broadcasting on a global scale, increasing viewing audiences giving more detailed coverage and more of the action, with referees miked up, and replays from different angles. Spectators can easily view at any point or dip into the action without losing the plot.

Media **technological innovations** are fuelling the insatiable appetite of the sports spectator. Tech innovations lend themselves well to social media as a means of communication and interaction, including **email**, **social networking**, instant **messaging** and chat via tech gadgets such as **tablets** and **phablets** (phone + tablet).

figure 10.14 – satellite technology

Fans can share sporting moments **instantaneously**. These high tech gadgets provide another outlet for the **commercial** sector to exploit. Historically, **television** broadcasting was the main source of **revenue** for elite sports teams, leagues and national governing bodies. In the twenty first century the **Internet** and **social media** are transforming **sports marketing**.

- The Internet has created new possibilities for the distribution and consumption of sporting events.
- The Internet creates new possibilities for **minority sport**s (such as netball) that are not large enough to attract significant revenue from mainstream television broadcasting.
- Can attract a new audience.
- Help clubs deliver behind-the-scenes access to fans on a cost-effective basis.
- Internet technology promises to challenge how sports rights holders, such as governing bodies, protect the value of the broadcasting rights they sell to TV companies.

The influence of technology

- **Social media** has taken the world by storm. It has impacted the way we receive and share all kinds of news. Sports news is no stranger to social media and has had a large impact on sports journalism.
- Social media is creating new forms of **communication** between fans, athletes, teams and sponsors.
- Strategies include '**buzz**' marketing which encourages existing fans to promote an event with offers that can be tracked through social media.

- **Enhanced digital media** aims to enhance the fan experience through multiple perspectives such as highlight repeats and commentary from pundits and experts who build ties with individuals and fan networks.
- The **marketing objective** is to develop **brand awareness** within sport and then go through the classic stages of adoption by developing an interest in participating in the sport, attending an event, buying a subscription or season ticket and ultimately developing close ties with the sports organisation and other fans.
- **Online sports media** (for example, **Digital Sports Group** - a UK digital network) connects sports fans and participants worldwide, featuring the latest news, expert opinions, results and fixtures and a variety of features. **sport.co.uk** is rapidly emerging as a major player in online sports media.

Sports journalists and social media

As sports journalists increasingly adopt social media so does the sporting industry. Sports news is no stranger to social media either and has had a large impact on sports journalism.

Three major global sports and sporting events with a lot of social buzz:

American football:
- There were 185 million interactions on Facebook about Super Bowl 2017.
- More than half of the commercials aired during the 2017 Super Bowl included some type of social hash tag.

figure 10.15 – SuperBowl 2017

Basketball:
- Two thirds of NBA players are on Twitter.
- 26 million tweets were generated about the NBA finals.

World Cup Soccer:
- 12.2 million tweets were generated by the opening game of the 2014 FIFA World Cup.
- 495 million posts, likes and comments were generated on Facebook.
- During the first week of the 2014 World Cup, Portugese soccer star Cristiano Ronaldo was mentioned 1.5 million times on Twitter between the US and Portugal.

Benefits of social media to the sports journalist

- Sports journalists experience many benefits from using social media outlets for reporting, such as interaction with their readers, listeners and viewers.
- Social media promotes the work of journalists.
- Social media can direct journalists to the stories that are the most important and most followed by sports fans.

Drawbacks of social media to the sports journalist

- There is **pressure** for the journalist to get information quickly and produce content through a variety of mediums.
- Sports journalists need to **check** social media regularly.
- There is increased **competition** from other journalist and bloggers.
- There is potential for **negative interactions** with readers, viewers, and listeners.
- There can be **inaccuracies** of data on social media outlets.
- There is a feeling of a **non-professional attitude** of journalist's handling stories/news via social media.

73% of all journalists use social media to monitor their competition.

The arrival of pay-per-view

In the early 1990s TV broadcasting was shaken up by the arrival of '**pay-per-view**' in the form of BSkyB. Their dedicated sports channels have since become the only place for some major sports to be seen.

Starting in 2006 the Irish company Setanta Sports emerged as a challenger to Sky Sports' dominance of the British pay-TV sports market. Setanta's UK channel went into bankruptcy administration and off the air in 2009. Between 2009 and 2013 **Entertainment and Sports Programming Network** (ESPN) made an attempt to challenge Sky Sports before its British operations were bought out by Sky's current main competitor.

Pay-per-view

- **Pay-per-view** (PPV) is a type of pay television service by which a subscriber of a television service provider can purchase events to view via private telecast.

- The broadcaster shows the event at the same time to everyone ordering it (as opposed to video-on-demand systems, which allow viewers to see recorded broadcasts at any time).

- Events can be **purchased** using an on-screen guide, an automated telephone system, or through a live customer service representative.

- PPV has been introduced by BT Sport, a subsidiary of the former national telecommunications monopoly BT. Customers pay a monthly subscription for full coverage of Champions and Europa League matches when they sign up for this TV bundle.
- Having paid £897m for the rights to all Champions League and Europa League matches over three years, BT will show all 351 games live on a new channel called BT Sport Europe.

- With the rise of the Internet, the term **Internet pay-per-view** (iPPV) has been used to describe pay-per view services accessed online.

- PPV is most commonly used to distribute combat sports events, such as boxing, mixed martial arts and professional wrestling.

- There is a clear shift from cable TV to direct streaming that is accelerating many industries worldwide. For example, World Wrestling Entertainment (WWE) has partially cut its cable and satellite TV contracts to embrace Internet television, and this presents the WWE fans with a cutting edge, subscription-only streaming video service.

- The smart shift to the live sports pay-per-view business could bring in millions in revenue.

Growth of pay-per-view

The growth of pay-per-view can only go in one direction, as discerning sports fans follow their teams and thus contribute to what is expected to be an increase in growth over the next few years.

The future of commercial sport

- Sports are **expensive** to run and so **sponsorship** deals and additional publicity, via the media, benefit both performers and spectators, a win-win situation.
- **Entertainment** and consumption will be the major **organising principles** for the future.
- Financial **profits** and economic **expansion** will be the goals of most sports and corporations.
- The emphasis on entertainment will fuel the success of **professional sports** in forms of '**sportainment**' TV which provides online streaming platforms.

The future of commercial sport

- **Corporate conglomerates** will buy teams and link them to their media, entertainment, and Internet divisions.
- **Sport equipment manufacturers** will continue to sell the idea that involvement in sports requires highly specialised and **expensive** equipment and clothing.
- **Wealthy people** will use sports as contexts for announcing their status and identities through **appearance**, and sport **ownership**.

But despite all such predictions it is to be believed that leisure pleasure sport will be an integral part of the **lifestyle** of masses of people to improve human **wellbeing** and **quality of life** as a form of everyday **healthy** activity compensating the demanding goals and objectives of our lives.

Commercialism, media and sport in today's world

Commercialisation creates employment opportunities in media, coaching, sport and event management, as well as stimulating businesses related to sport and benefitting the economy overall.

The following tables (table 10.1 and 10.2) set out the positive and negative impact on different aspects of commercialisation, sponsorship and the media on the performer, the coach and the audience.

Table 10.1 - **positive and negative impact of commercialism, sponsorship and the media on sport**

positive impact on sport	negative impact on sport
the elite performer	
increased income from sponsorship in return for using or wearing the sponsor's goods	sponsorship and the media can be over-demanding of a performer requiring interviews at inconvenient times
the media can increase the awareness of the public of the skill, excellence and peronality of the performer (a role model)	increased pressure on a performer to obtain or change lucrative contracts for playing
improved facilities for training, coaching, TID and competition available through increased funding for a sport	the media tend to sensationalise lifestyle and non-sporting life choices by a performer instead of sporting excellence
increased participation level due to exposure of major event, people want to have a go at a new sport (eg rugby after England's World Cup victory in 2003)	there are inequalities of coverage (minority sports don't get much exposure), thereby performer cannot attract sponsorship
media led developments lead to more variations to sport (e.g. twenty20 cricket - summer season for Rugby League) leading to greater opportunities for income to the performer and financial gain to the sport	exposure of deviance (fighting, diving to cheat, arguing with officials) lowering role model status caused by 'win-at-all-costs' attitude in media
increase of profile of performer and the sport	elite performers are often treated as commodities
competition sponsorship can nurture young talent/grass roots sport	
unprecedented earning power for male athletes in most popular sports and for females in a more limited number of sports	psychological pressure on high profile athletes through excessive media attention
performers can concentrate on training without financial worries	performers are under pressure to perform when injured
positive role models encourage mass participation	

positive impact on sport	negative impact on sport
the coach	
can award contracts to performers which in professional sport gives him or her control over everything to do with playing strategy	sponsorship and the media pressure can be over-demanding of a coach
sponsorship can include coaches and enable travel to support performers at coaching camps and major events	an imbalance of salaries paid to coaches/managers of top professional clubs, such as soccer, and professional coaches/managers employed in amateur sports
the audience	
increased investment improves quality of facilities, acquiring top players and entertainment eg cheer leaders to attract bigger audiences	excessive advertising could interrupt the viewing experience
certain sports (soccer, rugby, cricket, golf and tennis) are ring fenced into terrestial or free to view TV for primary events, therefore maintaining large audience for high status events (test matches, Wimbledon, cup finals etc.	pay-per-view TV can make some sports events expensive to watch
sports channels available (at a cost) for specific events	low attendance at events which are fully covered on TV
media led developments lead to more variations to sport (e.g. twenty20 cricket - summer season for Rugby League) leading to greater opportunities for fans and more exciting games	there are inequalities of coverage (minority sports don't get much exposure), thereby sports fans for that sport cannot see their favourite sport
technology, such as video screens and HawkEye for replays and match statistics, increase excitement, awareness and knowledge of the sport	more breaks in play can disrupt audience experience
commercial products are readily available for the spectator	player kit merchandise is regularly changed and disfavoured by some supporters due to expense
if the performers are able to work better with sponsorship, entertainment levels should rise	event schedules are planned to maximise USA viewing figures and so may not be timely for the UK arm chair spectator or athletes
	tickets to major sporting events are expensive
the growth of commercial sport through exposure/coverage in the media has increased participation and audience numbers	ticket prices go up due to the popularity of club/team
sports media can promote balanced, active and healthy lifestyles	incorrect umpiring decisions are highly published in the media and so can be questioned by fans
digital media such as newspapers, online outlets and social networking are creating a digitally savvy sports audience	social media ruins the element of surprise as media outlets get the news out faster
	media over-exposure may put some fans off from watching an event
	the media and fans can twist and exaggerate stories

Table 10.2 – **positive and negative aspects of media coverage of sport**

positive aspects of media coverage	negative aspects of media coverage
players or teams gain revenue from sponsors	sponsorship companies usually only focus on high profile players or teams
sponsorship can provide teams with improved facilities and/ or equipment	sponsors can control event timings to suit peak-viewing times
teams or players gain publicity and promotion	players or teams can be restricted as to what products they can use
sponsorship can elevate new sports into the limelight via media publicity	sports can be overrun with sponsors – thus losing the nature of the game
more money for grass-roots teams	NGBs forced to alter rules to make games more exciting - in order to generate sponsorship interest
	more exciting events given priority over other sport
raises profile of the sport	leads to a squeeze on amateur sport
	media will not support minority sports, or low profile sports such as badminton with less identifiable role models

Practice questions

1) Commercial sponsorships of sports are primarily motivated by commercial interest in:
   a.   promoting a way of life based on consumptions and consumerism.
   b.   developing a single worldwide standard of living.
   c.   finding new ways to train workers who will produce goods.
   d.   building sports that bring the world together for global competitive events.

2) The images and messages presented by sponsors of major sporting events tend to:
   a.   dictate what people think.
   b.   influence what people think about.
   c.   be ignored by nearly all spectators.
   d.   discourage consumption-based lifestyles.

3) Which one of the following does not represent positive aspects of media coverage of sport?
   a.   sponsor can provide teams with improved facilities.
   b.   more money for grass roots teams.
   c.   sponsors can control event timing to suit peak viewing times.
   d.   sportspeople gain publicity and commercial benefit.

4) Which one of the following best describes a positive impact of commercialisation on sport?
   a.   performers are under pressure to perform well when injured.
   b.   improved facilities for training and coaching through increased funding for sport.
   c.   officials may become too dependent on technology.
   d.   pay-to-view TV can make sports events expensive to watch.

5) A definition of sponsorship is:
   a.   the act of watching an event, especially a sports contest.
   b.   a means of communication with the users of a product or service.
   c.   when a person or organisation pays the cost of an activity or event.
   d.   a deal whereby a company will pay an individual for its brand to be associated with that individual.

6) Identify three factors that have influenced the commercialisation of sport within the UK.   3 marks

7) Discuss the advantages and disadvantages of commercialisation in sport.   8 marks

Practice questions

8) a)   Give a definition of sponsorship. Support your answer with an example.   2 marks

b)   Identify three factors that would influence a sponsor's decision to invest in a sport.   3 marks

9) a)   What conditions are required for commercial sport to develop?   4 marks

b)   Suggest two reasons why commercial sports have become global commodities.   2 marks

10) How are advertising and merchandising linked together within sport's marketing?   3 marks

11) Write an argument for and against the suggestion that the commercialisation of sport
has been beneficial for the performer and for the sport.   4 marks

12) a)   Describe three negative effects of media coverage on sport.   3 marks

b)   Describe three positive effects of media coverage on sport.   3 marks

13) Describe three ways that sport benefits TV.   3 marks

14) Many elite sports are now commercialised and seen as forms of entertainment.
Discuss the suggestion that an increase in the commercialisation of sport has been
beneficial for performers and the sport.   8 marks

15) Outline the positive and negative features of sponsorship for the sports performer.   6 marks

16) What is the role of the media in promoting healthy lifestyles and lifelong involvement in physical activity?   5 marks

17) Sport, commercialism and the media are all interdependent on each other for their
success and popularity. Discuss.   20 marks

18) How should a team or national governing body use high profile athletes to grow and promote their sport?   4 marks

19) a)   Identify some of the threats posed by the Internet and social media on the sources
of revenue for an international governing body such as the International Rugby Board   4 marks

b)   In minority sports, such as badminton and extreme sports, how can the Internet be
of use to promote the sport in a different manner to television broadcasting?   2 marks

20) Discuss the future of commercial sport.   4 marks

21) a) What is meant by the term 'pay-per-view?   I mark

b) Briefly describe how pay-per-view has grown over the past decade.   3 marks

Answers link: http://www.jroscoe.co.uk/downloads/a2_revise_pe_ocr/OCRA2_ch10_answers.pdf

CHAPTER 11: *Routes to sporting excellence in the UK*

Development of elite performers in sport

Excellence is defined as a '**special ability beyond the norm, to which many aspire but few go onto achieve**'. Excellence suggests a specialism of one activity and in sport is judged by international standards. **Talent** is a **natural ability to be good at something, especially without being taught**.

Talent identification is the **recognition** of talent in an individual.

Identification and development of talented individuals

The early identification and development of talented individuals is considered increasingly important. What is needed to become an elite athlete is a rare combination of **nature** (genetic makeup) and **nurture** (the process of socialisation - observing, watching and copying others). Elite athletes have **talent** in abundance, **work hard** and have the right **psychological** profile.

Identifying personal attributes that characterise exceptional performers can help talented individuals to progress from **participation** to **elite** level performance, as summarised in figure 11.1.

figure 11.1 – development of talent - personal factors

Social and cultural factors

Figure 11.2 provides a summary of the **social** and **cultural** factors that are required to support progressions from talent identification to elite performance, which will be discussed throughout this chapter.

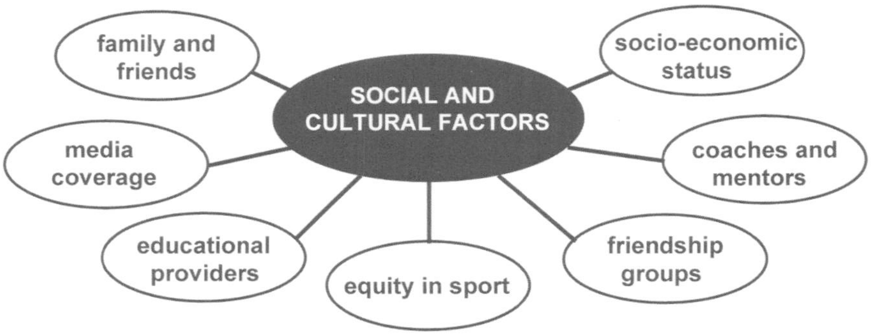

The role of schools, clubs and universities in contributing to elite sporting success

figure 11.2 – development of talent - social and cultural factors

Schools and clubs

Playing sport helps to keep people healthy and is good for communities. Playing sport at school or in a local club is also the first step to competition at the highest level. To make sure as many young people as possible are playing sport, the government and financial support from the National Lottery are:

*   Supporting **Sport England**, to help community sports grow, including helping 11 to 25-year-olds to keep playing sport throughout their lives through local agencies such as **County School Partnerships** (CSP). Also skateboarding has been a highly successful Sportivate activity.
*   Expanding the **School Games programme** (operated by the **Youth Sport Trust**) to increase opportunities for more young people to play competitive sport.
*   Investing in primary physical education and sport by providing specialists PE teachers to raise standards.
*   Providing **academic opportunities** to study PE and Sport at GCSE, BTEC and A level.

Schools and clubs

- Creating **links** between **schools**, **colleges** and **clubs** with access to specialist facilities and coaching (figure 11.3). This is where a talented individual can progress from **participation** to **performance** level. For example, in 2017 there are in excess of 6000 partnership links in major sports such as soccer, rugby and tennis.

- School or county sports organisations run trials to select county sports teams, who in turn select their most promising players for regional trials, who in turn recommend players for **national trials**.

- It is interesting to note that in the Rio Olympics 2016 just 7% of the medal-winning athletes attended state-maintained schools which educate 93% of all under 16 year old students.

figure 11.3 – coaches are important

Universities

Many British Universities offer an **elite sport strategy programme** that supports a student athlete alongside their academic studies. There are various opportunities available:

- **Talented Athlete Scholarship Scheme** (TASS) is a Sport England funded partnership between talented athletes, accredited education institutions, such as universities, and national governing bodies.

- A **university sports scholarship** supports talented athletes both financially and academically. For example, a sports scholar could opt for an extended university degree thereby creating more time for training and competitions.

- **BUCS Awards** recognise the contribution student athletes make to the overall performances in **British Universities and Colleges Sport** (BUCS) leagues.

- Additional **financial support to Athletic Union clubs** who are competing in BUCS Tier 1A or above and have demonstrated excellence across a number of areas.

- Specialist **facilities** and **coaches** to develop talented athletes.

- **Medical support systems** such as physiotherapists and psychologists, and **research services** that offer facilities including acclimatisation chambers and data technical expertise.

- **National UK hubs**, for example, Loughborough University HIPAC (figure 11.4) is the national base for UK Athletics funded by Sport England and containing support services provided by the English Institute of Sport (EIS).
- The centre provides a crucial all-weather training base for both Loughborough's students and many of the country's leading elite athletes.

figure 11.4 – Loughborough University HIPAC

Talent development and support services in the UK

The original Talent Identification and Development (TID) programme which operated in the UK began in 1998 following the start of **lottery funding** of which sport was a 20% part. Prior to this point, there were two years of zero exchequer funding (from central taxation) and near or total bankruptcy of several sports which relied on this funding for their NGB activity.

Some of these sports based their future TID model on the East German and Australian models. These new UK models included:

*   Grass roots **searches for talent** at ages 12 to 14 within major cities.
*   Development of **facilities** 'within reach of one million people at 30 minutes travel'.
*   Such facilities were centred around existing facilities where possible.
*   Usage of the 2002 Manchester Commonwealth Games facilities then being planned.
*   Provision of **coaching** and advice for selected groups.
*   Channeling of the selected young people into **local clubs** where it was assumed that coaching and competition could continue.
*   Development of a **UK Sports Institute** (UKSI) covering the scientific elements of sports training.

2017 development routes from TID through to elite performance

National sporting organisations, such as **UK Sport**, have increasingly recognised the limitations with traditional TID approaches which mainly emphasised 'genetic' determinants of talent and focus on age-group success rather than senior success.

More **contemporary developmental routes** to elite performance are highly structured with multi-dimensional approaches that take into account all the variables across all disciplines that are needed by elite performers.

Figure 11.5 traces the talent pathway that most NGBs use in 2017.

Perhaps the most important element is **lottery funding**, and as long as it lasts, it should sustain UK Sport programmes. Recently (2017), the sale of lottery tickets has fallen, resulting in decreased budgets for home countries.

The provision of funding (overseen by Sport England and the other home country Sports Councils) depends on the performance of a sport in the latest Olympic Games or World Championships according to the formula set out in the **Whole Sport Plans** proposed by the NGBs of the individual sports (page 178).

In the case of athletics, the gradual fall off of funding has led to the reduction of hubs to one centralised facility based at Loughborough University which is almost exclusively only available to those athletes in the National Squad who have achieved the top status.

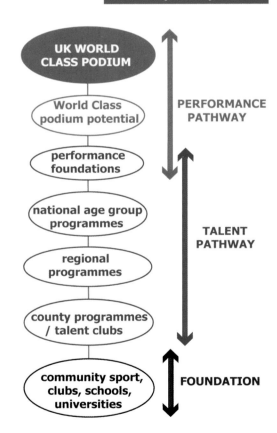

figure 11.5 – UK sport talent pathway 2017

At Loughborough, **medical** back-up, sport **psychology** advice, and **accomodation** and **life-style** support are provided to the athletes, as well as professional **coaching** and access to the best **training facilities** in the country.

The remaining 7 English hubs still exist and are mostly available to **regional** and club groups for training. The Welsh, Scottish and Northern Irish hubs continue to support athletes who are at elite **Commonwealth Games** level.

2017 development routes from TID through to elite performance

UK Sport and the respective home countries have far greater financial control over NGBs than in the past. **Lottery funding** is the mainstay in the development routes of the Performance Pathways, and as a result of Whole Sport Plans and NGBs (page 177). **Talent and Performance Pathways** have become far more uniform in structure and centralised in control.

Talent development and support services

Investment in elite sport within Britain has increased considerably since 1996. If such investment is to have a positive impact on British sport, it is apparent that some of it must be targeted towards athletes that have the greatest potential of producing successful performances at major international events.

There are two predominant methods that broadly capture athletes who are currently identified within sport:

- **Natural selection** is aimed at identifying talented individuals that are already participating within a sport due to the recognition of performance or scouting.

- **Scientific selection** is a more proactive procedure by which identification of the talented occurs as a result of testing individuals on values that are associated with expertise within a certain sport.
    - For example, the physical, physiological and psychological attributes that affect performers within sprinting or weightlifting.

- The English Institute of Sports' (EIS) talent development work aims to identify, recruit and progress the most promising young athletes and put in place the systems, pathways and support to facilitate their transition from **talented junior** to **elite international performer**.

The private sector - soccer and scouts academies

In soccer a strong **scouting network** works throughout the country looking for football talent. Their main priority is to recruit young players with a technical aptitude, mental and movement skills, and the right temperament. Very few of these young players will make it through the academies and achieve professional contracts (page 184 for further notes).

Strategies to address drop-out failure rates

There are many reasons why talented athletes drop out of sport:
- Over the years the development in **elite youth sport** has required increasingly more **strenuous** workouts, **early specialisation**, careful planning and the ability to handle tough competitions.
- Training programmes are too focused on early specialisation, and are often related to **stagnation** in athletic performance.
- Athletes with a **negative performance** development will experience lower self-esteem, poorer estimation of potential success and **lack of motivation**.
- **Inadequate training facilities** and **lack of experienced coaches** may influence the athlete's decision to drop out from sport.
- Drop-outs may be forced to quit because of serious **injury/illness**.
- Drop-outs may not be able to afford the **costs of participation** in competitive sports.
- Drop-outs may wish to engage themselves in **other interests** and activities.

The pathway to success in sport is often referred to as the '**10 year rule of attainment**'. Combined with handling the necessities of education, work and other interests, this demanding situation applies more pressure (physical, psychological and social) on the young athlete.

Models, such as the **Long-Term Development Plan** (LTAD), are aimed at addressing the drop out issue.

Long-Term Athlete Development (LTAD)

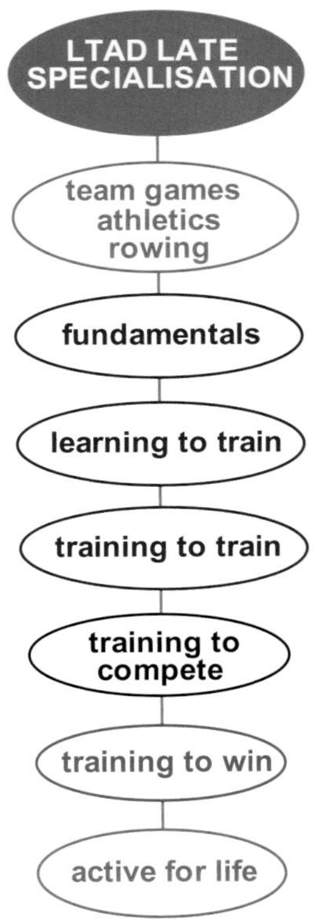

LTAD is a model used by majority of NGBs in the UK that was developed by Istvan Balyi in 2001. Figure 11.6 outlines the six stages of the late specialisation model.

The philosophy of this LTAD model is as follows:
- It aims to **retain** athletes for life as well as develop them.
- It hopes to match desire and talent of a performer to an appropriate training environment.
- In turn, this should lead to increased **retention** and increased **success**.
- It hopes to establish a **clear development pathway** for athletes.

The effectiveness of talent identification programmes (TIPs)

- Recruiting talented athletes on such schemes increases the chances of producing **more medals** on the world stage.
- Gives talented athletes considerable material benefits, **financial support**, including time to train, access to **professional coaches** who provide highly structured training programmes, and the use of top **facilities**.
- Access to high tech sports science and **sports medicine therapies**.
- Promotes the use of a system which is **scientifically** based in terms of screening, training, diet and sports medicine.
- Talented youngsters are directed towards sports that most suit their **strengths**.
- Selection is based on **natural talent** and not socio-economic background, thus ensuring equal opportunities to the talent pool.

Disadvantages of using TIPs

- Selectors/scouts need to be able to look beyond the immediate success and characteristics, and look at the components such as age-related speed and balance, which are better predictors of potential performance.
- There is the possibility that **late developers** are not spotted.
- Early versus late specialisation needs to be considered on an individual basis.
- Talented athletes have **no guarantee** of realising their potential.
- They could get injured on the way.
- Identifying future potential is difficult, as predictions are being made regarding how well an athlete may develop, rather than just assessing their current ability.
- **Growth** and **maturation** have a marked effect on an athlete's ability at a given time, and need to be taken into consideration.

The role of UK Sport and national institutes in developing sporting excellence

Figure 11.7 depicts the organisations involved in UK Sport.

UK Sport

- UK Sport is an agency that operates under **government** direction.
- The primary role of UK Sport is to strategically invest **National Lottery** and **Exchequer** income to maximise the **performance** of UK athletes in the Olympic and Paralympic Games and the **global events** which precede them.

figure 11.6 – LTAD model

LTAD LATE SPECIALISATION
- team games athletics rowing
- fundamentals
- learning to train
- training to train
- training to compete
- training to win
- active for life

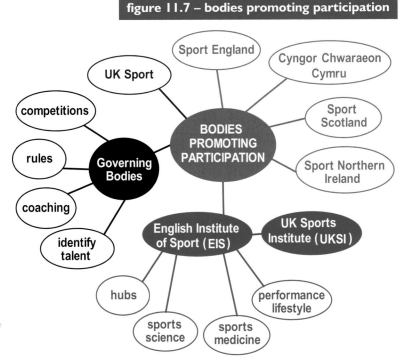

figure 11.7 – bodies promoting participation

UK Sport

- Decisions are made on a **four year basis** wherever possible to cover a complete Olympic or Paralympic cycle but are focussed on an **eight year performance development mode**l.
- **Central funding** for sporting **National Governing Bodies** (NGBs), enabling them to operate a **World Class Programme** (WCP)
  - Success is measured by the **medals won**, the number of medallists developed, and the quality of the systems and processes in place to find and support the nation's most promising **future champions**.

To achieve this UK Sport invests around 70 per cent of its income through two channels, World Class Podium, and World Class Podium Potential, (details on page 179 onwards).

- Ensuring athletes have access to outstanding support personnel and training environments to prepare them to compete against the best in the world.
- Funding is in the shape of an **Athlete Performance Award** (APA). This award, funded by National Lottery income, is paid directly to the athletes and contributes to their living and sporting costs.
- UK Sport also runs a number of world leading centralised **strategic** support services including the development of **world class coaches** and **talent identification** campaigns to fast track future medallists in to the right sports.

- The **UK Sport coaching team** seeks to ensure the delivery of quality coaching to athletes on **UK Sport's World Class Performance Pathway**, a system devised to identify, develop and refine talented British athletes.
- To achieve this, the **UK Sport World Class Coaching Strategy** must deliver targeted and innovative programmes specific to the needs of world class coaches.
- Coaching (figure 11.8) is one of a number of key elements of the high performance system, and alongside other key performance support services such as **Sports Medicine** and **Sports Science**, **Performance Lifestyle** and **Research** and **Innovation**, plays a crucial role in ensuring the ongoing success of British athletes.

figure 11.8 – sports coach UK

- UK Sport works in conjunction with partners, such as the English Institute of Sport (EIS), by providing trained and accredited **Performance Lifestyle** practitioners to work with athletes to develop the necessary skills needed to cope with the unique demands of being an elite performer.

- **Lifestyle Support** is designed to support, advise and mentor talented athletes in managing their personal development and lifestyle.
- **Performance Lifestyle** aims to help the individual to develop skills to effectively manage all their commitments including sport (training and competition) and non-sport (family, education and employment).

National governing bodies of sport

NGBs are tasked with **overseeing** their sport and **organising** their existing and future direction.
These bodies are responsible for:
- Establishing the **rules**.
- Organising **national competitions**.
- **Coaching** within each individual sport.
- Selecting individuals for **funding**.
- Picking **teams** for **international** competition.

NGBs, together with local partners, are working together to create a new **satellite club** at every school, linked to an existing community 'hub' club, and run by coaches and volunteers from that hub club.

By being located on a school site, the satellite club is within easy reach of young people, but is distinct from school physical education as it is run by community volunteers.

Whole Sport Plans and NGBs

Whole Sport Plans are the delivery contract between **Sport England** and each of the 46 funded **National Governing Bodies** for Sport (NGBs). Each NGB is required to produce a whole sport plan which should include everything relating to its particular sport, through the full range of abilities from **participation** at the basic level, to **elite** level.

The plan must state how that sport will achieve Sport England's '**start, stay and succeed**' objectives, and use 60% of NGB **funding** on the **14-25 year old age group**. The intention is to create a sporting habit for life.

figure 11.9 – Dina Asher-Smith

To be eligible for Whole Sport Plan funding, NGBs must also meet high standards of **governance** and **financial control**. Sport England has invested £493m into 46 sports between 2013 and 2017. Payment is by results, with withdrawal of funding to governing bodies that fail to deliver agreed objectives.

Of the £22 million received by UK Athletics, Sport England allocated £8.8 million of the total investment for UK Athletics to get more people involved in informal running. **Park run** is an example of a successful grassroots scheme which satisfied this criteria.

UK Athletics wants to increase the number of talented athletes who could go on to elite and world class level. For example, **Dina Asher-Smith** (figure 11.9) who went from bag carrier in London 2012, to fifth in the Rio Olympics 2016. This was achieved by focusing on increasing and enhancing **coaching**, as well as improving the domestic competition opportunities, (which also applies to talented **disabled** athletes).

UK Sports Institute (UKSI)

figure 11.10 – GB women's hockey, Rio 2016

UKSI provides world class facilities and coordinated support services. For example, the National Sports Centre at Bisham Abbey, where GB women's hockey (figure 11.10) is based.

Its **Athlete Medical Scheme** provides the UK's top Olympic and Paralympic athletes with **free medical care**. It also organises and sponsors world class coaching conferences, which present the UK's top coaches with opportunities to gain new insights and skills to develop future World, Olympic and Paralympic Champions.

UK Sport and UKSI devolve their regional responsibilities into the Home Country Institutes, for example, the EIS.

National Institutes of Sport - English Institute of Sport (EIS)

The EIS aims to develop and produce performers at the **elite level** of the sport development pyramid, and who will therefore become part of the lottery funded **World Class Performance Programme** (figure 11.11, page 179).

World Class Performance Programme (WCPP)

Funded by the **National Lottery** through UK Sport, the WCPP selection is based upon the potential to win medals at an Olympic or Paralympic Games and has two distinct levels.

World Class Podium (WCP)

WCP (figure 11.11) supports sports and athletes with realistic medal capabilities at global events.

This group of elite athletes should be standing on the medal podium at the next world or global games for their sport.

World Class Podium Potential (WCPP)

WCPP supports sports and athletes who are on the pathway immediately beneath WCP. Such athletes have demonstrated realistic medal winning capabilities for future Olympic or Paralympic Games. Athletes at WCPP level are typically four to six years away from the podium.

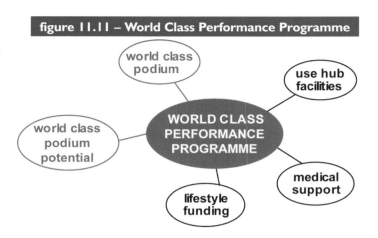

figure 11.11 – World Class Performance Programme

world class podium

use hub facilities

world class podium potential

WORLD CLASS PERFORMANCE PROGRAMME

medical support

lifestyle funding

Membership of a WCP group or National Squad carries great intrinsic and extrinsic esteem (in terms of adulation from the press and people who follow the sport) and ensures high **motivation** to succeed.

EIS has a network of world class services that support athletes on the WCP.

EIS Performance Pathways

Performance Pathways build and sustain highly effective systems for talented athletes to ensure success at future Olympic and Paralympic Games.

The EIS Performance Pathways work in partnership with UK Sport World Class Programmes to identify and develop talented athletes and to construct the underpinning support systems through the following four work areas:

- **Pathway Frontline Technical Solutions**: delivery of tailored solutions to identify and develop talented athletes that meets the needs of each individual sport such as talent recruitment, talent transfer and development of curriculums.

- **Pathway Education**: provision of educational opportunities for development of coaches and managers covering topics unique to the elite developing athlete.

- **Pathway Analytics**: the use of diagnostic tools that robustly measure and benchmark the effectiveness of their performance pathway. This includes the **Performance Pathway Health Check** (PHC) which provides a support system that provides a set of procedures that can be used to review current systems and practices which support the development of world class athletes and future medal winners.

- **Pathway Strategy**: assists individual sports to develop and implement an aligned pathway vision and strategies from foundations level to elite podium level.

EIS initiative

An example of an EIS initiative is the **Army Elite Sports Programme** (AESP) - a joint collaboration with the British Army and UK Sport. Launched in 2014, AESP aims to identify future Olympic medallists for the Tokyo 2020 Olympics and beyond (figure 11.12). The AESP is funded by a £1.4m donation the British Army received for providing some of the security at the London 2012 Olympic and Paralympic Games.

figure 11.12 – soldiers practise shooting

In terms of impact, the EIS Performance Pathways have worked in partnership with 20 Olympic and Paralympic sports, over 100 world class coaches, run 12 national athlete recruitment campaigns and assessed over 7000 athletes.

The UK is keen to promote **sport participation** for many reasons: **health** benefits, **societal** benefits and as a feeder to sporting **excellence**.

Regional multi-sport hub sites

- The 'hubs' (multi-sports High Performance Centres) provided by the Institutes of Sport for elite sportspeople, are intended to be located within 1 hour travel time of a million people, and 30 minutes travel time for 250,000 people.
- Governing bodies are insisting that members of the World Class Performance groups locate themselves near to a hub, so that coaching and medical support can also be provided simply and at less cost. For example, UK Athletics have created their national hub for elite athletes at Loughborough University (figure 11.4, page 173).
- There is an evolving network of **satellite centres**.

Lifestyle funding

- The **Performance Lifestyle Programme** which provides supplementary career and education advice.

Sports science and medical support systems.

- Top quality support by **strength and conditioning** specialists, medical support teams such as **physiotherapist** and **sports massage** personnel (figure 11.13).
- **Sports science** specialists, and sport psychology experts assist and advise on most situations facing the aspiring talented performer.

figure 11.13 – medical support

These systems have been put into place by the EIS to provide a **worry-free environment** for the sportsperson to train for up to **6 hours per day for 6 days of the week** (allowing for some rest and recovery time).

In terms of sporting excellence, pre-supposing an individual has the talent to achieve excellence, then he or she must have the **opportunity** provided by facility **provision** near enough to be feasible for regular **travel**.

By using scientific research to identify the optimum environment for nurturing these criteria, resources can be targeted at those individuals that have the greatest potential of becoming outstanding performers.

Working in partnership, UK Sport, National Institutes of Sport and NGBs are tasked with **identifying** and **developing** sporting talent.

England pathway for netball – a case study

Satellite academies (figure 11.14): County Netball Associations (on behalf of England Netball) manage and deliver about 15 sessions per year. Young netballers learn how to train on their own, and to understand, experience and practice some of the different components required in a training programme.

County academies: County Netball Associations manage and deliver the training programmes set by England Netball (15-30 sessions per year) providing athletes with the support and skill set they need to progress to the next level of the pathway, the Regional Academy.

Regional Academies: are located across the country and operate year round individualised training environments for athletes, delivering between 3-4 hours per week of coaching.

There will be up to 20 athletes in each of the Regional Academies, some of whom will also attend National Academy training and may be part of the U19/U17 England Squads.

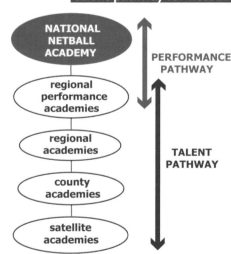

figure 11.14 – England talent pathway for netball

England pathway for netball – an a case study

Regional Performance Academies: are located across the country and operate year round individualised training environments for athletes, delivering between 5-7 hours per week of coaching. There will be up to 20 athletes in each of the Regional Performance Academies, some of whom will also attend National Academy training and may be part of the U19/U17 England Squads.

The **National Academy** operates via centralised and weekend camps, bringing together the best U17 and U19 players in England for extra coaching and training. It also provides athletes with an opportunity to access similar support services that are available to senior athletes, for example, individualised strength and conditioning programmes, on-site physiotherapy, performance lifestyle and medical services.

U19 and U17 squads will be selected from the National Academy, prior to tours.

Practice questions

1) A definition of talent is:
   a. possessing a deep need to always improve.
   b. having a feeling of trust in one's own abilities.
   c. pushing the body to the limits.
   d. having a special ability beyond the norm.

2) Which one of the following is part of the UK talent pathway?
   a. community sport.
   b. national age group programmes.
   c. world class podium potential.
   d. UK Sports Institute.

3) Which one from the following strategies would not be considered responsible for drop-out and failure rates in elite sport?
   a. sustaining a serious injury.
   b. not be able to afford the costs of participation.
   c. having a suitable training facility.
   d. peer pressure to socialise.

4) What is the function of the World Class Performance Programme?
   a. to win medals at global sporting events.
   b. to develop grass roots participation.
   c. to provide science and medical support systems.
   d. to pick teams for international competition.

5) Which of the following choices outlines the correct sequence for the six stages of the long-term athlete development model (LTAD) as proposed by Istvan Balyi?
   a. team games/fundamentals/learning to train/ training to compete/training to train/training to win/active for life.
   b. team games/fundamentals/learning to train/training to train/training to compete/training to win/active for life.
   c. team games/fundamentals/learning to train/training to win/training to train/training to compete/active for life.
   d. active for life/team games/fundamentals/learning to train/training to train/training to compete/training to win.

6) a) Differentiate between excellence and talent.   2 marks

   b) Describe some of the personal factors needed for the development of sporting talent.   4 marks

7) a) What is talent identification and what strategies are currently in place to develop it in the UK?   6 marks

   b) Discuss the effectiveness of talent identification programmes within the UK.   6 marks

Practice questions

8) Which organisations are concerned with developing excellence in the United Kingdom?   4 marks

9) What are the core elements of the World Class Performance Programme and what are the main aims of each one?   6 marks

10) What is meant by Sports Science and what contribution can it make to the development of excellence in sport?   4 marks

11) Describe a talent identification programme implemented by a UK governing body of a sport.   5 marks

12) Explain how the structure of sporting organisation in the UK is able to develop talent.   5 marks

13) There are two methods of talent identification: natural selection and scientific selection. Define and explain positive and negative aspects for each method.   6 marks

14) Describe the administrative system (institutes of sport) underpinning elite sport in the UK and account for its structure.   6 marks

15) Briefly identify and describe what you think UK Sport is doing to satisfy the needs of elite British performers.   4 marks

16) a) One of the key roles of a national governing body is to produce a Whole Sport Plan. Outline the key features of a Whole Sport Plan.   3 marks

    b) Select a sport and explain how this NGB has implemented a Whole Sport Plan.   3 marks

17) Early identification of talented individuals is considered increasingly important. Discuss the contributory factors required to support progression from talent identification to elite performance.   10 marks.

18) What does TASS stand for and how does it help to develop sporting talent?   3 marks

19) Discuss the role of National Agencies in the development of an elite performer.   10 marks

20) The English Institute of Sport (EIS) aims to develop and produce performers at the elite level of the sport development pyramid. How does the EIS achieve these aims?   10 marks

21) The UK World Class Programme that supports elite athletes, relies on the services of the three main areas of sport science, namely physiology, sport psychology and biomechanics. Discuss the ways in which an elite athlete can use these services to improve his or her sporting performance?   20 marks

22) Models of an athlete development programmes, such as the Long-term Athlete Development (LTAD), were developed by Istvan Balyi in 2001. What is the philosophy behind such models?   3 marks

Answers link: http://www.jroscoe.co.uk/downloads/a2_revise_pe_ocr/OCRA2_ch11_answers.pdf

CHAPTER 12: *Modern technology in sport*

Technology and engineering are making an impact everywhere, from goal-line technology to detailed analysis of performance data, to biomechanics of how the body moves, sports equipment and clothing, and the impact of technology on drug testing and spectators.

Modern technology at elite performance and general participation levels

Analytics represents the new frontier in the sports data industry. From the rugby pitch to the race track, an increasing reliance on **data**, **science** and **technology** is reshaping the world of sport as we know it.

Functions of sports analytics

Sports analytics is the provision and understanding of feedback to performers and coaches in an attempt to get a positive change in performance using a variety of data collection. It is also used to provide extensive data information for keen spectators.

Sports analysts (figure 12.1) are involved in **spectator entertainment**, **talent identification**, **player recruitment**, **nutrition**, and **rehabilitation** from injury. Video and data, captured or displayed on iPads and other devices, are used to give real-time **feedback** to coaches during a sports performance.

The **feedback information** they provide and the insights they bring can give a team a truly **competitive** edge. As well as providing fans with useful statistics for after game banter, data also helps team players and individual athletes to improve their individual performance and fitness.

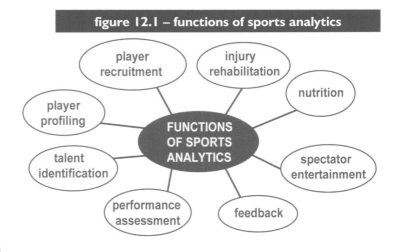

figure 12.1 – functions of sports analytics

player recruitment

injury rehabilitation

nutrition

player profiling

FUNCTIONS OF SPORTS ANALYTICS

spectator entertainment

talent identification

performance assessment

feedback

Analytics data can have a valuable impact for the **assessment** of performance, when it provides objective information that sits alongside other sources of information provided, for example from scouts who have an innate understanding of the game.

The most important aspect that coaches and players need to consider when selecting and using sports analytics software is that the raw data can be **trusted**, is **reliable** and that it has a **meaningful** impact on the individual and team performances.

An example would be the use and application of drilling down data on psychological and sociological **profiling** that would give insight into individual aspects of personality and decision making processes, resulting in KPIs (**Key Performance Indicators**). The danger is that clubs and the individual could be swamped and overwhelmed by the sheer volume of data that could have a negative impact on performance.

The use of technology in the monitoring of fitness for performance

A GPS tracking unit is a device that uses the **Global Positioning System** to determine and track its precise location and hence that of its carrier. This device is normally carried by a moving vehicle or person.

The recorded **location data** can be stored within the tracking unit, or it may be transmitted to a **central location database**, or Internet-connected computer, using a cellular (**GPRS** or **SMS**), radio, or satellite modem embedded in the unit. This allows the device's location to be displayed against a **map backdrop** either in real-time, or later when analysing the path moved by the device.

The use of technology in the monitoring of fitness for performance

Data tracking software is available for smartphones and tablet devices.
Examples of these applications include:
- **MyFitness Pal App**, which is a calorie and diet tracker.
- **Strava App**, GPS tracking system for cycling and running.
- **MapMyRun** – a running and walking GPS app that tracks distance, pace, speed, elevation, calories burned, and route travelled on an interactive map.
- **Instant Heart Rate** is the most accurate heart rate monitor app.

The use of analytics in talent identification (TID)/scouting

Sports analytics provides the quantitative and qualitative data needed to create a **profile** that can be used to assess the suitability of the talented performer to the demands of the sporting activity. It is critical to **define the TID tests** when determining these key performance indicators required by the sport.

Pathway Analytics enables sports to robustly measure and benchmark the effectiveness of their performance pathway using specialist diagnostic tools.

Talent identification programmes usually examine, judge and assess a performer by **watching** him or her **perform** in a competitive situation. If the player is deemed 'good enough' he or she is invited to an **academy** for a trial period.

Academies are special training centres set up by clubs to help them develop young players.

The TID system used by **professional football clubs** involves the use of scouts who work for or are attached to the clubs monitoring competitive matches. The criterion typically used assesses players on their techniques, balance, personality and speed.

Once recruits have entered the club system, clubs can build up a sustainable system that enables talent transfer within an aligned pathway vision (delivering tailored solutions to build sustainable programmes) that will develop talent from novice to elite performers.

This process can be supported by pathway analytics, such as the **Pathway Health Check** (PHC) devised by Sport England, which reviews the athlete's progress, fitness levels achieved and whether the athlete is transitioning well between junior and senior levels.

Equipment and clothing

Safety standards provide benchmarks that are used in the design of equipment and facilities. For example, helmet construction in cycling, cricket and lacrosse (page 66).

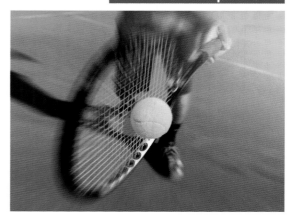

figure 12.2 – composite tennis racquet

For some sports, high tech equipment is important in injury prevention as discussed from page 58. For example, compression clothing, bespoke footwear, wicking fabrics and energy absorbing plastics.

The use of composites in sports equipment is relatively recent. For example, modern day tennis rackets (figure 12.2) are made from a high modulus **carbon fibre**, which is used to keep the frame lightweight and stiff for increased racket head stability and give players more control.

These carbon fibre materials allow for more aerodynamic shapes to be made which increases the speed at which a racket can travel.

The use of these materials in racket manufacture, allow the tennis rackets to be strung at higher stringing tensions without weakening the frame. High string tensions are used by tennis players to gain more control and feel from their tennis rackets.

Adaptive technology

Bespoke sporting equipment has radically changed the opportunities for disabled athletes and an ageing population to participate in sporting activities, but there is a fine balance between improving the functionality of the sport and turning individuals into robots.

figure 12.3 – Oscar Pistorius, blade runner

The aim of researchers is to effectively match the technology with the athletes' requirements, known as **assistive** and **adaptive technology**.

Assistive technology refers to any item, piece of equipment that is used to increase, maintain, or improve functional capabilities of individuals with disabilities.

Adaptive technology covers items that are specifically designed for persons with disabilities and would seldom be used by non-disabled persons.

Given the opportunities for participation in sports for persons with a limb deficiency, the demand for new, innovative **prosthetic designs** is challenging. Made from carbon, flex-fibre, 'Cheetah Flex-Foot' blades enabled Oscar Pistoruis (figure 12.3) to break 26 world records. In 2008 he started a debate within the athletics community by petitioning to be able to compete at the Beijing Olympic Games, against able-bodied competitors.

Paralympic long jump champion Markus Rehm had a dream of competing at both the Rio Olympics and Paralympics in 2016. The 27-year-old set a world record of 8.40m in winning the T44 long jump event at the IPC World Championships in Doha in October 2015, a distance that would have given him gold ahead of Britain's Greg Rutherford at the 2012 London Olympics. The German track and field federation (DOSB) did not select him as it was felt that his prosthetic take-off foot and leg gave him an **unfair advantage**.

This case raises issues about **equity** of performers and performance as well as technology.

Throwing frames are individually designed assistive devices which are scaffold-like chairs made of metal bars and plates welded together. The main purpose of the throwing frame is to assist in weight bearing, thus enabling a seated disabled athlete to throw.

A range of **wheelchairs** have been developed for disabled athletes, evolved to suit the specific needs of that sport, including wheelchairs for basketball, rugby, tennis, racing and dancing.

The chairs are usually non-folding (in order to increase rigidity), with a pronounced negative camber for the wheels (which provides stability and is helpful for making sharp turns), and often are made of composite, lightweight materials. Built to the individual's width, height and seating preference, the design team create a scan from the disabled athlete sitting in his chair, then create a computerised model that can be used as a template to manufacture the wheelchair.

The major barrier of this adapted technology is expense in the design and manufacturing of the wheelchairs that are often in excess of £2000.00.

figure 12.4 – racing wheelchairs

Racing wheelchairs (figure 12.4) provide bucket seats, angled wheels to increase stability and a **'t' shaped frame** that gives precision steering and balance. **Specialist gloves** are used to protect the hands used in striking the push rim.

Wheelchairs, used for wheelchair **rugby** and wheelchair **basketball**, are designed to withstand heavy impacts and be easily manoeuvrable. **Tennis** wheelchairs have extended wheels in the front that would allow athletes to reach as far out to return shots.

Adaptive technology

Hiking poles offer increased support and stability on unfamiliar ground and uneven surfaces, help improve posture and increase confidence for the individual. Walking is the most popular activity within the retirement population.

Wheelchairs offer mobility to the elderly to travel and access sports centres and pursuits such as **wheelchair bowls**. This sport follows exactly the same rules as for able-bodied players, and so offers the opportunity of integrating ageing immobile individuals with able bodied performers.

Assistive devices can help to improve the **quality of life** for both the disabled and elderly and maintain their sense of independence.

Equity legislation has helped to improve the infrastructure needed to increase participation rates. For example, improved physical access to sporting facilities for people with reduced mobility, coupled with close parking spots, good lighting and innovative programmes using a range of high tech equipment.

Technology and facility development

Modern technology has improved **facilities** for elite performers (able and disabled-bodied) and the active general population. Construction of facilities such as those built for the London 2012 Olympic Games, have left a legacy (figure 12.5).

figure 12.5 – the Olympic Park

The biggest technical London legacy involved the development of **ICT systems** needed to deliver pictures, texts, phone calls and video, which created the most digitally enabled Games ever, thus enhancing the viewing experience then and now.

Most sports are now played on low maintenance, synthetic or **artificial sports surfaces** at both competitive and recreational levels.

Hockey, netball, basketball, and athletics are almost exclusively played on synthetic surfaces at a competitive level, and other sports such as tennis, volleyball, cricket, and badminton have also benefitted from the development in sports surface technology.

figure 12.6 – artificial sports surface

For example, **multi-use games areas** (MUGAS), such as 3G/4G turf technology, are great for schools and sports clubs as they offer a more cost effective sport space for multi-purpose use (figure 12.6). There is no evidence of a greater risk of injury when matches are played on artificial turf compared with natural grass.

Although the initial cost of installing a synthetic pitch could be up to £400,000, a big advantage is that **maintenance costs are low** and the all weather qualities enable sport to be played throughout the year, thereby offering the potential for greater participation.

Some playing surfaces are tailor made to meet the demands of the sport. For example, **rubberised cushioned hard courts** have been developed to provide a more yielding artificial surface. This surface is played on at the USTA National Tennis Centre in New York City, home of the U.S. Open, and its yielding properties have reduced chronic injury rates and so more professional tennis players are able to extend their playing careers.

Climate chambers

Climate chambers are utilised for testing performance clothing, equipment and research into the studies on the effect of hypoxia (page 39) and heat stress, on the human body in a safe local environment.

Climate chambers are very specialist testing facilities that are normally sited at national hubs and universities. The use of such facilities is costly and hence may only be available to elite performers. In addition elite performers from poor countries are at a disadvantage over those countries where finance is available for the development and installation of such facilities.

Nutrition and fitness

Nutrition and fitness are probably the most important features which can affect an athlete's performance in sport. Software programmes, for example **Precision Nutrition**, are being used to monitor and analyse an athlete's nutrition and fitness levels in much more accurate ways than previously.

Fair outcomes

Within the sporting arena there are many examples of technology that have been developed to improve the game and add excitement for the viewing public.

Electronic timing devices

- **Timing devices** include **timing gate systems** (for example, as used in alpine skiing), provide real time feedback as the skiers pass through infra red photocells that record splits that can be instantaneously displayed on large public screens. This technology adds to the speed and drama that makes alpine skiing events so popular.

- **Electronic timing devices** are used in sports such as swimming. Touch pads mounted on the wall of each swimmer's lane register instant split and finishing times.

- **Photo finish devices** are high-definition cameras mounted on poles to provide a reliable photo finish system that can provide a rapid and accurate results service for both the media and spectators, either in printed form or by TV screen.

HawkEye and goal-line technology

figure 12.7 – HawkEye in action

HawkEye has been an integral part of tennis since 2002 and continues to deliver innovative solutions for federations, tournaments, broadcasters, and sponsors that truly enhance the game for players and fans alike. HawkEye is an extremely **objective** and **reliable** sports analytics tool, thus ensuring high pressure points do not fall prey to the **subjective opinions** of umpires and line judges.

The **electronic line calling** service takes the doubt out of close line calls by using the most sophisticated millimetre accurate ball tracking cameras to identify whether a ball has bounced in or out (figure 12.7).

HawkEye's Smart Replay technology can deliver **instant video replays** to assist officials with close decisions on foot faults or line calls on clay courts, and provides **entertainment** to live and armchair spectators across the globe.

In football, goal-line technology has recently been introduced to give a clear indication to the referee as to whether the ball has crossed the line or not. This is similar to HawkEye in that the ball is portrayed via computer simulation and not action replay.

Action replays

Action replays are used to help referees make the right call. In international rugby, TV replays are available to the television match official (TMO) who can assist the referee in making the correct decision if there is doubt whether the ball or player went into touch, or if the ball was properly grounded to score a try. The TMO is able to advise the central umpire or referee on producing fair results.

The downside to these technologies is that the media can highlight an official's mistakes that could increase anxiety levels for the officials as the live viewing audience criticise the umpiring decision. In turn the authority of the official is weakened.

Technical aids can usefully assist officials, but their value depends strongly on how they are used. Technical aids will never replace the personality of an official and their communication and social skills that are necessary to turn a competition into a great event. Even the best technical systems may develop a tendency to fail in important moments.

New technologies and doping

New technologies raise the feasibility of doping which will be **undetectable**. On the other hand, the **Athlete Biological Passport** (ABP) is based on the personalised monitoring of biomarkers of doping that can be used to detect doping. The main advantage of the ABP is that it is based on the stability of the physiology of the human being. In addition to its original aim of providing proof of a doping offense, the ABP can also serve as a platform for an ethical **Rule of Sport**.

Screening

Screening has already been discussed on page 61 within the context of the prevention of sports injuries. Technologies, such as **running kinetics technology** (page 60), provide instantaneous feedback on performance motion analysis. **Biometric health screening** can detect health risk factors. For example, UK Athletics has worked with **Cardiac Risk in the Young** (CRY) for several years, providing a screening service to athletes on the World Class Performance Programme.

Entertainment

Modern technology and entertainment

As already discussed in Chapter 10, modern technologies have been a major driving force in the sports entertainment industry and the changes they bring have never remained the same for long. Audiences can now choose from a variety of contents, choose where they want to see it and choose when they want to see the contents. The technology and capabilities of these **smart devices** have encouraged **video on demand** (VOD) platforms to develop **apps** that can transmit instant sporting results and educate and entertain millions of users regardless of geographical location.

*   **Smartphones**, **phablets** (the smartphone/tablet hybrid, figure 12.8) and tablets have become tools to accessing video contents online without being limited by location or time.

*   Contents once limited by linear TV are now accessed by '**consumers on demand**'. Internet has broken all communication barriers and social media has made it even much easier for the public to view and share sports coverage.

*   The British media is dominated by national outlets, with local media playing a much smaller role.

*   High tech equipment is expensive to buy for the average spectator.

figure 12.8– a phablet is a hand held computer and phone

Modern technology and entertainment

Multi camera rigs let fans watch any angle they want. When placed over a field at a stadium the rigs work together to create a panoramic view of the action, theoretically letting the viewer pan or simply select the specific angle.

- **Mini cameras**, called action cameras, are associated with outdoor sports, and are often attached to helmets, handlebars and on the front, inside and rear of racing cars, giving the audience a more intimate view of the action.

- As a result of miniaturised video cameras (hence multi-camera angles, and player carried cameras), the armchair spectator may develop more interest, passion and understanding of the sporting event.

- **Action replays** also provide spectators with improved analysis and understanding of the game.
- Slow motion action replays **on-demand mobile technology** is coming soon and will enable sport fans to control frame rate clips at a selected pace that can be shared on social media.
- They also can help diffuse audience aggression and frustration, if pressure points do not fall prey to bad umpiring decisions.

- **Electronic scoreboards** (figure 12.9) engage the viewing audience with action, statistics, instant replays and results.

- Immediate statistics and replays can be distracting, but in reality are inevitable.

- A wider range of sports are accessible and visible through the development of technology, for example glass walled squash courts.

figure 12.9 – electronic scoreboards give immediate statistics and replays

Punditry

- **Punditry analysis** offers opinion and commentary on a sporting event, often led by popular media sports personalities, for example Sue Barker and Gary Lineker. Pundits may be asked for their knowledgeable opinions whilst action is ongoing, or during breaks in the play whilst replays are being judged. A negative for this process is that it may be irritating for the spectator to miss bits of an event (such as a global athletics meeting), or breaks in play which slows down the action and increases the playing time. This could lead to spectator frustration.

- Televised sporting events are often preceded by a pre-match show involving pundits. Within relaxed digital studios a pundit often provides a personal touch along with his or her critical analysis of the forth coming event. Although entertaining and informative, the pre-event show may not be of interest to some armchair spectators.

Sports TV

Pay-per-view and audience entertainment has already been discussed on page 167. There is also a dedicated UK version of Eurosport, called British Eurosport which runs a similar scheme.

Sky Sports Pass lets you watch all seven Sky Sports channels for 24 hours. Sports organisations (federations, leagues and clubs) are pretty enthusiastic about going direct to the consumer for **self-distribution**.

The development of TV technologies may encourage the viewing public to stay at home as opposed to attending a stadium event. This is a much cheaper option and may result in a decline in live attendances.

Positive and negative impacts of sports technology

Table 12.1 - **positive and negative impacts of sports technology**

Positive impacts	Negative impacts
electronic timing provides instant and accurate results	modern technologies, such as bespoke wheelchairs, may only be available to those athletes/countries who can afford them
force platform measures ground reaction force	modern technology can also support an unfair 'playing field' with such things as the development and use of ergogenic aids, for example, oxygen tents, where cost is an important factor
HawkEye has greatly enhanced sporting knowledge	technological aids may have a placebo effect that boosts performer's confidence, as opposed to actually benefitting the performer
fibre reinforced tennis racket frames has resulted in larger racket heads and an increase in the sweet-spot area of the racket which has increased the speed of the game	officials may become too reliant on technology systems and so lose skills such as time-keeping and the ability to make quick and marginal decisions
high tech equipment at elite level has made sport a global product benefitting sports business	

Table 12.2 - **positive and negative impacts of technology on the coach**

Positive impacts	Negative impacts
sports analytics make it possible for coaches to provide their athletes with the best possible opportunities to achieve maximal performance	coaches may become too reliant on technology and not use their intuitive coaching instincts
enables effective and informed team selections and player substitutes during a match and rest and recovery	software data may get corrupted and become unreliable
the video camera is perhaps the single most important development in coaching in the modern era of sport	as sports technology continues to evolve, will sports technology replace the coach?
software such as Dartfish, provide the coach with detailed technique analysis and the biomechanical tools that can compare and monitor skill development	using motion capture analysis is very time consuming, expensive and needs the technical understanding of how to use it to best effect
smartphones and ipads are cheap accessible technologies coaches can use to analyse real-time performances in terms of strengths/weaknesses and/or tactics/strategies	coaches need to be aware that their athletes don't become 'guinea pigs' in the experiments of the technology industry
smart equipment can be used to measure performance such as exercise stress testing and cardiovascular assessment	coaches sometimes find video difficult to use while an athlete is performing, it may be better to observe by eye and interpret rhythms and corrections from the performance
electronic timing devices provide the coach with specific, detailed recording of performances such as gun reaction time and lap split times	
nutrition and fitness software programmes are used by elite coaches to accurately monitor and analyse an athlete's nutritional needs, and fitness levels	

Table 12.3 - **positive and negative impacts of technology on the performer**

Positive impacts	Negative impacts
development of nanotechnology (study and application of extremely small things) has created a variety of products aimed at improving and increasing athletic performance	footwear and clothing are generally chosen more for comfort and sometimes fashion and injury avoidance rather than performance enhancement
faster injury rehabilitation	protective equipment, such as helmets, can create a more aggressive playing environment
the use of hypobaric and humidity chambers can recreate competition environments	the growing use of drugs in sport has led to many high profile athletes cheating the system
sporting equipment, such as helmets and body protection, are used for example in cricket and hockey to help prevent injuries	PEDs are part of the win-at-all-costs ethic, and can lead to over-aggressive behaviour in addition to detrimental physiological side effects
smart clothing e.g. sports socks that are absorbent, flexible and breathable and wick away sweat	
compression clothing, such body suits, increases venous return and $\dot{V}O_{2max}$ during high intensity exercise and aids recovery as the effects of DOMS is reduced	
footwear can be made to match the shape and mechanics of feet on an individual basis to make movement more efficient and improve performance	affordability is an issue unless the individual is sponsored
prosthetics have also been made for those athletes with a specific disability	prosthetics are very expensive
wheelchair devices used in sporting activities have also become more sophisticated	wheelchair devices are very expensive when tailor-made
improvements in the design of sport equipment and clothing have both aerodynamic and physiological benefits for sports performers	at what point does technology enhance performance unnaturally?
GPS and associated apps, linked to Google Earth, provide KPIs such as position, distance covered and speed of player's performance	elite athletes could see a pay decrease during salary negotiations not based on their performance, but on sports analytics data
quantitative data from GPS technology, can be used to create training programmes, monitor progression and recovery during and between training sessions, and injury prevention and rehabilitation	data analysis can be time consuming and at times overwhelming
nutrition analysis and menu planning software assess energy expenditure and dietary intake used to create meal plans to achieve performance goals	
advances in stress management techniques that can redirect attention away from failure or perceived failure	

Table 12.4 - **positive and negative impacts of technology on the audience**

Positive impacts	Negative impacts
sports are a form of entertainment, and providing new technologies such as HawkEye can increase their engagement and knowledge of the game	breaks in play, whilst replays are being judged, slows down the action and increases the playing time and may lead to spectator frustration
the armchair audience has access to enhanced experience in the home through the use of more cameras/player cam, as a result of miniaturized video cameras	commercial adverts disrupt playing schedules for the armchair spectator
technologies can help to diffuse audience aggression and frustration, when pressure points do not fall prey to with bad umpiring decisions	commercial advertising of sports clothing may be fashion led, as opposed to what is best
a 'miked up' referee further facilitates the involvement of live and armchair fans to engage in real-time play	high tech equipment is expensive to buy for the average spectator/participant
spectator interest and excitement are enhanced by broadcasting and in-stadium replay screens scoreboards that can very quickly communicate results to an audience	some people decry the use of technology to improve sports performance but in reality it is inevitable
a wider range of sports are accessible and visible through the development of technology, for example, glass walled squash courts	
the research and development of sport equipment and clothing is an industry in itself which creates opportunity for investment and employment	

Practice questions

1) Modern technology has been said to increase participation in sport.
   Which one of the following has had the greatest impact?
   a. the design of sports clothing.
   b. the use of composite materials that make sports equipment lighter and stronger.
   c. the development of climate chambers that can mimic different environment conditions.
   d. the provision of sporting facilities.

2) Which one of the following definitions does not describe the benefits of modern technologies on fair outcomes?
   a. electronic timing devices provide instant results.
   b. official's mistakes are exposed.
   c. modern technologies expose foul play.
   d. modern technologies improve sport provision.

3) The efforts to control the use of performance enhancing drugs in sports will only be effective if they:
   a. appeal to personal values of athletes themselves.
   b. provide education programmes emphasising the dangers of drug abuse.
   c. appeal for fair play within sports.
   d. recognise that most use of drugs is a form of deviant overconformity.

4) The Athlete Biological Passport is part of modern technology. What is its main function in elite sport?
   a. it profiles biological markers of doping and results of doping tests.
   b. it is an excellent alternative to ensure fair outcomes.
   c. it is administered to establish whether an athlete is manipulating his/her physiological variables.
   d. it serves as a platform for an ethical Rule of Sport.

Practice questions

5) Sports entertainment in the twenty first century has seen the emergence of the sports pundit. Identify from one of the following, the key role of a sports pundit:
   a. to provide spectator interest and excitement.
   b. to communicate results to an audience.
   c. to offer his or her opinion or commentary on a particular subject area.
   d. to provide constant interruptions during a sporting contest.

6) How can sports analytics assist in the development skill and technique?   4 marks

7) How can adaptive and assistive technology increase access to sport for the disabled?   4 marks

8) Identify and describe a modern technology that aids analysis and feedback for improvements in sporting performance.   4 marks

9) Identify the disadvantages of using technology in assisting officials in their decision making.   3 marks

10) Discuss how increased technology has helped officials in their decision making and its impact on the sporting event.   3 marks

11) Discuss the notion that sports performers are only as good as the technology that supports them. Use examples from global sports to support your answer.   20 marks

12) What is meant by the Athlete Biological Passport and how does it function in the detection of drug abuse in sport?   2 marks

13) Sports are a form of entertainment. How have contemporary technologies enhanced the entertainment value for both live and armchair spectators?   5 marks

14) Discuss the negative and positive impact of technology on the performer.   10 marks

15) Modern technologies can enhance and limit sports entertainment. Discuss.   10 marks

16) Discuss the use of modern technologies in talent identification programmes.   4 marks

17) a) What is sports punditry?   2 marks

    b) How does sports punditry enhance spectator entertainment?   3 marks

Answers link: http://www.jroscoe.co.uk/downloads/a2_revise_pe_ocr/OCRA2_ch12_answers.pdf

OCR A Level Physical Education Examination Papers

The A level examination structure consists of three written papers:

Paper 1: Physiological factors affecting performance

- Applied Anatomy and Physiology.
- Exercise Physiology.
- Biomechanics.

This is a 2 hour written paper worth 90 marks, representing 30% of total A Level.

Paper 2: Psychological factors affecting performance

- Skill Acquisition.
- Sports Psychology.

This is a 1 hour written paper worth 60 marks, representing 20% of total A Level.

Paper 3: Socio-cultural issues in physical activity and sport

- Sport and Society.
- Contemporary issues in physical activity and sport.

This is a 1 hour written paper worth 60 marks, representing 20% of total A Level.

Each paper includes multi-choice, short and 20 mark extended questions.

Our answers to short and extended practice questions (located at download link www.jroscoe.co.uk/downloads/a2_revise_pe_ocr/) have been presented in bullet format to enable clear identification of the point being made.

Bullet point responses can be used when command words 'state', 'name', 'identify' and 'list' have been used. Otherwise, you must write your answers in continuous prose and paragraphs.

It is advisable to sketch out a short plan (such as a spider diagram) for the extended questions.

OCR Assessment objectives for A Level OCR Physical Education are included in the introduction to the questions and answers electronic file at www.jroscoe.co.uk/downloads/a2_revise_pe_ocr/

It is important that you use correct terminology, accurate knowledge and its application, supported by relevant examples in sufficient detail, when answering a question.

Key command words used in examination papers

Your first task when answering a question is to understand what the question is actually asking. Underline the key command words (within the question) and its interpretation, to maintain focus in your answer.

Advantages and disadvantages
Clear statement of why one condition is better that another. Would normally need justification and/or qualification relevant to the question.

Analyse
Break down into component parts and identify their characteristics.

Apply
Using the information provided, link it directly to practical and relevant situations within sport.

Assess
Judge the relevance and accuracy of information provided.

Calculate
Be able to enumerate and evaluate data in numerical form.

Characteristics
Common, agreed factors for a situation, structure or process.

Comment
Present a written evaluation of the worth of a situation in the context of sport or physical education.

Compare
Identify similarities and or differences between two or more situations.

Consider
Look at the information given and give an opinion as to its worth in its context.

Contrast
Identify differences and draw attention to the significance of these differences.

Define/What is meant by....?
Formal and precise description frequently of a technical term/less formal by definition.

Describe
Use of quantitative or qualitative information to explain a statement or a relationship between factors. This term is maybe qualified as 'briefly describe'. Examples are frequently used.

Differences
A comparison between two states in the question. You should be precise and not be tempted to wander.

Discuss
Presentation of both sides of an argument, seeking an opinion based on knowledge and analysis with a justified conclusion.

Evaluate
Estimate the worth of something either qualitatively or numerically quantitatively.

Explain
Justification beyond simple statement or descriptions required (the why). Will frequently require examples, sometimes qualified as explain briefly. Consider number of marks allocated.

Give
Provide an answer from recall.

Identify and explain
Linking of cause/problem and effect/solution. Marks awarded only if links are made.

Interpret
To explain and translate information into a simpler form.

Justify
To explain based on evidence or detailed examples, the accuracy of a statement or opinion. The more detail the better.

List
A number of points or features, frequently only a single word. No description required.

Name
No explanation required or credited. Will normally require use of a degree of technical language. One or two words.

Outline
Briefly state a plan of a situation.

Plot, Sketch and Label
Used for graphical presentation. For a sketch, graph paper is not required. Important factors are correct labelling of axes and shape of graph. Plotting requires the use of appropriate scales on axes and accurate plotting points.

Principle
Theoretical concept underpinning a practical example.

State
Express clearly and briefly.

Suggest
More than one option available which require a justification linked to a question. Not to be answered from pure recall.

C

D

H

haematoma, 49
haemoglobin, response to altitude, 36, 38, 39
HawkEye, 187, 190, 192
HBOT benefits, 76
HBOT, hyperbaric oxygen therapy, 29
headgear, protective, 66
heat acclimatisation, 43, 44
heat energy transfer, 39
heat stroke, consequences, 42
heat therapies following injury, 68
Heathens, Newton Heath Football club, 158
heat-shock proteins, 68
helmets, protective, 59
high glycolytic enzyme activity, 18
hiking poles, 186
homeostasis, 26
hooliganism, 151, 156
hub sites, 180
hubs, 173
hydration, pre-exercise, 43
hydrogen ions, 15
hydroplaning, 98
hydrotherapy, 69
hyperbaric oxygen chambers, 78
hyper-mobility, 55
hyperthermia, 40
hypobaric chambers, 39, 76, 78
hypothalamus, 40
hypoxia, 35, 36, 37, 39
hypoxic stimulation, 76

I

ice jackets, 43
ice therapy, 50
ice water immersion, 70
ideal-self, 120
IHT, intermittent hypoxia training, 39
illegal betting industry, 153, 154
illegal drugs, 141, 155
imagery, 123, 138
imagery relaxation, 134
immune suppression at altitude, 38
inflammation, 77
inflammatory process, 25
injuries, 48
injuries, hard tissue, 52
injuries, overuse, 58
injuries, soft tissue, 49, 53
injury prevention, 54, 77
injury prevention, stages, 61
injury risk, 77
injury, rehabilitation, 66
Instant Heart Rate, 184
institutes of sport, 182
interactionist theory, leadership, 127

internal factors, Weiner's model, 116
internal, Nideffer's attentional styles, 132
Internet, 171
Internet pay-per-view, 167
Internet, influence on sport, 166
intrinsic risk factors, sports injuries, 54
IOC, international Olympic committee, 146
ipads, 190
IRB's recognise and remove 6 Rs, 65

J

joint injuries, recovery, 74
joint mobilisation, 71
joint sprains, 77
joint sprains and tears, 50
journalists, sports, 166

K

KPI, key performance indicators, 183
kinaestheic cues, 108
kinetic energy, 12
KISS, keep it simple stupid, 111
Kreb's cycle, 15

L

lactacid oxygen recovery, 24
lactate dehydrogenase, 14
lactate/aerobic threshold, 23
lactic acid, 19, 71
lactic acid removal, 24, 25
lactic acid system, 12, 14, 17, 19
laissez-faire style, leadership, 126
laminar flow, 96, 97, 103
Lance Armstrong, 145
lateral epicondylitis, 53
leader characteristics, 128
leader effectiveness, 128
leadership, 126
leadership styles, 137
learned helplessness, 117, 118, 124, 125
legal supplements, 155
lifestyle funding, 180
lifestyle support, World Class Performance Pathway, 177
lift, aerodynamic, 100
ligament grafts, 51
ligament injuries, grades, 50
ligament tears, 50
longitudinal axis, 87
long-term memory, 106, 109, 112
lottery funding, 175, 178
Loughborough University HIPAC, 173
LTAD, long-term athlete development, 57, 175, 176, 181, 182
luck, Weiner's model, 116

M

N

O

S

safety hazards in the environment, 60
safety measures, to avoid injury, 61
sagittal axis, 87
SALTAPS, 64
scalars, 80, 91
schools, role of identification and development of talent, 172, 173
scientific selection, 175, 182
screening, injury prevention, 61, 78, 188
secondary therapy, HBOT, 76
selection, 175
selective attention, 107, 108, 112, 113, 131
self-confidence, 120, 121
self-efficacy, 122, 123, 125
self-efficacy, strategies for building, 123
self-esteem, 117, 120, 121
self-image, 120
self-serving bias, 117
semantic code, 106
semantic level, Craik and Lockhart, 110, 112
sensory memory, 106, 112, 113
shear thickening materials, 59
shin splints, 53
short-term and long-term recovery from exercise, 28
short-term memory, 106, 107, 108, 109, 111, 112, 113
side-spin, Magnus effect, 101, 102, 104
simulation, 154
situational factors leadership, 128
sleep and recovery, 29
slow twitch muscle fibre type, 18
smart clothing, 191
smartphones, 188, 190
social factors, role of identification and development of talent, 172
social learning theory, leadership, 127
social learning theory, leadership, 136
social media, 157, 166
social support behaviour, leader, 129
somatic relaxation techniques, stress, 130
somatic techniques, stress, 136
specific learned helplessness, 118
spectator violence, 151, 156
spectator violence, causes of, 151, 152
spectatorship, 157, 158, 161
speed, 80, 83, 84, 93
speed or velocity against time graphs, 85, 92
spin, applying to a ball, 102
sponsorship, 157, 162, 163, 170, 171
sport (1940-today), 159
sport between the wars (1918-1940), 159
Sport England, 184
sport equipment manufacturers, 168
sportainment, 167
sport-confidence, 121
sports analytics, 183, 193
sports betting syndicates, 154
sports boats, 97, 98
sports drinks, 46

sports entertainment, 193
sports injuries, 48
sports labour, 161
sports science support systems, 180
sports surfaces, artificial, 186
sports technology, positive amd negative impacts, 190
sportsmanship, 155, 160
sportsmanship ethic, 152
sprain, 77
sprains, 50
sprains, recovery, 74
sprinter, 85
stability, locus of, Weiner's model, 116
state anxiety, 138
state sport-confidence, 121
static stretching, 62
steady state - maximum, 27
steady state - oxygen consumption, 16
stimulants, 145
stimulus identification, 107
Stoke City FC, 162
strains, 50
strapping, to avoid injury, 59, 60
Strava App, 184
stress, 130, 137, 138
stress fractures, 52, 73
stressors, 130, 136
stretching as part of rehabilitation after injury, 67
stretching as part of warm-up, 62, 63
stretching, injury prevention, 77
stroke volume in cardiovascular drift, 41
structural level, Craik and Lockhart, 110, 112
Sue Barker, 189
superficial heat therapies, 68
supplements, legal, 141
surgery, 72, 73, 78
sweat gland activity response to high temperature, 40
sweat rates during exercise in the heat, 42
symptoms of stress, 130

T

tactics and strategies for recovery, 30
talent, 181
talent identification, 181, 182, 183
talent identification programmes, 184
talented individuals, identification and development, 172
task difficulty, Weiner's model, 116
task-centred leadership, 127
TASS, talented athlete scholarship scheme, 173, 182
technique, risk factor for injury, 58
technology and drag, 97
technology and recovery, 30
technology, influence on sport, 166
temperature regulation in a warm climate, 46
tendinopathy, 53
tendon, 51
tendon overuse, 77
tendon, total ruptures, 51
therapy, massage, 67